Anatomy of Printing

Anatomy of Printing

THE INFLUENCES OF ART AND HISTORY ON ITS DESIGN

John Lewis

Watson-Guptill Publications
New York

First published in 1970
by Faber and Faber Limited
24 Russell Square, London, WC1

Published in 1970
by Watson-Guptill Publications
165 West 46 Street, New York, N.Y. 10036

Library of Congress
Catalog Card Number: 78-114197

International Standard Book Number 0-8230-5025-4

Designed and produced by John Lewis

Printed in Great Britain by W. S. Cowell Limited
at their press in the Butter Market, Ipswich

Acknowledgements

In writing this book and collecting the illustrations, I have had the help of many people. I am particularly grateful to Mr Denis Richards, Mr James Mosley and Dr Berthold Wolpe for reading the text and making many helpful suggestions and to Mrs Helen Wodzicka for help in collecting many of the illustrations. Illustrations from public collections have acknowledgements printed in their captions. I would like to express my gratitude to the Trustees of the British Museum and the Directors of the National Gallery (London), the Tate Gallery and the Victoria and Albert Museum for permission to reproduce many of the illustrations. The illustrations without acknowledgement are from my own collection and the collections of friends.

Finally my thanks to my wife Griselda, without whose help this book could not have been completed.

Dedication

To Berthold Wolpe, Hon. Dr. R.C.A., R.D.I. whose work has made him a part of the anatomy of printing.

Contents

List of Illustrations: colour and monochrome plates

9

Line illustrations in the text

12

Introduction

This book started, as did my *Printed Ephemera*, with the discovery of the Palgrave scrap-book. This was a collection of old printed pages and printed fragments, compiled in about 1820 by the University Librarian at Cambridge. Because I am a designer, I was interested in the purely visual aspects of these faded bits of paper, but interest deepened in my trying to discover exactly what these pages were. This led me to museums and libraries and inevitably to reading history, both specifically and in general. A pattern in depth began to emerge and printing revealed itself as a reflection of the art, architecture and fashion of its time, showing the fluctuations of style in these background changes.

This interaction between the printing press and the artistic, social, religious and economic backgrounds of the Western World became of compelling interest. As I was at that time a tutor in typography at the Royal College of Art, I used this material for the substance of a series of lectures. To a generation of students nurtured on a diet of 35mm slides, the effect of handling actual pieces of history was interesting. A Jenson page, a Caxton colophon, a Baskerville book or a nineteenth-century playbill, held in the hand, brought history to life. These old printed pages helped towards an understanding of quality and may have provided a yardstick for judgement. For me they also began to develop another dimension.

My often rather unscholarly research led me into some extraordinary byways. Not the least interesting of these were the records of the men who actually printed these pages and, even more so, of the people who worked with them and influenced them, men such as Erasmus and Rabelais, Holbein and Rubens, Morris and Ricketts, and Moholy-Nagy and Lissitzky. This was the added dimension. I was reminded of something Ruskin wrote in *The Stones of Venice* ' . . . with that love of change, that strange disquietude of the Gothic spirit, that restlessness of the dreaming mind.'

'That love of change' showed itself in the recurring conflicts of style in printing, when, from the earliest days, black letter was in conflict with the roman typeface, to four hundred years later, when the roman old style letter was overwhelmed by the bold brashness of nineteenth-century display typography; and to the end of that century, when William Morris's Kelmscott medievalism was in conflict with both the Jensonist manners of the succeeding private presses and the *art nouveau* typography of Charles Ricketts; and to twenty years later, when the battle was joined between Dada and Constructivism, to be followed by the enduring rivalry of the classic English book style and *Die Neue Typographie*. The tensions set up by these recurring conflicts provide something of the substance of this book.

Printing is communication. That methods of communication are changing at a great rate and that computer setting is a long jump ahead of hand composition does not alter the fact that the result is a thing seen.

This is what this book is about — things seen. Inevitably it reflects a personal viewpoint. Some things — and some people — interest one more than others but the field is wide. There is room in the story of printing for every kind of interest.

JOHN LEWIS
WOODBRIDGE 1970

'The invention of the printing press and movable type marks the dividing point between the arts and crafts of the Middle Ages and modern technology'.

Opposite: A page from 'The Squire's Tale' from Caxton's 1483 edition of *The Canterbury Tales*. This was one of the first books to be printed in the English language; without the printing press, it might never have survived.

The Squire's tale from *Canterbury Tales*, the second edition printed by Caxton (1483) but the first with illustrations.
British Museum

The Squyers tale

Here begynneth the squyers tale

At surrey in the londe of Tartarye
There dwellyd a kyng that warryd russhy
Thorolw whyche there dyd many a doughty man
Thys nobyl kyng was cleppyd Cambuscan
Whyche in hys tyme was of so gret renoun
That ther was nowhere in no regioun
So excellent a lord in alle thyng
He lackid nought that longed to a kyng
As of the secte of whyche he was born
He kepte hys lay to whyche he was sworn
And therto he was hardy wyse and ryche
Pytous Juste and alwey y lyche
Soth of hys word benygne and honourable
Of hys corage as ony centre stabyl

1 The *Lindisfarne Gospels* A.D. 698 – 721. Page showing interlaced
patterning and zoomorphic forms. *British Museum*

The Background to Printing

Printing was established in Germany as an already fully-formed, highly sophisticated medium of communication by the middle of the fifteenth century. Its nature and its appearance were governed by both Gothic and Renaissance cultures. Printing in its turn influenced both these cultures. This interaction between the printing press and the artistic, social, religious and economic background of the Western World has produced tensions that have done much to shape the appearance of books and the style of printed ephemera.

The prelude to Gutenberg's successful invention lay in several hundred years of slow, often hesitating, progress in the form of language and the shape of letters. This growth was largely due to the spread of Christianity, which had reached Britain before the beginning of the fifth century and the withdrawal of the outposts of the Roman Empire. The evangelising of the Celtic pagan tribes had started with St Patrick's mission to Ireland in A.D. 432. For the next hundred years the Irish monasteries became the only protectors in Northern Europe not only of the Christian faith, but also of the written word, in a world that had largely forgotten how to read or write.

The Roman tongue slowly degenerated and became modified over the centuries into the Italian dialects and into French, Spanish and Portuguese. The Irish monks, however, continued to write their copies of the Gospels and to speak their sermons in a classical Latin.

Such writing as was done at this time was in rustic capitals or in roman uncials. Both rustic capitals and uncials were capital-letter alphabets that had become modified by the use of a square-edged pen. They continued in use for fine book work until the eighth century. The characteristic letters of the uncial alphabet are the rounded A, D, E, H, M and U (or V). The need for speed brought further modifications with the so-called half-uncials. This cursive hand was developed by the Franks and used by the Roman missionaries who visited Ireland. The Irish in their turn formalized this roman half-uncial into a beautiful if angular script, more slowly written and with the horizontally cut quill.

A century after the Roman missionaries had established themselves in Ireland, the Irish S. Columba helped the spread of the faith and learning by establishing a monastery at Luxeuil near the Vosges and another on the Island of Iona, which lies a mile or so from the south-west corner of the Isle of Mull, off the west coast of Scotland. This evangelising crusade was carried a stage further under the inspiration of Pope Gregory, when Augustine's mission arrived in Kent in A.D. 597. In the north, Bishop Aidan travelled from Iona across the Lowlands of Scotland to establish some four miles north of the 'royal city' of Bamborough a monastery at Lindisfarne, where in the words of the Venerable Bede: 'As the tide ebbs and flows, this place is surrounded by sea twice a day like an island and twice a day the

Uncial handwriting from a sixth-century manuscript

Rustic roman capitals, third or fourth century

Half-uncial handwriting, seventh century

Irish half-uncial handwriting, eighth century

sand dries and joins it to the mainland.'[1]

In this somewhat bleak northern sanctuary, Aidan built up his monastic community, with a scriptorium, where his monks wrote in their fine Irish uncials on vellum, copies of the Gospels, in a classical Latin. These scribes also began to decorate their pages with curious strapwork designs and animal forms. The Northumbrian script slowly evolved and developed certain subtle differences from that used by the Irish scribes.

The monastic scriptorium, such as that at Lindisfarne, was the forerunner of the modern printing press. It was concerned, as is the modern press, with the multiplication of texts. The medieval scribe, however, had to be the equivalent of compositor, reader and pressman. On some occasions, he was the illustrator as well. The mass-production copying of the late Middle Ages, where the arts of illumination were usually carried out by outside craftsmen, often itinerant monks or friars, can hardly have been in practice in these early years at Lindisfarne and at the other Northumbrian and Irish monasteries.

Soon the monasteries were producing increasing numbers of copies of the scriptures. The books that the missionaries Hadrian and Theodore had brought from Rome, where the libraries were rich in manuscripts, were illustrated in a classical tradition. This implied that the artists were interested in narrative rather than pattern, and that their representations of the human figure were naturalistic.[2] However before this classical tradition could bite very deeply, a copy of the Gospels now known as the *Book of Durrow* was produced. This was about A.D. 670. It rests today, in company with the *Book of Kells*, in the library of Trinity College, Dublin. It is probably a copy of an Irish manuscript, written in a Northumbrian monastery and its style of decoration is certainly Northumbrian (or Hiberno-Saxon). The strapwork and other decoration is very like that on the jewellery and gold work that was found in the Sutton Hoo burial ship, which was buried in a mound overlooking the upper reaches of the River Deben in Suffolk only a few years before the *Book of Durrow* was produced. Designs incorporating the strapwork interlacing could have been found in may places in the Roman Empire. It was a common feature in mosaic pavements. Not so the interlaced animal forms which have nothing to do with Roman art. They are essentially Anglo-Saxon.[3]

The barbaric Anglo-Saxon form of decoration combined with the classical Roman handwriting (in capital letters) which evolved in Northumbria was further enriched and modified with a mixture of Anglo-Saxon and Celtic influences. Where Anglo-Saxon styles begin and Celtic end it is hard to say for Irish and Northumbrian monks were working together in monasteries in both countries. Books of the Gospels from these times show both Irish and Northumbrian handwriting, in both uncial and half-uncial scripts, as well as texts that belong to

1. *A History of the English Church and People*, Bede, Trs. Leo Sherley-Price. Penguin Books, 1955.
2. *The Sequence of English Medieval Art*, Walter Oakeshott, Faber, 1950.
3. Ibid.

both traditions.[4] The half-uncial was a further development in a search for a more quickly written script.

In A.D. 673, Bede, the greatest scholar of the early Middle Ages, was born at Wearmouth, on the lands of the joint monasteries where he was to spend the whole of his life.

Whilst Bede was writing commentaries on the scriptures, as well as between thirty and forty other works, including his five-volume *History of the English Church and People*,[5] some forty-five miles north of Wearmouth, the monks and illuminators of the monastery at Lindisfarne were writing and decorating the greatest book (at least to survive) of the early Middle Ages. This was the *Lindisfarne Gospels*. An inscription in the book tells us it was written and presumably illuminated, by Eadfrith, the Bishop of Lindisfarne from A.D. 698 to 721, and was bound by Aethelwold, Bishop from A.D. 724 to 740. Whether these worthy bishops actually did the work themselves or merely took the credit for it is debatable. The point has been argued, but it seems more likely that it was their talented monks who did the actual writing, the illumination and the binding. It is a monumental book, to be seen today in its glass case in the prosaic surroundings of the King's Library in the British Museum. In spite of a tradition that it had been dropped in the sea, the vellum pages show little evidence of this. The intricate, entwined animal and abstract decoration follows the manner of the *Book of Durrow*, but the portraits of the Evangelists are Byzantine in character, superbly formalized creations yet with a slight discord of some spindly, broken-backed Greek letter forms, giving the names of the individual characters. This meretricious use of Greek (a language little understood in the West) was due to Irish and not to Byzantine influence.

Northumbrian and Irish books were widely distributed through Western Europe. Copies of the Gospels and other works written in Ireland or Northumbria have rested to this day in the libraries of such monasteries as St Gall in Switzerland, as well as in various other monasteries in Germany and Italy.

In Gaul, Byzantine influences were still effective. The use of Byzantine stylisms and highly decorative drawings of reptiles, birds and fishes, to make up initial letters was commonplace. These zoomorphic initials were used with great effect in the *Sacramentary of Gellone*, which was written in the second half of the eighth century.

On occasions, drawings of human figures, such as that of John the Baptist, appear in these initials, in stiffly formalized positions and coloured like enamelled jewels. The letter forms that lie behind these contorted creatures were haphazardly based on both roman and uncial alphabets.

During the eighth century, and almost entirely through the work of English missionaries working among the heathen Franks (the Germanic tribes that lived between the river Main and the North Sea), Britain established a close relationship

4. Ibid.
5. *A History of the English Church and People*, Bede. A Translation by Leo Sherley-Price. Penguin Books, 1955.

with Pepin the Short and his Frankish court. Pepin's son Charles (Charlemagne, A.D. 742–814) followed his father's lead and maintained these connections with the English. The Frankish court was not exactly a cultural centre and Charles grew up barely able to read or write. However he was a man of Utopian vision and, as a result of a visit to Rome in A.D. 774, he set himself the task of spreading Christianity and learning among his peoples. To do this meant establishing a common written language and a script that could be easily learned and read. It also meant the transcription and preservation of the classics.

Charlemagne's renaissance of learning was the result of calculated intentions, put into effect by court orders and decrees and also by attracting to his court scholars from Britain, Ireland and Italy, countries where monastic schools had survived. Their scholarship was limited to the Latin tongue, for the Greek world had become completely cut off from Europe. Charlemagne's visiting scholars included the Italian grammarians, Peter of Pisa and Paul the Deacon, and Paul's friend Alcuin of York.

Charlemagne's empire was ultimately to stretch from the Bay of Biscay to the Elbe and from the Eider river to the river Ebro in Spain, and also to include the Northern part of Italy. It covered much the same ground as the modern European Common Market.

Before Charlemagne could take any active steps in forwarding this educational programme, he was approached by three Saracen chiefs from Spain, who came asking for help against the tyrannical Caliph of Cordova. An extension of Charlemagne's boundaries was to be the reward for this military aid. In A.D. 778 Charlemagne marched his armed forces across the Pyrenees into Spain and took Pampaluna. The expedition met with some reverses and as a result of little local support came to a stop before Saragossa. Here news of a Saxon revolt along the banks of the Rhine caused Charlemagne to withdraw.

As the Franks were marching back through a narrow pass in the Pyrenees, near Roncesvalles, the rearguard was ambushed and wiped out by a detachment of Basques. One of those killed was Roland, the Margrave of the Breton March. This relatively very minor foray resulted in one of the greatest epics of the Middle Ages, the eleventh-century *Chanson de Roland*.[6]

Charlemagne's chief agent in his educational programme was the Abbot Alcuin, who had been born in York in A.D. 735. When Alcuin was still only seventeen or eighteen years of age, he accompanied Aelbert, his school master, to Rome in a search for classical manuscripts. These two scholars must have travelled by packhorse and on foot along the old trade routes down the Rhone valley and then either through the Ligurian Alps, or they may have sailed direct from Marseilles to Ostia. On their return to York, Aelbert was made Archbishop and Alcuin succeeded him as headmaster of the Episcopal school.

6. The *Chanson de Roland* is a French *Chanson de geste* of about 4,000 lines; the oldest known text of it is in the Bodleian Library, Oxford. This text was first printed in 1837, by Francisque Michel in Oxford. The scene of the disaster is thought to be the Val Carlos on the road from Pampaluna to St Jean Pied de Port.

B*

3 The eighth-century *Sacramentary of Gellone*, written in a
Merovingian script, during the last years of Pepin the Short and
decorated with zoomorphic initials. The letter L in the form of
an ox and the letter I in the form of a man with an eagle's head.
Bibliothèque Nationale

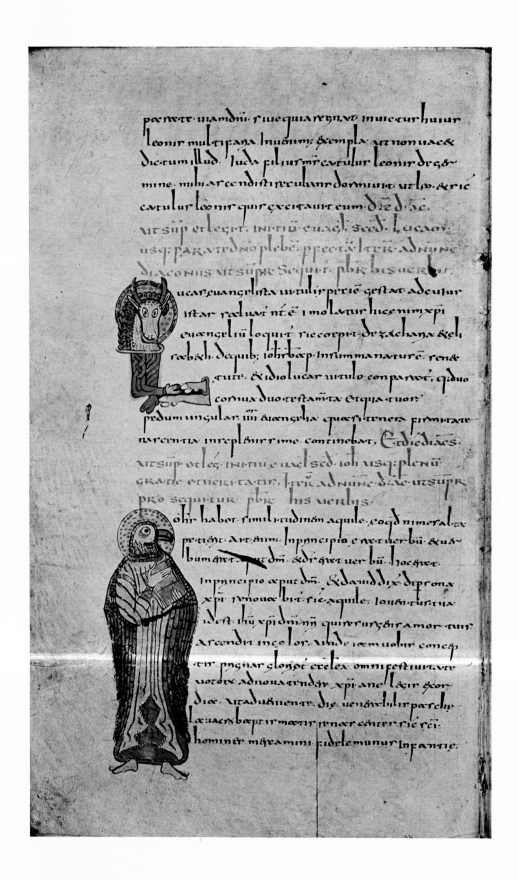

4 Decorated initials from the eighth-century *Sacramentary of Gellone* with the letter I in the form of a saint and two versions of the letter E made up of fishes. In this prayer book the initials are not only in the form of saints, birds, fishes and oxen, but also are made up from drawings of snakes, rodents, horses, sheep and dogs. *Bibliothèque Nationale*

In A.D. 780 Alcuin again visited Rome. On his return journey, at Pavia, he was presented to Charlemagne.

Charlemagne was impressed with this much travelled school-master-cleric and persuaded him to come to his court. On Alcuin accepting, Charlemagne made him the Abbot of the Abbeys of Ferrières and Troyes. He was to make sure that divine service was properly conducted and that the Gregorian chant was sung; he was to produce a definitive text of the scriptures, to create schools, to revive learning and to establish classical Latin as the written language. Alcuin organized his first school in the palace for the royal children and their friends and then founded another school at Tours. These were to be the forerunners of many other and similar schools.

Alcuin suited the teaching programme to the needs of his students, dividing up the spheres of study into reading, writing, singing, the liberal arts and the Holy Writ. The first need for his educational programme was a supply of books. Alcuin sent to Britain and to Ireland, to Italy and to Spain for books for his scriptorium to copy. These were not limited to books of the liturgy or to comments on the scriptures, but also included such classical writings as had survived from ancient Rome. In time the more precious of these books were copied, decorated and illustrated with ever-growing splendour.

In A.D. 789, Charlemagne sent out an edict to his bishops, that schools on the model of the one at Tours should be established in every diocese declaring: 'Because it is our duty at all times to improve the state of our churches, we are concerned to restore with vigilant zeal the teaching of letters, which has fallen into abeyance through the negligence of our ancestors.'[7]

The teaching methods established by Alcuin were influenced by the traditions originated by Bede and made use of both biblical and classical texts. A text would be read by the student, or his master, and would then be analysed for grammar, rhetoric and dialectics. Such discussion and reasoning provided the basis for all schools not only in Carolingian times, but throughout the Middle Ages. 'It was a determining factor in the development of the human mind.'[8]

By A.D. 790 the first phase of Alcuin's work was completed and he returned to Northumbria. However he was quickly recalled, for Charlemagne needed his help in dealing with various heresies in which his clergy were beginning to indulge. A year or so later, Alcuin returned once again to his beloved north country. This visit was but a short one, for disturbances in Northumbria made it advisable for him to return to the Continent. Not long after his return, the Danes landed on the Northumbrian coast and sacked and plundered Lindisfarne Abbey.

Charlemagne meanwhile had presented Alcuin with the great Abbey of St Martin at Tours. Here Alcuin worked at his abbey school and in the scriptorium, where he had manuscripts

7. *The Civilization of Charlemagne*, Jacques Boussard: World University Library, Weidenfeld and Nicolson, 1968.
8. Ibid.

femper prole fecund&·fida·fpa.
&caritatif uof munere repleat·
&fuae muobif benedicaonifdo
na infundat· A M E N

Carolingian script

9. *The Awakening of Europe*. Philippe Wolff, Penguin Books, Harmondsworth, 1968.
10. The term 'Merovingian' originated with a barbarian king, Clovis (A.D. 481–511). Clovis, the leader of the Salian Franks, a Germanic tribe, married to a Burgundian princess, who was a staunch Christian, was the founder of the Merovingian dynasty and of Christian supremacy in Europe. Clovis put himself at the head of the Church, the only existing literate body of men who could understand the ways of Roman government and Roman law. He, a Teuton, set the seal on the Mediterranean character of medieval France.
11. Philippe Wolff.

of the Gospels and other works copied. In attempting to produce a definitive text of the Bible, Alcuin had to cope with a number of conflicting texts. However, he was able to sift from much material the only reliable original text, that of St Jerome, which had been compiled at the end of the fourth century. Alcuin's final text has provided the textual basis of the Bible until the publication of *The New English Bible* in 1970.

At the Abbey of St Martin, Alcuin had over two hundred monks, many of them working in the scriptorium. The French historian, Philippe Wolff, describes such a workshop: 'We can picture the studio, a biggish room, its size depending on the number of copyists, although not all of these would be working at the same time. The monk in charge, who was the librarian as well, dealt out the work. It was rare for a whole manuscript to be entrusted to a single scribe . . . generally the sheets of the text to be copied would be distributed amongst the scribes, who had to take great care with their spacing in order to finish the page on the same word.'[9] Wolff also tells of a 218-page, 20-lines-to-the-page, copy of St Augustine's *Commentary*, which in A.D. 823 had been written in 7 days and corrected on the eighth by the same scribe. This is at the rate of 30 pages per day. The scriptorium at Tours became the equivalent of a modern printer, publisher and bookseller all under one roof. The manuscripts were accurate, the texts were carefully collated, the spelling was consistent and so was the actual handwriting. The calligraphy that Alcuin's scribes used was a great improvement on the confused and cluttered Merovingian script[10], or on the angular Irish hand. It was a combination of two alphabets, the Northumbrian half-uncial book hand of the *Lindisfarne Gospels* used for the rapidly written but extremely legible, rounded and separate small letters; and formal, slowly-made roman capitals. This hand, now called the Carolingian script, is the basis of all modern European printed letter forms. However much doubt the typographers of the twentieth-century Bauhaus may have had about the need for two alphabets, Alcuin's standardized double alphabet has proved its worth for over a thousand years. His was the greatest contribution before the age of printing to the arts of communication, for he had established Latin as a general written language and had formed a script that could be universally understood wherever man could read or write. The introduction of Alcuin's combined alphabet can rank with the invention of printing as one of the two most important events 'in the growth of a civilization based on the written word.'[11]

As for the decorations in the Carolingian books, these to some extent followed the pattern of the Charlemagne classical revival. The texts were copies of classical manuscripts, the decorations were also in the classical style. Alcuin's *emigré* Northumbrian illuminators had to forget their interlaced strapwork and intertwined animal forms and turn to the formal but naturalistic classical style of illustration. Art gave substance to ideas which the limited intellects of the time found difficulty in understanding. Art became an essential feature in education. A comparison with today's use of visual aids in teaching is very striking. The style of illustration had nothing to do with aesthetics. It was to bring reality, by following Byzantine and classical models, into pictures of events in the scriptures. The abstract designs of the illustrations in the *Lindisfarne Gospels* were set aside. The Carolingian artists breathed life into their pictures with much greater success than their Roman, Greek or Byzantine predecessors had ever done. The workshops that produced this work were attached to great monasteries such as those at Aix-la-Chapelle, Rheims, Salzburg, St Gall and Tours. The finest surviving example of the work of the Tours scriptorium was the Bible of Charles the Bald, written and decorated in the mid-ninth century. It was Irish in the style of its decoration yet it used classical roman capitals for the richly decorated initials, and had vividly realistic illustrations. At Lindisfarne and York, and Iona as well, the old barbaric style continued and was to persist for the next hundred years.

After Alcuin had returned to Tours, he continued to correspond with Charlemagne. Over two hundred of his letters have survived, many to Charlemagne, some to his friends in England and also to his friend and pupil Arnulf of Salzburg. These letters were first collected and published in 1617 and a fuller and better edition was issued by Froben from Ratisbon in 1777. These letters describe graphically the social and literary problems of the time. Alcuin also wrote Latin grammars and works on rhetoric and poetry, including a history in verse of the Church at York. Alcuin spent his last days peacefully at his Abbey at Tours. Blind and full of years he died on Whit Monday in A.D. 804.

Charlemagne's renaissance was a conscious reaction against barbaric anarchy. It was based on an understanding of the Holy Writ and a belief in the civic virtues of classical Rome. There was a parallel renaissance in Byzantium where the natural leaning of the Macedonian dynasty towards Oriental art was upset by a revival of interest in the work of ancient Greece and in the Greek language and literature. At the same time, an explosion of learning happened in Baghdad to add further lustre to Haroun-al-Raschid's reign. The capture of Turkestan by the Arabs in A.D. 751 led to the introduction of the Chinese art of paper-making to Baghdad, which, because of its relative cheapness, proved to be a vital factor in book production.

In Europe, Charlemagne's schools, Alcuin's stabilizing of Latin, the Carolingian script and the ubiquitous monks were dominating intellectual life. New monasteries were built in every part of the empire where the new and civilized ways of life could be taught afresh.

The prevailing religious order was Benedictine. Northumbrian and Irish Benedictine monks were teaching, studying, writing and establishing libraries at various monasteries, including Reichenau and St Gall. The libraries were the essential element in this renaissance of learning, though the process of actually borrowing books was complicated, for it was only by hearsay or enquiry that a scribe would know that a certain text that he needed was in such and such a monastery.

By the time of Alcuin's death, the various European languages had become consolidated. Those within the boundaries of the old Roman Empire (excluding Britain) were based on Latin, but with variations as diverse as modern French is to Portuguese or Italian to Spanish. In Britain, with the departure of the Roman legions, Latin as a spoken tongue ceased to be used in everyday life. However, the monks continued to learn Latin as a language to write and in which to say their religious services. This Latin remained reasonably unadulterated, unlike the Continental vernaculars which were subject to the constant change of daily use by illiterate people. It was this relatively pure classical Latin that Alcuin taught to Charlemagne's priests and monks. It became and remained the international language of educated Europeans until the time of Queen Elizabeth I. It remained in use in the Catholic Church until 1968.

Within a few decades of Charlemagne's death in A.D. 814, his empire began to crumble as the result of invasions, in the east from the Hungarian plains, and in the south because of the devastation caused by Saracen pirates. In A.D. 853 Norman ships came sailing and rowing up the Loire to Tours, and like their Viking forbears proceeded to pillage and rape. Alcuin's great monastery with its archives and library was burned to the ground. Many other monasteries, mostly built of wood, went the same way, but a few survived. History was repeating itself and once again the Benedictine monks became the only guardians of the written word, of culture and of the scriptures. England, meanwhile, was again coming under pressure from the Picts in the north and from the piratical Norsemen on the east coasts. The marauding Viking longboats came from the Norwegian fjords, from Jutland and from the Friesian Isles. They penetrated the Suffolk and Essex estuaries and sailed up the Thames, laying waste the riverside villages. Panic spread before them, for, after about two hundred years of freedom from invasion the terror of the 'sea wolves' was present again. Slowly over three-quarters of a century the invaders were absorbed by the conquered. Christian worship reappeared, government was re-established but, when Alfred came to the throne of Wessex, he bemoaned the fact that Britain, in Carolingian times the leader of Europe in culture and scholarship, now, not much more than a century afterwards, had to send to the Continent for Frankish teachers and preachers.

But it was King Alfred, not his Frankish schoolmasters, who did most for English culture. He either translated himself, or ordered the translation, editing and expansion with comment of Bede's *History*. Alfred's version of Bede's great work was the forerunner to the *English Chronicles*, itself the first Northern European history to be written in the speech of the country. A national literature had already begun. Alfred only ruled a southern England that reached in the east up to the Suffolk Stour, in the middle to the Thames valley and in the west to the Bristol Channel and the borders of Cornwall. A rough and ready political order prevailed, but after Alfred's time, as a result of the fears and insecurities aroused by the various invasions, men increasingly turned to a feudal system for protection. From the arrival of the Danish King Canute (1016), a period of peaceful and orderly government began. For the next two and a half centuries, apart from the painful episode of the Norman Conquest and some disturbances under King Stephen, there was in England a time of growing prosperity and peace. Farming increased, forests were cleared, marshes drained.

London had long been a busy centre of commerce. The ports of Lynn, Boston and Ipswich on the east coast and Rochester on the Medway began to import a wide variety of goods from Scandinavia, the Low Countries and even from the Near East. The main export was wool. The great East Anglian wool trade was already established, though it had by no means reached its zenith.

In Gaul, the estuary of the Seine had fallen to the Viking longships. France ceded this piece of the coast which became the Northman's Land or Normandy. Slowly, Norse leaders were absorbed, eventually into becoming feudal French nobles. They adopted Christianity, at first with reluctance, then avidly. They built churches and monasteries and they invited schoolmasters from abroad. In 1045, Lanfranc, a Lombard from Pavia in Italy, founded a school at Bec, which became famous throughout Europe. Lanfranc might be considered as one of the outriders of the Renaissance. The rebirth of learning was beginning. Lanfranc was succeeded as Prior of Bec by an even more famous scholar, another Italian called Anselm, who came from Aosta. Anselm was one of the first to lay the foundations of the theology of the late Middle Ages.

At the same time, the building of monasteries and indeed of cities developed at a great pace. The Romanesque church of this time was a structure that owed its unity to its function, its order and its proportion. Its design was based on arithmetical proportion. Transepts were the same width as the nave; the nave twice the width of the aisles. The plan was that of a cross, the structure massive with great circular pillars supporting semi-circular arches and a semi-circular vaulted roof. Such ornament as these buildings had, when not limited to geometrical shapes, made use of formalized vegetable and animal forms; the influence of the Lindisfarne style persisted.

The Norman Conquest of Britain in 1066 introduced the French
language to court and government and led to new Gothic
styles in building, but it made little difference to the appearance
of English illuminated manuscripts. What has been called the
Age of Innocence was coming to an end, to be succeeded by an
age of learning, as well as an age of town and city building. The
Norman Conquest also brought in its train a considerable
immigration from the Continent of traders, artisans and artists.
Amongst these traders were colonies of Jews, who did much
to enrich English life, helping to finance the building of great
cathedrals.

Winchester, the capital of Anglo-Saxon England, had two
monasteries, the Priory of St Swithun and the New Minster.
The church of the Priory of St Swithun was rebuilt after the
Conquest and after many alterations and additions, is the great
cathedral of today. Beautifully illuminated books survive from
both these monasteries. The drawings that decorate them range
from the severely classical to the lively and humanistic. They
are witty and cartoon-like in style and so could be read without
difficulty.

The early medieval artist did not have to worry about how
unrealistic his pictures were, for in an age of faith, the faithful
needed only the lightest props, or the most formalized figures,
to remind them of whatever story the picture had to tell. As
people became more sophisticated, pictures became more
naturalistic, the artists treating their subjects as though they
were part of everyday life. They made little demand on the
imagination, but were often revealing representations of the
life of the times.

The first phase of the illuminated books from Winchester is
represented by the *Benedictional of St Aethelwold*, written by the
scribe Godeman, who later became Abbot of Thorney. This
was produced between the years A.D. 963 and 984. The pictures
are a development from the Carolingian style, yet Hiberno-
Saxon influences are here and abstract decoration overpowers
classical illustration. It is a rich, almost indigestibly florid book,
with a text written in black, red and gold. Forty or fifty years
later there is a complete change of style. The *Liber Vitae* from
the New Minster is filled with line drawings of smiling angels
and such illustrations as a happy free-for-all contest, with St
Peter giving the Devil a poke on the nose with his outsize key.
These lively drawings are in sepia ink, sometimes with the
addition of a little local colour. Yet, a century later, the heavy
solemnity of the Romanesque period is casting a gloom over
the illustrations in a bible from the Old Minster. These are
superbly formalized line drawings of battles, deaths and en-
tombments and there is not a smile on any face. Apprehension
seems to be the dominant note. They probably had not much to
smile about.

Until this time all the works of the scriptorium, texts or

illuminations, were done by the monks themselves. From the twelfth century onwards, much of this work was carried out by freelance scribes and artists, who used to travel from monastery to monastery and town to town for this purpose.

In the first years of printing, most of the texts used had been written long before Gutenberg's invention. Many of these texts were tales of chivalry, of troubadours and Courts of Love. In *Cligés*, the twelfth-century French poet Chrétien de Troyes describes the troubadourish, Courts of Love existence of the French aristocracy in the late Middle Ages. It was a world of pretty make-believe. In the tale, Cligés, the hero, has as a servant, John, who was a prototype of the Pre-Renaissance artist, skilled beyond belief both as a sculptor and painter, world-famous and yet without any social status and ranked as a serf, on the same level as the farm hands and kitchen maids. It seems an improbable state of affairs.[11]

The golden age of the troubadours lasted until the early years of the thirteenth century. Provence was their happiest playground, for it was also a golden age for the Provençal nobility. Courts of Love were established at places such as Les Baux, which lies high in the Provençal hills, some twenty kilometres south of Avignon. At such courts, the noble ideals of chivalry were practised amongst much pageantry. These gentle influences drifted northwards and became a part of the life of the courts of Burgundy and England. The Arthurian legend played a recurring part in this romantic movement.

An interest in the heroic exploits of Roland and Oliver or the courtly love of Launcelot and Gwenever went hand in hand with all the fanciful trappings of tournament and court life. It is comparable in many ways to the Italian Renaissance; in fact, as Johan Huizinga wrote: 'It is a naïve prelude to it. In reviving chivalry the poets and the princes imagined they were returning to antiquity. (It was) a world disguised in the fantastic gear of the Round Table.'[12]

This belief in the practice of chivalry and tournaments and courtly love was further strengthened when in 1280, the *Roman de la Rose* was published. The *Roman* had been begun by Guillaume de Lorris in 1240 and was finished by Jean Chopinal forty years later. This book of lyrical and erotic poetry exercised a remarkable influence on aristocratic life, not only when it first appeared but for the next two hundred years. It confused most happily apparent saintliness with lusty sensuality. The book is full of allegory, with such characters as *Bel-Accueil*, *Doulce Mercy* and *Humble Requeste*. *Danger* represented a very jealous husband.

To match the chivalry and the romance of court and tournament, the extravagance of the Gothic movement in architecture was spreading from France across northern Europe. And it was in a Gothic manner that printing was first to appear.

Romanesque art was, in its essentials, an attempt to recreate

11. *Gothic*, George Henderson. Penguin Books, 1967.
12. *The Waning of the Middle Ages:* J. Huizinga. First published in 1924. Penguin Books, 1965.

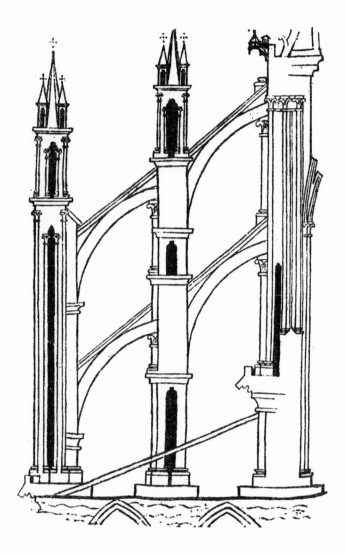

Architectural drawing of Rheims Cathedral, showing flying buttresses by Villard de Honnecourt, the architect possibly in charge of the building of the churches at Cambrai and St Quentin. *Bibliothèque Nationale*

the formality and order of the designs of ancient Rome. Gothic art, in complete contrast to Mediterranean rationalism, was romantic, yet paradoxically scientific, a flight of fancy inspired by nature. With reference to Gothic architecture, the rather boring simile of 'Nature's Cathedral' had more than a little truth in it.

Though the Gothic style might appear to have come out of the forest walks, its architects must have been engineers with some training in strains and stresses. This often apparently frivolous style, of much be-pinnacled flying buttresses, towering slender shafts and soaring steeples, was basically functional.

The hundred and forty-five foot nave at Amiens or the four-hundred foot steeple at Salisbury (both buildings were started in the same year of 1220) are relatively sophisticated constructions, unmatched by anything until Eiffel built his tower or the first skyscrapers appeared on Manhattan.

The first great centre for this Gothic style was the Ile-de-France, an area of countryside around Paris, bounded in the north by Picardy, in the west by Normandy, in the east by Champagne and in the south by Orléanais and Nivernais. Gothic cathedrals were built here at Paris, Bourges, Chartres and beyond these borders at Amiens and Rheims. In the earliest of these buildings, to add to the feeling of height, windows were tall and narrow, but during the fourteenth and fifteenth centuries, glass began to replace the stone of the walls so that through great windows, filled with richly coloured glass, the buildings were flooded with light in all the colours of the spectrum. The familiar comparison between the coloured glass, heavily leaded, of a cathedral such as Chartres and a manuscript of the late Middle Ages is reasonable enough. The leading has an affinity to the compressed textura letters, the coloured glass to the rubrics and illuminations. The cathedral at Chartres, with something like eight thousand sculptured or painted figures, was certainly intended to be 'read' by the illiterate as if it was a great book. This building is a reflection of a new awareness both of the ancient worlds of Greece and Rome, of Plato, Aristotle and Pythagoras and of a search for a new order of design.

The Carolingian script changed with the times, slowly evolving into a Gothic mould. The letters became narrower and more angular. In the fourteenth century, with the greatly increased use of paper (instead of parchment), manuscripts proliferated and the writing varied from hurried scribbles to superb, formal scripts. New fashions for rounded, tall, condensed or spiky letters came and went in different localities. In Italy there was the Gothic-roman of the early humanists, and in the north, the rotunda. In Germany scripts became more rounded, reverting a little to the Carolingian model. In the Netherlands, the vertical textura was widely used, showing a marked similarity to the vertical stresses of Gothic architecture.

6 *Courts of Love:* a sixteenth-century Flemish conception. *April* illustration from the *Kalendar* of Simon Benninck (1483 – 1561). *Victoria and Albert Museum*

7 Lindisfarne Abbey, Northumberland, a nineteenth-century engraving of the ruins of the late Norman Abbey, which are on the site of St Cuthbert's monastery. *National Monuments, Crown Copyright*

8 *Lindisfarne Gospels:* portrait of St Matthew with 'broken-backed' Greek titling. *British Museum*

9 The Chinese *Diamond Sutra:* illustration and part of the text. A.D. 868. *British Museum*

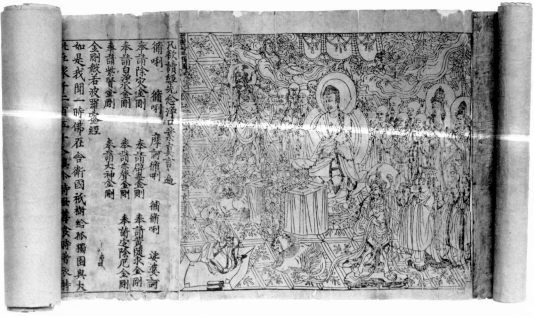

10 The Lion of St Mark from *The Book of Durrow*. Northumbrian c. A.D. 670. Showing interlaced strapwork borders. *Trinity College Library, Dublin*

11 Geometrically patterned mosaic pavement from the Roman villa at Bignor, Sussex

12 Purse-lid made of gold and inlaid with garnets and glass from the burial ship at Sutton Hoo, Suffolk. Seventh century A.D. *British Museum*

13 Incised roman capitals from Trajan's Column

16 South Nave, Durham Cathedral, built between 1099 and 1133.
Tomb of Lord John Neville. *Edwin Smith*

17 The 106-foot-high Nave of Chartres Cathedral, re-built between 1194 and 1260. *French Tourist Office*

19 *Roman de la Rose*, c. 1500. Flemish manuscript: the illustration shows Venus in a cart pulled by doves. *British Museum*

20 A detail from a stained glass window in La Sainte Chapelle, in Paris (c. 1244). *Draeger*

21 Textura script. c. 1400

Details from the sketchbook of Villard de Honnecourt. c. 1225–50. The architect attaches a note to these drawings in which he says: 'Here begins the method of drawing as taught by the art of geometry to facilitate working.' *Bibliothèque Nationale*

The textura script had tall, narrow, black letters, spaced with immaculate precision – hence the name – for it could be thought to resemble the texture of a woven cloth.[13]

The Gothic movement in France came in with an age of restless excitement. It was an age of agricultural development and urban expansion. The Gothic artist liberating himself from a stylistic preoccupation with the past could look afresh at the world around him. In sculpture, the carved images of saints and of Christ and Virgin, were changing in the most subtle manner. The severely formalized, hieratical figures of the Romanesque were becoming more human, gentler and often smiling. It was a reflection of the new age. The artist was looking for his models at pretty girls in the street, rather than gloomily repeating symbolic figures and conventional poses, previously used as memory aids for the illiterate.

The architects of the Ile-de-France and their artists and craftsmen were inventing a new language of design. By logical thought and careful analysis of the vault and the pointed arch, they designed and built buildings that could satisfy the emotional needs of man so that he could, at least in his imagination, soar heavenwards in company with the towers and the steeples.

Paris had become the intellectual and book centre of the Western World. Saint Thomas Aquinas had been teaching at the University since 1257, the year in which the College of the Sorbonne was established in the Latin quarter. St Thomas Aquinas through his knowledge of Greek literature sought to bridge the gap between the classical thought and the Christian teaching of the late Middle Ages. But his *Summa Theologica* was only one of the stream of religious books that were pouring out from the University.

The Gothic architectural style spread quickly across Europe to find its most powerful expression in Germany and its most pleasant in England. Of all the countries of Europe only Italy had no use for it, for already by the mid-thirteenth century there was in Italy a fresh preoccupation with the culture of ancient Rome and Greece. This was nothing new, there was no invention here but only a renewal of the old classical traditions. Yet here was the great divide. The Florentine doctrine of humanism was soon to banish the Gothic to northern fastnesses where it was not to reassert itself with any effect until the nineteenth century. It was then, however, to provide a springboard in those northern countries for a counter-renaissance – the modern movement in architecture, design and lettering.

By the end of the thirteenth century, European contacts with Asia were being made. The Venetian traveller, Marco Polo, in 1271 whilst still a boy had set off on his travels to the Far East. His itineraries sound like something out of the *Arabian Nights*. Marco Polo found a China incomparably more civilized than

13. *Die Schriftentwicklung.* H. E. Meyer. Graphis Press, Zurich, 1958.

the Europe of his time. China also had had her dark ages, largely coinciding with the anarchy that prevailed in Europe after the decline of the Roman Empire. Buddhism in north China, like Christianity in the West, had managed to survive through these years. With the establishment of the T'ang dynasty (A.D. 618–906), peace and prosperity came to the empire. Buddhism spread and art and learning flourished. The T'ang emperors acted in much the same way as Charlemagne, extending and consolidating their empire, which reached from Korea to East Turkistan, and included the whole of China and most of Indo-China. Expeditions crossed the Himalayas into Kashmir and in order to contain the growing territorial ambitions of the Arabs, a Chinese army travelled as far west as Samarkand.

Like Charles the Great, the T'ang emperors were good patrons of religion, learning and the arts. T'ai Tsung (A.D. 627–649) built a library to contain between 50,000 and 60,000 manuscript rolls of paper, at a time when paper was an unknown commodity in Europe. It had already been in use in China for five hundred years. Tradition has it that in the year A.D. 105, the eunuch Ts'ai Lun reported the invention of paper to his emperor. Eunuchs, with little to occupy their minds, seemed to have been prone to intrigue. Ts'ai Lun was no exception and became involved in some squabble between the Empress and the aged grandmother of the Emperor. Finding himself too deeply involved with these royal ladies and to avoid any further embarrassment 'He went home, took a bath, combed his hair, put on his best robes and drank poison.'[14] Perhaps it may be some posthumous consolation to Ts'ai Lun that he has been deified as the God of Papermakers.

Paper was made in China from many materials, including plant fibres, hemp and rags; it was sized and loaded with filling; it was coloured and made in many weights and textures; it was used for writing, for wrapping and for domestic purposes.

In the eighth century, the secrets of papermaking reached the Arabs at Samarkand in Turkestan, the methods of manufacture being taught to the Arabs by Chinese prisoners. Mills were soon established in Turkestan and the papers of Samarkand became widely famous. Mills were also started in Baghdad. Haroun-al-Raschid imported Chinese workmen experienced in the craft to work in these mills. The craft of papermaking finally reached Europe in the twelfth or thirteenth centuries when the Moors passed the knowledge to the Spanish. The paper that Gutenberg printed on at Mainz in the fifteenth century was made in the same manner as that in use in China a thousand years earlier.

In the West, when we talk of the birth of printing, we think of the fifteenth-century printers of the Rhine Valley and above all of Gutenberg who perfected a method of casting the letters of our alphabet into movable type. In the Far East, the birth of

14. *Essai sur L'histoire du Papier.* Blanchet, Augustin, Paris, 1900.

rinting happened the first time anyone made an impression rom a clay or wood block, which was about six hundred years efore Gutenberg was born.

n China, with over forty thousand different symbols or ideoraphs, the production of movable types was unlikely to ntecede the wooden block on which could be cut a whole page f words.

he first printed impressions, however, were little more than he equivalent of the modern rubber stamp. They were made rom wooden charm seals, originally used for stamping in clay. hese were dipped in red ink and impressed on paper. This was ne precedent for printing; the other was ink-rubbing. The Chinese used to take impressions from carved stone inscriptions y laying damp paper over the surface of the stone, brushing it vell into the letters and then wiping ink over the back of the aper so that the text stood out white against the inked paper. he first Chinese printers had a ready supply of block cutters, or the Confucian classics were usually cut in wood but were not ntended for printing.

he invention of block printing is attributed to Fêng Tao. The nk he used was comparable to our Indian ink or the more ppropriately named French *l'Encre de Chine*.[15]

t was quite unlike European printing ink, which depends on n oily base. It gave a clean, crisp impression from the woodlock, which was of pear or jujube wood, but was unsuitable or printing from metal.

A skilled block printer could take about 2000 impressions in a lay. The oldest known printed text is the Chinese *Diamond utra*, dated A.D. 868. It was printed from large wood blocks on sheets 30 inches by 12 inches, which were pasted together to nake a roll 16 feet long. The text is based on 'a section of the Buddhist scriptures, which was a favourite subject with early rinters consisting of discourses of Buddha on the subject of he non-existence of things.'[16] The *Diamond Sutra* was probably rinted in the province of Szechwan which was the centre of rinting in western China in the ninth century.

Of the many wonders Marco Polo recorded, the most revealing o our purpose was his description of the printed paper money n common use in China since the latter part of the tenth entury. He was clearly intrigued not only by its use, but also oy the possibilities of unlimited riches that it offered to the Great Khan. Marco Polo says the actual paper used for the noney was made from the bark of the mulberry tree. It was a olack paper and was impressed in red ink with the official seal. Anyone found forging these notes was promptly executed.[17]

What printed texts Marco Polo may have seen he does not tell us, nor does he mention the actual printing process. Printing rom movable types, cast in earthenware, had been invented by a certain Pi Shêng, in the middle of the 11th century and though ome experiments had been made in the use of tin types, the

15. *L'Encre de Chine* was made from lampblack, collected from an iron funnel placed over a bowl of oil in which were several lighted wicks. The lampblack was mixed up by means of pestle and mortar with gum or gluten. The paste was then put into moulds. It hardened into sticks. To use it, the stick was rubbed in water against a smooth stone. The procedure for printing from the woodblocks was as follows: the surface of the block was rubbed over with paste made from boiled rice or size; the writing on very thin paper was pasted to the block, the block was then cut and a printed impression was taken by a man who held in his right hand two brushes, fixed at the opposite ends of the same handle. With one brush he inked the face of the block, with his other hand he laid the paper on the block, then he ran the dry brush over the back of the paper to make the impression.

16. *The Invention of Printing in China, and its Spread Westward*. T. F. Carter. 2nd. edn. revised by L. C. Goodrich. The Ronald Press Company. New York, 1955. Also see *Harunobu and his Age*; D. B. Waterhouse. British Museum, London, 1964.

17. *The Book of Ser Marco Polo the Venetian*. Sir H. Yule, London, 1903.

material in general use was wood, probably boxwood.

In spite of their technological expertise, the Chinese made no
use of the printing press. All their printing was done by brushing or burnishing the backs of the sheets of paper, placed on
the inked types. This method of block printing certainly
reached Europe before the time of Gutenberg.

In northern Europe, the fourteenth century was a time of
commercial growth. The greatest trading company of the time
was the Hanseatic League, which had been founded in Lübeck
and in Hamburg to safeguard the route that connected the
Baltic with the German Ocean. Soon the Hansa traders con-
trolled the Lower Rhine, the main trade artery of northern
Europe, on the banks of which river a century later the first
German printers were to establish themselves. All trade with
England, to the ports of Lynn and Boston, Hull and York,
Norwich, Ipswich and London, and as far west as Bristol, came
under the League's control. In 1343, the League established its
most northerly trading post at Bergen. The towns of the League
reached from Krakow in the east, to the Zuider Zee port of
Amsterdam in the west, to Reval in the north and Göttingen in
the south. The centre of this Hanseatic European trade was
Bruges in Flanders. The system was based on a huge monopoly
intended to cut out any possible competition. It was the tail-end
of medieval town economy. The League reached its peak of
prosperity between 1360 and 1377, in spite of an unsuccessful
war with Holland and the breaking of its Baltic monopoly. The
Dutch, with larger ships, captured the Baltic grain trade and
the French salt trade. They also greatly increased their share in
the North Sea herring fisheries.

The middle classes of Europe were growing in wealth and
status. Geoffrey Chaucer describes them and every other class
of English society in his *Canterbury Tales.* This is life in the raw,
described with zest and truthfulness for the first time in English
literature. His characters range from knight and squire to
weaver, dyer and ploughman, from buxom housewife to parson
and clerk, from wanton friar to carpenter and haberdasher.
Chaucer came from the middle classes. His father was a wine
merchant in Thames Street and Chaucer spent most of his life
in London. At sixteen he became a page to Lionel of Clarence;
he served in the campaign of 1359 and returned to Court under
the patronage of John of Gaunt. He was sent abroad on various
diplomatic missions, including three visits to Italy, in the years
1372, 1374 and 1375. It has been suggested that Chaucer may
have met Boccaccio in Florence, where the memory of Dante
was still alive, and in Padua heard the story of *The Patient
Griselda* from Petrarch himself.

The *Decameron* was the inspiration for the *Canterbury Tales* and
the particular form they should take. Chaucer started work on
the tales soon after his return from his last visit to Italy. The
Peasants' Revolt flared up in 1381 and in the same year John

And at a knyght thennes wille begynne

knyght there was a worthy man
That fro the tyme that he first began

32

Wyclif, the Master of Balliol, started his verbal assaults on the Papacy, and particularly against the Pope's extortionate greed. As a result of the prolonged wars, the University of Paris had lost its intellectual supremacy which had moved to Oxford. And of all the Oxford dons at this time, John Wyclif was the most brilliant. Wyclif's formal pronouncement ridiculing the doctrine of Transubstantiation was the beginning of the Reformation. He became (like Martin Luther) a pamphleteer, demanding the right of every man to read the Bible for himself. Unlike Luther, he did not have the printing press.

The first of Chaucer's tales appeared in 1384, the last in 1391. This brief burst of literary genius was curiously isolated. William Langland's sober poem *Piers Plowman* had appeared in 1377, Froissart's *Chronicle* in 1373. For the next hundred years in England, there was a literary drought. It was a time of civil strife and restraint of political freedom.

In Europe things were moving. It is a pleasant fancy to think that Chaucer on his first visit to Italy may have talked with Francesco Petrarch, who was then an old man. Petrarch had been born in Arezzo in 1304. When Petrarch was nine years old his family had settled in Avignon, in the south of France, which had been the residence of the Popes since the insults to Pope Boniface VIII in the previous year. As a boy he must have watched the building of the Palace of the Popes, one of the great fortresses of the late Middle Ages.

In 1337 Petrarch began a period of solitary study at Vaucluse. However his fame as a poet and a philosopher was spreading. In 1341 he was invited to Rome and was crowned with a Poet's Crown. His oration on this occasion was based on Virgil's words 'Sed me Parnassi deserta per ardua dulcis raptat amor'. The ancient world and the modern world met. This moment could be considered as the beginning of the Renaissance.[18]

Petrarch's great contribution to this new age was to bring his contemporaries into sympathetic contact with the worlds of ancient Greece and Rome. He was a collector of books and old manuscripts and showed that such a collection was more than mere acquisitiveness, that it could lead to serious scholarship. The humanism of Petrarch, the spiritual impetus of Wyclif and his followers known as the Lollards,[19] the counter propaganda of the Catholic Church, the commercial expansion in northern Europe of the Hanseatic League and its successors and the searching for knowledge of the scholars of the Renaissance led to one common medium, the printing press.

The invention of the printing press and movable type marks the dividing point between the arts and crafts of the Middle Ages and modern technology. The printing press was the greatest accelerator of ideas, the greatest propagandist and the greatest selling agent the world had known up to that time. The age when man read the cathedrals like a book was passing, for now he demanded a book of his own.

18. *A Short History of the English People*. J. R. Green, Macmillan, London, 1874.
19. This was a term of abuse, 'lollard' meaning a babbler.

A woodcut illustration of the east bank of the Rhine, showing the
City of Cologne. From *The Cologne Chronicle*. 1499

Printing began amidst the Gothic culture and the busy commerce of Mainz, one of the oldest cities in Germany. Mainz is situated on the west bank of the Rhine at the widest point of its upper course, where it is joined by the Main. This position ensured the city's commercial success, for the Rhine was, and still is, one of the great trade routes of Europe. Every year millions of tons of goods are carried along this river, but before the railway age, in the hundreds of years of trading from the time when the Romans had a fortified camp where Mainz now stands, the Rhine provided the only satisfactory means for the transport of goods up to Basel and the Swiss Cantons or down to the Low Countries, the Hanseatic ports and the North Sea. When the snow was melting in the high Alps of the Grisons, where the Rhine has its source, the river at Mainz could not have been easily navigable, and in the narrows below Mainz navigation against the stream must have come to a stop. Even under normal conditions all ships and barges travelling up stream from Coblenz to Mainz were dragged along by teams of horses.

By the middle of the thirteenth century Mainz was the centre of a powerful federation of Rhenish towns. Its prosperity was so great, that it was known to its neighbours as *goldene* Mainz. Mainz was still a prosperous city when in 1450 the so-called 'Father of Printing' established his press there. By this date, and possibly earlier, Johann Gensfleisch zur Laden, known as Gutenberg after the name of his family home, had solved the problems of casting movable types and printing from them. An astronomical calendar, calculated for the year 1448, had already appeared. This was the first dated piece of European printing. To support his publishing ventures, Gutenberg had borrowed eight hundred guilders from Johann Fust, a Mainz lawyer and moneylender. Gutenberg, after carrying out experiments at Strasbourg, set up his presses at Mainz which was his birthplace, famous for its goldsmiths and fine metal workers.

The technical ingredients for printing and type-founding were at hand. Goldsmiths and jewellers were accustomed to use punches for decorations and for their personal marks. Spherical shot moulds and other similar casting arrangements must have been familiar to the craftsmen of Mainz, though Nuremberg was the main centre for metal manufacturing. Mainz was also between two of the greatest of the Rhine wine districts, the Rheingau in the north and the Rheinhessia in the south.

Wine presses in plenty were at hand, as a source for the mechanical principle used in printing presses. For ink there was the oil paint that had been introduced into picture making by Jan van Eyck some twenty years before Gutenberg first started experimenting. Van Eyck had succeeded in producing a varnish medium for painting by boiling up linseed and nut oils. This, combined with pigment, 'lit the colours up so powerfully that it gave a gloss of itself' (Vasari's *Lives of the painters*, 1550). For printing the only necessary addition to this painting medium was soap, to prevent the type from sticking to the paper. Gutenberg's genius lay in taking these familiar ingredients, amalgamating them and virtually perfecting his craft, with the production of the adjustable type-mould as his great invention. But it was left to others to exploit this invention with its infinite potentialities.

In 1455, or thereabouts, Gutenberg completed the printing of his great 42-line Bible at the very moment when Fust sued him for repayment of his money. This superbly printed Bible, which even included a second colour, a fine vermilion in the first pages of each section, may well have been mistaken for a hand-written manuscript. One of the reasons for this was because of the number of ligatures and variants of character that Gutenberg cut. It was as if he had said to himself, 'anything a scribe can do, I can do'.

From the surviving documents that deal with the complicated wrangles between Gutenberg and Fust, the only salient point to emerge is that Fust failed to get back his capital but succeeded in ending the partnership with Gutenberg. Whether Fust actually bankrupted Gutenberg it is hard to say. The 'Helmer-sperger Instrument', as George Painter says, 'apparently con-demns Gutenberg to forfeit all his equipment . . . like so many medieval documents, is, in fact, not a verdict subsequently executed, but merely a procedural cover for a mutual agree-ment.'[1] So, though on the face of it, it looked as if Fust had bankrupted Gutenberg and deprived him of all his typefaces, punches, matrices and presses, in fact no such thing happened. The partnership was terminated and Gutenberg moved to new premises, taking with him at least a couple of presses and much of his type matter, punches and matrices. He remained in busi-ness at Mainz until 1458 when he moved to Bamberg. A year later he returned to Mainz for a further six years of successful and energetic print production.

In 1465, he retired with a generous 'Civil List' pension from the Archbishop of Nassau which included an annual allowance of two tuns of wine. He enjoyed his pension for only a short while for he died in 1468, aged about 70.

In spite of much investigation, we know tantalizingly little about what went on between 1450 and 1455, the year when the lawsuit brought to an end the Gutenberg-Fust partnership and when about half of Gutenberg's plant was handed over to Peter Schöffer of Gernsheim. Schöffer worked for Fust and later married his daughter, so establishing a precedent of marrying the master's daughter or his widow, that was to recur with monotonous regularity in the printing trade.

Whether Gutenberg's inability or refusal to repay his loans was due to unforeseen expenses in the production of the first of the great bibles that he planned and worked on, or whether Fust's foreclosure had anything to do with the unsettled state of

Der Buchdrucker.

Ich bin geschicket mit der preß
So ich aufftrag den Firniß reß/
So bald mein dienr den bengel zuckt/
So ist ein bogn papyrs gedruckt.

1. 'Quincentenary': George Painter. *The Book Collector*, Spring 1968.

The paper maker. From Joost Amman's *Book of Trades*.
St Bride Printing Library

Germany at that time is not at all clear. In 1448, the Concordat of Vienna was signed by Frederick III and the Pope, healing the schism with Rome and aggravating the unrest that finally led to the Reformation. From 1449 to 1453, a series of tough local wars were fought by a confederation of Swabian and Franconian cities, led by the city of Nuremberg, against a number of princes under the leadership of the future Elector of Brandenburg. These were very much local affrays, between city and local princeling. On the whole, the princes held the balance of power. In 1462, Mainz was devastated in one of these battles through a squabble between two archbishops, Dietrich II of Isenburg and Adolph II of Nassau. The Mainz citizens backed Dietrich, and backed the wrong archbishop. Adolph won and many of the Mainz citizens who had thrown in their lot with Dietrich were exiled. Amongst these were most of Gutenberg's and Fust's pressmen, compositors and foundry workers.

Whatever one may think about Johann Fust and his litigation, he had found in Peter Schöffer a very able printer. The first book to include the name of the printer and to be dated, was a psalter produced by Fust and Schöffer in 1457. It was a most sophisticated piece of work, set in two different founts of type, printed in black and red, with a great number of initial letters, printed separately in red and blue and red and grey. It was 'a full dress performance in which typography was going all out to show what it could do in rivalry of the copyists.'[2]

The craft had been born fully fledged. Jobbing printing now ran side by side with book work. There was a heavy demand for Papal indulgences, pamphlets and calendars. The revenue successes of the Roman Church's mass production of these indulgences was to boomerang in the next century, when Martin Luther used the printing press to propagate his arguments against what he considered was their scandalous misuse. When the first printing presses were established in Germany, the country had already passed through a marked social change. As in France the age of chivalry had passed. The epic poems of Arthur's Round Table, the stories of Parzival and of Tristan, or the Rhenish legends of Siegfried meant nothing to a new reading public, largely made up of the commercially-minded middle classes. There was a demand for popular literature which the printing press was not only to satisfy but to increase to an extraordinary extent by the end of the century. Marshall McLuhan has promoted the intriguing idea that printing created the 'Renaissance Man', whose outlook was personal, and based on visual judgements – a man who read and perhaps believed what he read. This is a thought-provoking, but hardly a fully tenable hypothesis. 'Renaissance Man' was well on the way to finding himself when Francesco Petrarch was crowned in Rome with the Poet's Crown in 1341.

The Italian Renaissance was essentially a Mediterranean culture. Germany still lived in, and remained with, the Gothic culture

2. *Fifty-Five Essays*. Victor Scholderer. Amsterdam, 1967.

of the late Middle Ages. McLuhan substantiates this when he writes: 'The same urge to translate the tactile skills of the Renaissance rituals provided an aesthetic medievalism in the north, and in Italy inspired the recreation of ancient art, letters and architecture. The same sensibility that led the Dukes of Burgundy and Berry to their *très riches heures* led the Italian merchant princes to restore Rome'.[3] The urges may well have been the same, the cultures were fundamentally different. This dichotomy provides an underlying theme in the development of printing. For over five hundred years these two visual cultures have been in conflict, though at times the Gothic has been overwhelmed and has lain submerged, only to struggle to the surface again. With Gutenberg we reached a watershed. Printing began in a Gothic form. The German printer converted into type the Gothic black-letter script in common use. In Germany, as we have noted, these were of different forms and were used for different purposes: the close-knit, appropriately named *textura* for bibles and other liturgical books, the dagger-shaped cursive *bastarda* for the law, and the *rotunda* which was a rounded form, nearer to the original Carolingian scripts on which all these letter forms were based, was used for a wide range of works in the vernacular.

The textura developed into the modern German black letter called Fraktur, the other two – the cursive bastarda and the rotunda – combined to become by the end of the fifteenth century the Schwabacher, originally used like the rotunda, for printing texts in the vernacular. These rich black types were to remain in common use in Germany until well into the twentieth century.

The spirit of humanism which was the essential factor in the life of Renaissance Italy was stoutly resisted by the Germans. The humanist doctrine had led to the rediscovery of the Carolingian hand. This, wedded as it was to the incised capital letters of ancient Rome, provide the basis for the roman hand and the first roman typefaces. S. H. Steinberg explained this enduring use of black letter in Germany, and in the Scandinavian and Slavonic countries in cultural dependence on her. He wrote – 'The original reason for the prevalence of the black letter (in these countries) . . . may be found in the preponderance of theological over humanist writings in Germany. This was backed first by the strictly Thomist teachings of Cologne and later by the Lutheran theology of Wittenberg, two University towns which at the same time were busy centres of printing.'[4] With the sacking of Mainz, the printing craftsmen scattered along the trade routes of Europe: to Cologne in 1465, up the Rhine to Basel in 1466, over the Alpine passes and into Italy, first to Subiaco in 1467, then to Rome and Venice in 1469. After that the trade spread like a bush fire to Nuremberg, Utrecht, Paris, London and Stockholm, and to numerous other cities as well. These itinerant printers went to commercial

Rotunda

Bâtarde

Textura

3. *The Gutenberg Galaxy*: Marshall McLuhan, University of Toronto Press, and Routledge and Kegan Paul, London, 1962.
4. *Five Hundred Years of Printing*: S. H. Steinberg. Penguin Books, 1955. The 'Thomist' teachings referred to are those based on the writings of St Thomas Aquinas.

Glos appellatur mariti foror: atꝗ idem fratris uxor.
Leuir dicitur frater mariti:quafi leuus uir.
Fratriæ appellantur quafi fratrum inter fe uxores.
Amitini fratrum & matris & fœminæ filii.
Patrueles matrum fratrum filii.
Côfobrini ex duabus editi fororibus:de quibus exempla mul╱
ta funt in antiquis auctoribus:& maxime in Affranio:& ui╱
ris uetutiffimis fcriptoribus.

•

NONII MARCELLI PERIPATETICI TIBVRTICEN
SIS COMPENDIOSA DOCTRINA AD FILIVM DE
PROPRIETATE SERMONVM IMPRESSA VENE
TIIS INDVSTRIA ATQVE IMPENDIO NICOLAI
IENSON GALLICI. .M.CCCC.LXXVI.

centres, and not to centres of learning. An exception to this rule
was the ancient Benedictine monastery at Subiaco, near Rome
where Conrad Sweynheim, who may have worked for Fust
and Arnold Pannartz of Cologne, set up a press and printed
four books before moving to Rome in 1467. There they started
printing with a roman typeface, at the same time as the printer
Adolf Rusch began using a roman fount at Strasbourg. Apparently Sweynheim and Pannartz did not prosper. Rome was
of little importance as a commercial centre and they had to
turn to the Pope for assistance.

The introduction of the roman typeface in Italy was hardly
surprising for the roman hand was in common use. It was
apparently unthinkable for the Italians that their humanist
writings should be printed in, to their eyes, the archaic black
letters of the north. The gothic letter was fit only for the
writings of the Church. The strongly humanistic Renaissance
needed the open round letters to express the Florentine's new
open-ended thoughts. Yet these German and French printers
were equally at home with both gothic and roman typefaces.
Jenson, so praised for his fine roman typefaces, used two
gothic faces for *Gratianum Decretum*, the first definitive book
on canon law, which he printed in Venice in 1474. In this work
a large face was used for the text and a small one for the marginal
commentary. The book is a superb piece of printing and just
as handsome as his edition of Cicero's *Epistolae ad Familiares*
which, set in a roman typeface, he printed in the following year.
Apparently there had been some over-production of the
classics by the Venetian printers, for after 1473, they began to
search for other texts to occupy their presses. Mathematics and
the law provided material for these and Jenson presumably
felt that the archaic phraseology of the law needed the archaic
gothic typeface. This use of black letter in legal documents has
continued at least in part until today.

Though in Italy the craft of printing was first established in
Rome, it reached its full flowering not, as one might have expected, in Florence, the centre of humanism, but in the great
trading port of Venice. Venice in the latter part of the fifteenth
century was a bustling exciting place, where speed of production counted for more than leisurely quality. The centre of
the city, from the Doge's Palace and the Piazza di San Marco
to the Ca' d'Oro looked much as it does now.[5] Whilst Renaissance styles were changing the appearance of Rome and
Florence, Venice was still a Byzantine-Gothic city, unique in
the Western world in its amalgam of the two cultures. When by
the end of the fifteenth century the influence of the classical
renaissance began to be felt, Venice produced an architecture
that was peculiarly her own – a halfway stage between
Byzantine-Gothic and a fully classical style. The Venetians
called it Lombardesque after the family of architects, the
Lombardi, who came from the Lake of Lugano and were really

5. The façade of the Doge's Palace dates from 1424; the Ca' d'Oro was
built in 1436.

responsible for this crossbred style. The superb houses that line the Grand Canal and the other waterways were built by the merchant princes, whose fortunes came from the trade with the Levant and with the countries of Northern Europe.

Venice by her victory over the Genoese in 1380 had established her supremacy over the Adriatic and the Mediterranean. She had gained complete control of the trade with the East and had become the shipping port and market for goods both for the Indies and the Near East. By 1420 she had annexed a slice of the mainland to give her control of her landward approaches, her frontier finally running from Monfalcone on the sea coast to the Alps in the north and as far west as the River Po. Constantinople fell to the Turks in 1453 and within a dozen years Venice was at war, trying to protect her trading ports in the Levant. She began to lose ground and had to concede some of her possessions and also to pay dues on goods shipped through the ports. Her prosperity, however, was still very considerable in 1469 when the first printers established themselves there. The first press was set up by John and Wendelin of Speier, who obtained a monopoly for printing in the city-state. However, the monopoly expired on John's death in 1470 and the way was cleared for that most prolific publisher-printer and superb type-cutter, the Frenchman Nicolas Jenson. Before the end of the fifteenth century there were something like 150 separate printing establishments at work, most of them of little note, learning or technical capability. The kind of ambience Jenson was working in was vividly depicted by Vittore Carpaccio whose paintings of the 'Miracle of the Cross at the Rialto' and the 'Story of St Ursula' (Accademia, Venice) are brilliant pictorial reportage of the daily life of fifteenth-century Venice.

To what extent the early Venetian printers divided their printing output between books and job work, it is impossible to say. Obviously, there must have been an ever-increasing demand for the latter, ranging from ships' manifests to notices of sailing times, or from legal documents to leaflets advertising the printers' own books. As for the kind of books they actually printed, John and Wendelin of Speier's first book was Cicero's *Epistolae ad Familiares*, with a first edition of 300, which sold out immediately, to be succeeded by another edition of 300 a few months later.[6] They also published the first edition of Petrarch's *Canzoniere* in Italian.

How Nicolas Jenson reached Venice is not clear. He was born at Sommevaire, near Bar-sur-Aube, and had been Charles VII's Mint Master at Tours. Charles sent him to Mainz to learn how to print. When he arrived in Venice he found backers amongst the German merchants of the Fondaco dei Tedeschi. He soon set up his presses and his foundry. All these early printers had, perforce, to be their own type-founders. His roman typeface is very fine, though the capitals are over large and tend to jump from the page.

6. *Five Hundred Years of Printing*, S. H. Steinberg, Penguin Books, 1955.

39

Præclariſſimus liber elementorum Euclidis perſpi/
caciſſimi:in artem Geometrie incipit quáfoeliciſſime:

Unctus eſt cuius ps nó eſt. ℂLinea eſt
lógitudo ſine latitudine cui⁹ quidé ex/
tremitates ſt duo púcta. ℂLinea recta
é ab yno púcto ad aliũ breuiſſima exté/
ſio í extremitates ſuas ytrũq₃ eoꝝ reci
piens.ℂSupficies é q̃ lógitudiné z lati
tudiné tm h₃:cui⁹termi quidé ſút linee.
ℂSupficies plana é ab yna linea ad a/
liã extéſio í extremitates ſuas recipiés
ℂAngulus planus é duarũ linearũ al/
ternus ꝓtactus:quaꝝ expãſio é ſup ſup/
ficié applicatioq₃ nó directa. ℂQuádo aũt angulum ꝓtinét due
lince recte rectiline⁹ angulus noíaf. ℂMñ recta linea ſup rectã
ſteterit duoq₃ anguli ytrobiq₃ fuerit eq̃les:eoꝝ yterq₃ rect⁹erit
ℂLineaq₃ linee ſupſtás ei cui ſupſtat ppendicularis yocaf.ℂAn
gulus yo qui recto maioꝛ é obtuſus dicif.ℂAngul⁹yo minoꝛ re
cto acut⁹appellaf.ℂTermin⁹é qð yniuſcuiuſq₃ finis é. ℂFigura
é q̃ tmino yl'termis ꝓtinef.ℂCircul⁹é figura plana yna q̃dem li/
nea ꝓtéta: q̃ circũferentia noíaf:in cui⁹medio púct⁹é : a quo'oés
lince recte ad circũferétiã exeũtes ſibiinicez ſut equales. Et hic
quidé púct⁹cétrũ circuli dr.ℂDiameter circuli é linea recta que
ſup ei⁹centꝛ trãſiens extremitateſq₃ ſuas circũferétie applicans
circulũ í duo media diuidit.ℂSemicirculus é figura plana dia/
metro circuli z medietate circũferentie ꝓtenta. ℂPoꝛtio circu/
li é figura plana recta linea z parte circũferétie ꝓtéta: ſemicircu/
lo quidé aut maioꝛ aut minoꝛ. ℂRectilinee figure ſũt q̃ rectis li/
neis cótinenf quarũ quedã trilatere q̃ trib⁹rectis lineis: quedã
quadrilatere q̃ q̃tuoꝛ rectis lineis: q̃dã mltilatere que pluribus
q̃z quatuoꝛ rectis lineis continenf. ℂFigurarũ trilaterarũ:alia
eſt triangulus hñs tria latera equalia.Alia triangulus duo hñs
eq̃lia latera.Alia triangulus triũ inequalium laterũ. Naꝛ iterũ
alia eſt oꝛthogoniũ:ynũ.ſ.rectum angulum habens.Alia é am
bligonium aliquem obtuſum angulum habens.Alia eſt oxigoni
um:in qua tres anguli ſunt acuti. ℂFigurarũ aũte quadrilateraꝛ
Alia eſt q̃dratum quod eſt equilaterũ atq₃ rectangulũ. Alia eſt
tetragon⁹long⁹:q̃ eſt figura rectangula : ſed equilatera non eſt.
Alia eſt helmuaym: que eſt equilatera : ſed rectangula non eſt.

De principijs ꝓ ſe notis:z ꝓmo de diffini
tionibus earundem.

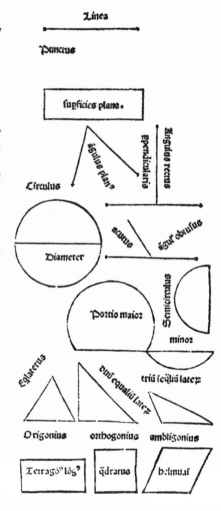

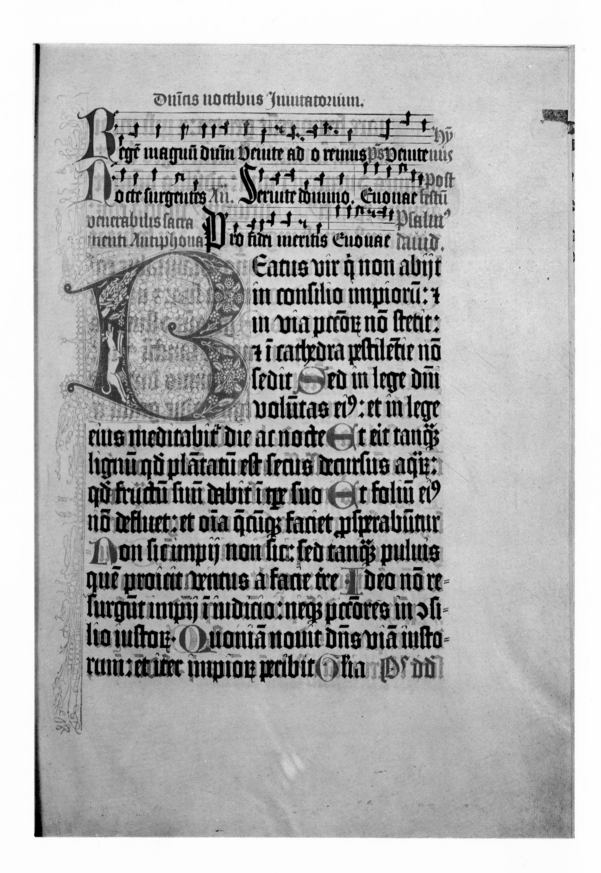

22 A page from the Mainz *Psalter* of 1457. Printed by Johann
Fust and Peter Schöffer. It is the first printed book to state the
name of its printer, the date of printing, and to give a note on the
method of production. *Printing and the Mind of Man*

25 30-line Indulgence printed by Gutenberg, issued by Paulinus Chappe, Proctor-General of the King of Cyprus, to contributories to the war against the Turks. Issued 29 April, 1455. *British Museum*

forma plenissime absolutionis et remissionis in vita

forma plenarie remissionis in mortis articulo

Jenson later cut the two gothic types used in his edition of
Gratianum Decretum. Various type designers have tried to re-
model Jenson's roman, amongst them William Morris and
Bruce Rogers.

Erhard Ratdolt was the most expert of the fifteenth-century
Venetian printers. He came from Augsburg, where his father
was a carpenter. It is more than likely that he worked as a
journeyman in one of the Augsburg printing houses.[7]
In 1476 he was established in Venice as a partner in the firm of
Maler, Löslein and Ratdolt. By 1480 he was in sole possession
of the business. Ratdolt's books are interesting, particularly for
their decoration and illustration work. He used woodcuts for
illustrations and ornamental borders; he printed large initials in
colour and skilfully drawn mathematical diagrams. He printed
Euclid's *Elementa* in 1482 and in the same year, the thirteenth-
century astronomical treatise of John Holywood (Sacrobosco)
of Halifax. This small quarto in its first edition had forty
diagrams, nine of which were coloured by hand; in the second
edition published three years later, most of these diagrams were
actually printed in colour. Ratdolt also made a quite successful
attempt at printing in gold[8] which he used for a dedicatory
letter in his *Euclid,* directed to Giovanni Mocenigo, the Doge
of Venice. He made his gold ink by substituting gold dust for
lamp black in the printing-ink formula. (Modern gold inks,
based on bronze powders, certainly will not match up to
Ratdolt's gold, even a year after printing, let alone five hundred
years later!) The *Euclid* had a beautifully printed black-letter
text with open line diagrams in the margin. The dedicatory
copy also has elaborate illumination with pictorial initials.

In 1486, Ratdolt returned to Augsburg and worked there for
the rest of his life. His roman typefaces were not very distinguished but his gothic letters were full of vitality.

Four years after Ratdolt had returned to Germany, the first
great Italian printer, Aldo Manuccio, arrived in Venice; he was
already forty years old. He had been born in 1450 at a place
called Bassiano, on the edge of the Pontine Marshes. He was a
scholar-printer, who loved the Greek language. Aldus had lived
for a while on Capri, under the patronage of the ruling Count,
Alberto Pio. Here he had worked as a tutor to the Count's
children. With the financial support of his former pupils, he
set up his press in Venice, with the object of publishing Greek
literature. Venice was still a prosperous city, but her decline as a
great trading port had been settled in 1487–88, when
Bartholomew Diaz pioneered the Cape route to India. From
that time onwards, practically all European seaborne trade to
India and beyond was to follow this route, and the carriers
were to be the Portuguese, Dutch and finally English ships.

By the time Aldus had become established in Venice, printing
presses were operating in over fifty German towns. In the
south, the main centres of printing were Nuremberg, Stras-

7. *A Guide to Exhibition of the King's Library,* British Museum, 1939.
8. *Colour Printers and Colour Printing.* R. M. Burch, Pitman, London,
1910.

E*

bourg and Augsburg and the Swiss frontier town of Basel; in the north, Cologne, who had far outstripped her local rivals, and the Hanse port of Lübeck; and in the Low Countries, the city of Bruges, where presses were established before 1475. All these towns were thriving manufacturing or commercial centres, successful in part no doubt because of the lack of competition from the French towns. As a result of the Hundred Years War, France had lost her pre-eminence in Europe. The neighbouring Dukes of Burgundy greatly benefited by this. They gave liberal commissions to artists, and under their benevolence, Flemish art developed at a great pace. Indeed Flemish painters by the end of the fourteenth century had revolutionized the craft by the introduction of a new realism. The brothers from Limbourg who illustrated the exquisite *Très Riches Heures du Duc de Berry* between 1409 and 1416,[9] produced a crystal-glass view of the last years of the Middle Ages, introducing quite unstylized scenes of peasants working in the fields as well as pictures of courtly pageantry. Art was still very much a part of daily life, serving a definite purpose – never wanted for itself alone. The object of art was to elucidate and to illustrate 'the rich efflorescence of the liturgy, the sacraments, the canonical hours of the day and the festivals of the ecclesiastical year',[10] and to decorate the pattern of daily life.

Huizinga describes how the artists at the Courts of Berry and Burgundy were artisans, whose work extended beyond picture painting or illuminating manuscripts, to designing scenery and costumes, decorating furniture and even repairing household goods and carriages. Apparently Jan van Eyck was engaged on painting maps for his patron and Hugo van der Goes has an additional claim to fame in being one of the earliest of poster artists: he designed a poster to advertise a papal indulgence. The Church and the court provided the pageantry that people needed, for life for the common man was still rigorous. The excitement provided by church festivals or court marriages was appreciated in direct ratio to the dreariness of everyday life. Apart from the luxury of the trappings and the gorgeousness of the clothes, all kinds of contrivances for amusement were in use. Caxton reports seeing one such device at the Castle of Hesdin and Jan van Eyck is known to have produced similar ingenious things. Huizinga records that when Isabella of Bavaria entered Paris in 1389, she crossed the bridge by Nôtre Dame and an angel descended 'by means of well-constructed engines'. This was just such a device as the one in Florence, where every Easter multitudes of people come to watch a dove launched from the High Altar of the Duomo down a wire leading outside to an archaic engine, bristling with fireworks, which, if all goes well, it ignites. It is a somewhat naïve proceeding, but would not have appeared so to the people of the late Middle Ages.

A decade or so after the brothers from Limbourg painted the

9. *Les Très Riches Heures* was unfinished at the time of the Duc de Berry's death in 1416. The manuscript came into the possession of Charles I, Duc de Savoie, who in 1485 on the occasion of his marriage, commissioned Jean Colombe, brother of the famous Bourges sculptor, to complete the work.

10. *The Waning of the Middle Ages*, J. Huizinga, 1924, Penguin Books, 1965.

illuminations for the Duc de Berry's *Book of Hours*, the brothers Van Eyck invented the craft of oil painting. It is impossible to say if they turned to this medium as being more durable, more damp resistant than either water colour or fresco, or because it gave their work greater depth. Certainly the pursuit of naturalism is typical of the declining years of the Middle Ages. The Van Eyck's were the last great medieval artists.

In Germany, on the Rhine and in the south, Burgundian and Flemish styles of painting were fused into a national style, and in the engravings of artists such as Michael Wolgemut, the German artist was finding the perfect outlet for his interest in craftsmanship, foreshadowing the complex and intricate detail of the work of Albrecht Dürer.

Printing reached France in 1470, when Johann Heynlin, the Rector of the Sorbonne and Guillaume Fichet, the Librarian, invited Ulric Gering and two other German printers to set up a press in the University. Fichet's objective was to maintain textual accuracy which the copyists seemed unable to do.

At the end of the Hundred Years War, France was depopulated, weakened and bankrupt. The country settled into a life of impoverished peace. Louis XI was on the throne. He was a devious and ignoble creature, who brought the Burgundian influence to an end and succeeded in making France to some extent the country she has been ever since. He achieved this by diminishing the power of the nobility, taxing the peasantry into the ground and building up the strength of the bourgeoisie.

In the arts, France was beginning to reject the Gothic. Jean Fouquet, her only considerable painter at that time, was much nearer to the Italian *Quattrocento* painters than to the contemporary neighbouring Flemish painters. Italian writing about architecture gave a new and different impetus to French building. The Renaissance was entering into French cultural life. The minor arts developed and French literature was to burst into song with the arrival of the printing press. The Sorbonne was renowned not only as a centre of learning, but also for the authority of its clerics. The whole Catholic world, even the Roman Curia, turned to them for dogmatic discussion and judgement in difficult points of canon law.

The autocratic dons at the Sorbonne were just as insistent about the manner and style in which their German printers should print as they were about theological doctrine. They had no use for textura or any other gothic face. Only the roman face would serve their needs. Within a dozen years other printers had set up in competition to the Sorbonne press. The two most important were Jean Dupré and Antoine Vérard. Both specialized in illustrated editions and Dupré was soon virtually in control of the French book market.[11] But the great age of French printing had not yet arrived. It was to come after the turn of the century with the Estiennes, Tory and de Colines.

coactiꝗ aſſentiremur habere · Qꝝ ſi uidemur belli fortuna ſecum participare⸱cōſultius eſſe ſato,opponere ſe illis q humilioꝛibus dnānꞇ⸱ q̄ uirum ſocium a finibus eꝛigere ⸳ ac ſe ultro romanis hoſtes oſtendere ⸴

⸢Brutus trallianis ⸴

Nꝰnciatū mihi eſt ꝗ menedotius ueſter⸳ dolobellę inimico meo hoſpes · ＆ amicuſ exiſtens⸳effecit⸳ut intra loca nꞇa caſtra metanſ inde abire nō urgerēꞇ · ＆ nūc quæꝛit ut intra urbem cū exercitu recipiaꞇ·Qꝝ dolobellæ pꝛo deſſe ipſe uel quis alius operatus ſit⸳id mihi

11. See *Five Hundred Years of Printing*. S. H. Steinberg.

Heynlin, the sponsor and initiator of the Sorbonne press, left
the University in 1473 to become an editorial consultant to the
Basel printer, and incidentally his former pupil, Johann
Amerbach. One of Amerbach's apprentices was Johann Froben
who afterwards worked in partnership with him. The Frobens,
father and son, were among the greatest of the late fifteenth-
and early sixteenth-century German printers. The standard of
their scholarship and their artistic judgement is indicated by
the fact that not only had they the ex-Rector of the Sorbonne
as a consultant at Basel but also had Erasmus of Rotterdam as
their chief editor and the Holbein brothers as illustrators.
Their productions included Erasmus's *Institutio Princeps
Christiani* and his *Epigramata* and also Thomas More's *Utopia*.
Both their typesetting and their presswork were exemplary.

44

A double-spread from the second edition of *Canterbury Tales*, printed by William Caxton in 1483. *British Museum*

The first English printing press was set up in Westminster in 1476, when William Caxton put up his 'Sign of the Red Pale'[12] in a shop near the Chapter House, on the route between the House of Lords, in the Palace of Westminster, and the House of Commons, which was then meeting in the Chapter House. It must have been both a convenient and a profitable site for a printer. It had taken something over fourteen years from the sacking of Mainz for the trade to reach Britain. Caxton was born in the Weald of Kent, it is thought at Tenterden, about the year 1422. His parents were well-to-do people with useful connections, for when Caxton was sixteen, he was apprenticed to Robert Large, a rich silk mercer, who became Lord Mayor of London. Large must have been fond of the boy, for when he died only three years after Caxton had joined his household, he

12. 'Red Pale' is a heraldic shield with a red bar down the centre.

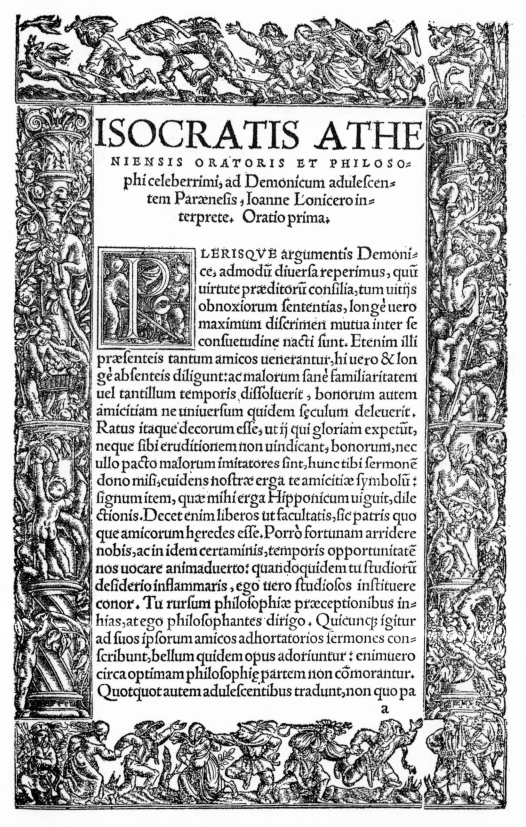

ISOCRATIS ATHE

NIENSIS ORATORIS ET PHILOSO=
phi celeberrimi, ad Demonicum adulescen=
tem Paraenesis, Ioanne L'onicero in=
terprete. Oratio prima.

PLERISQVE argumentis Demoni-
ce, admodū diuersa reperimus, quū
uirtute praeditorū consilia, tum uitijs
obnoxiorum sententias, longe uero
maximum discrimen mutua inter se
consuetudine nacti sunt. Etenim illi
praesenteis tantum amicos uenerantur, hi uero & lon
ge absenteis diligunt: ac malorum sane familiaritatem
uel tantillum temporis dissoluerit, bonorum autem
amicitiam ne uniuersum quidem seculum deleuerit.
Ratus itaque decorum esse, ut ij qui gloriam expetūt,
neque sibi eruditionem non uindicant, bonorum, nec
ullo pacto malorum imitatores sint, hunc tibi sermonē
dono misi, euidens nostrae erga te amicitiae symbolū:
signum item, quae mihi erga Hipponicum uiguit, dile
ctionis. Decet enim liberos ut facultatis, sic patris quo
que amicorum heredes esse. Porrò fortunam arridere
nobis, ac in idem certaminis, temporis opportunitatē
nos uocare animaduerto: quandoquidem tu studiorū
desiderio inflammaris, ego uero studiosos instituere
conor. Tu rursum philosophiae praeceptionibus in=
hias, at ego philosophantes dirigo. Quicunq; igitur
ad suos ipsorum amicos adhortatorios sermones con=
scribunt, bellum quidem opus adoriuntur: enimuero
circa optimam philosophie partem non cōmorantur.
Quotquot autem adulescentibus tradunt, non quo pa

a

left him a small legacy and apparently he also left directions to his executors as to how the apprentice was to complete his term.

Soon after his master's death, Caxton was sent to Bruges, which was the main foreign market for Anglo-Flemish trade and also the home of the Burgundian court. Caxton presumably completed his term of apprenticeship and then set up business as a merchant on his own account between 1445 and 1450. Bruges was a northern counterpart to Venice and was still at the height of its prosperity when Caxton went there to live. It was the centre of the wool industry, and when Philip the Good, Duke of Burgundy, had married Isabel of Portugal in 1430, he founded there the famous Order of the Golden Fleece. Bruges at that time still had access to the sea, but the river Zwyn was fast silting up. Burgundy had been allied to England since Philip had signed the treaty of Troyes in 1420, even though the relationship had not run smoothly. Philip and Isabel's son was Charles the Bold, who married Margaret of York, the sister of the English King Edward IV. This was the same Margaret who was later to become Caxton's patron.

Bruges was not only at the height of its commercial prosperity, but was also a great centre for Flemish art. The greatest of the Bruges painters was Hans Memlinc, who was a contemporary of Caxton's. Born near Frankfurt-am-Main, he lived in Bruges for most of his life. Memlinc, in spite of his origins, was essentially a Netherlander and expressed both the piety of the late Middle Ages, and the assurance, even the comfortable self-satisfaction, of the northern European renaissance.

Caxton's career in this busy medieval city appeared to have progressed most successfully. In 1463, he was made acting-governor of the Company of Merchant Adventurers in the Low Countries. This company came under control of the London Mercers' Company of which Caxton had become a liveried member in 1453. In 1464 he was confirmed as Governor and in the same year was appointed to represent English interests with Duke Philip of Burgundy, over the renewal of a treaty in connection with the wool trade. The negotiations were unsuccessful, but four years later the treaty was successfully re-negotiated with Charles the Bold. In the second diplomatic affair, Caxton had as a fellow negotiator Lord Scales, afterwards Earl Rivers, who was to be one of his chief patrons when he started printing.

In 1469, Caxton, who was by this time a leading citizen of Bruges, entered the household of the Duchess Margaret. What his appointment was is not clear. It may have been a sinecure to allow him to pursue his interests of translating and writing, for he was by now in his late forties, and could well have felt that he had had enough of commercial and diplomatic life.

In the often quoted prologue to *The Recuyell of the Historyes of Troye*, which he printed at Bruges, Caxton described how,

Of the chesse borde in genere how it is made capitulo   j

The draught of the kyng and how he meueth hym in the eschequer capitulo   ij

Of the moeuyng of the quene and how she yssueth out of her place capitulo   iij

Of the yssue of the Alphyns capitulo   iiij

Of the meuyng of the knyghtes capitulo   v

Of thyssue of the rokis & of her progresse capitulo   vj

Of thyssue of the comyn peple whom the pawnes represente capitulo   vij

Of the epilogacion and recapitulacion of thys book capitulo   viij

13. *A New Light on Caxton and Colard Mansion* by L. A. Sheppard. *Signature* N. S. No. 15, 1952.

having nothing very much to do, he took a French book and began to translate it into English, but got bored with it. However the Duchess Margaret seeing it, urged him to complete 'whos dredefull commandement y durst in no wyse disobey ... but forthwyth wente and labouryde in the sayde translacion.'

In the epilogue to the same book, he explains that as various friends wanted copies of it, he had learned 'at my grete charge' to print, and so the book was not 'wreton wyth penn and ynke as other books'. He actually finished his translation of *The Recuyell* in Cologne in September 1471.

His quite prolonged visit to Cologne lasted from July 1471 to towards the end of 1472. It would seem that the object of his visit was to learn to print, but in what printshop is not certain. Wynkyn de Worde's edition of *De Proprietatibus Rerum* in 1495, has in the prologue some lines stating 'Caxton first printed this book in the Latin tongue at Cologne'.

In England the Wars of the Roses were nearing their end, though at that moment of time the Lancastrians had restored Henry VI to the throne, and Margaret's brother Edward IV had had to take refuge at Bruges; it was not to be long before the Yorkist Edward was back on the English throne. Caxton must have been presented to Edward during his exile, for after the King's return to England, he was employed by the King on various missions. On Caxton's return to Bruges, he assembled material for a press, bought type and set to work, presumably assisted by a few craftsmen for presswork, casting type and all the other relatively menial jobs that a prosperous gentleman, now over fifty, would hardly be likely to do himself. Colard Mansion, the Bruges scribe turned printer, has frequently been credited with having taught Caxton the craft. It would now appear that far from this being the case, Caxton almost certainly taught Mansion; and though Mansion ultimately printed over twenty books, Caxton printed six titles for which previously Mansion had been given the credit.[13]

Caxton found conditions in Bruges were somewhat unsettled, for Charles the Bold was beginning to overreach himself. Charles unsuccessfully tried to annexe more territory, in order to re-unite Flanders and Brabant with the rest of his possessions. The tyranny of his lieutenant, Peter van Hagenbach, caused an insurrection in Upper Alsace. The Alsatians, finally helped by the Swiss, defeated Charles the Bold, who died in battle at Nancy in 1477. Whether it was because of these impending troubles, or because Edward IV had suggested such a course, Caxton after thirty years in Bruges, and just a year before Charles died, returned to England equipped with type and matrices and, at the age of fifty-four, set up the first English printing and publishing house.

Before the year was up, Caxton had started work, having established his press and foundry in a group of buildings which finally included almshouses and a chapel near the west end of

26 Book list issued by Peter Schöffer from Mainz in 1470, headed with *Primo pulcram bibliam in pergameno* (referring to the 'beautiful' 42-line Bible, printed on parchment). *Bayerische Staatsbibliothek, Munich*

27 The Miracle of the Possessed Man (Detail); from *The Legend of the Cross* by Vittore Carpaccio. c. 1495, the picture shows the Rialto bridge and the Grand Canal in Venice. *Galleria dell' Accademia, Venice*

30 '. . . a world disguised in the fantastic gear of the Round Table'.
The jousts of St Ingleuerch from Froissart's *Chronicle*. French, late
fifteenth century. *British Museum*

estminster Abbey. His first work was not as a book printer,
ut jobbing work. He printed an indulgence, which has been
ated by hand, '13 December 1476'. Within two years twenty
ooks had come off his press; by his death in 1491, he had
rinted nearly a hundred.

axton returned to an England wearied with the Wars of the
oses, yet where villages, towns and cities were virtually un-
uched. The damage was to the persons involved and not to
e places, to the great Lords and their unfortunate retainers.
the towns business was as usual, trade was booming and
hilst York and Lancaster knocked each others heads off in a
ccession of battles, comparable to a series of singularly
oody football matches, law followed its usual course.
dward IV, in spite of abandoning himself, as Green says 'to a
luptuous indolence, to revels with the city wives of London
d caresses of mistresses like Jane Shore . . . or idling over the
w pages from the printing press at Westminster . . .',[14] was
olitically astute. He was quietly making sure of absolute power
r himself. Though freedom of parliament was heavily cur-
iled during his reign, Edward can hold a place in history as
e patron of William Caxton – and so indirectly, because of the
wer of the press, as a supporter of intellectual freedom.

axton found the nearby City of London a prosperous, busy
ace. The liveried City Companies, the Mercers, the Grocers,
e Fishmongers, etc. ran the City. The ships belonging to the
ompanies packed the Pool of London, loading up with
nglish cloth, as well as wool and other English goods des-
ned for the ports of Europe.

he merchant classes were sending their sons to grammar
chools and universities, and there was a growing demand for
ooks. In the universities new colleges were built for the stu-
ents to live in. Many of these students were destined for the
hurch and, before college discipline became firmly established
the beginning of the fifteenth century, they were known to be
awless, lewd and licentious'. Their unrest has a parallel today.
was a capitalist society but there were no factories. In the
oth trade, the weavers worked at their own private looms in
eir own houses. The mercer commissioned them, paid them,
erhaps in advance, so that they could buy the raw material,
e wool, then he collected the goods and stored them in his
arehouses. In other trades, such as the metal-working and
ood-working industries, a master craftsman, assisted by
urneymen and apprentices, all sleeping under the same roof,
ould work on contract for shopkeepers or private buyers.
uch tradesmen had their craft guild, which on occasions acted
a federation to represent the employers' interests as well as
at of the employees. The whole pattern of the printing in-
ustry was to follow this medieval scheme of master-journey-
an-apprentice.

hen Caxton first started printing at Westminster, his aim was

14. *A Short History of the English People*. J. R. Green, 1874.

49

Top: An advertisement issued by Caxton about the year 1477.
Bodleian Library

Below: A woodcut from *The Game and Play of the Chesse* printed by
William Caxton, 1481 (second edition). *British Museum*

Jf it plese ony p man spirituel or temporel to bye ony
pyes of two and thre comemoracõs of salisburi vse
enpryntid after the forme of this preset lettre whiche
ben wel and truly correct, late hym come to westmo/
nester in to the almonesrye at the reed pale and he shal
haue them good chepe. .˙.

Supplico stet cedula

to provide a lay public with something lighter to read than th
lives of saints, though the educated classes still read wit
eagerness manuscript copies of Chaucer's *Canterbury Tales* ar
William Langland's *Piers Plowman*, as well as the endless
boring verse chronicles of England and France. To kill th
long, dreary winter evenings, men and women still practised th
art of story-telling. Many husbands must have grown tired o
their wives', and worse still their mothers-in-law's, oft-tol
tales. Here was a ready, eager market for the publisher of ligh
literature.

Caxton's problem was not so much what to print as in wha
language or at least in what vernacular. Though Latin was
universal language in Europe, people were beginning to want t
read works in the language they used every day of their live
There were no dictionaries of the vernacular, and local dialec
were numerous. Caxton, as a man of Kent, would have ha
some difficulty in understanding a man of the Essex marshe
About the Kent dialect he says: 'In Kente in the Weeld where
doubte not is spoken as brode and rude englissh as is in on
place of Englond.' However, he stuck to his last, and by s
doing, helped to form the modern English tongue. Of th
texts he printed, his greatest love was for his editions o
Chaucer; and in all he produced some seven books of Chaucer
works. The Chaucer he printed in 1478 is, typographically, a
attractive book. It is set in single columns in a lively *bâtard*
the second typeface he had had cut, modelled on the bookhan
used by the scribes in Bruges for the vernacular at the Burgur
dian Court. The text has hand-drawn rubrics and altogethe
makes a pleasant impression. It is a covetable book, not onl
because of its value and rarity.[15] He also published Malory
Le Morte d'Arthur, and in 1484 a translation of *Aesop's Fable*
with woodcuts based on those printed by Philippe and Rein
hardt at Lyons in 1480. These cuts were probably made by th
block cutter who did the illustrations for Caxton's *The Game an
Play of the Chesse* which he had printed at Bruges, befor
coming back to England.

Other works followed, including the *Order of Chyvalry* and *Th
Golden Legend*. The latter was a book of 900 pages, which
Caxton not only printed but translated as well. For the editio
of Higden's *Polychronicon*, which he printed in 1481, to brin
the history up to date he actually wrote the copy for the last hun
dred pages. Apart from all his literary achievements, he wa
also a good business man, as well he should have been afte
thirty odd years experience in the continental markets. H
concludes an advertisement of his wares with the words '. .
he shall have them good chepe', a phrase that William Morri
was often to repeat with delight.[16]

Caxton used eight founts of type, six bâtardes and two textura
He printed well, but not nearly as well as Fust and Schöffer
His typographic tastes were a little behind the times. If on

15. In the King's Library, British Museum.
16. The first memoir of Caxton was an octavo, *The Life of Mayster
Caxton, of the Weald of Kent* by John Lewis, Minister of Margate, Kent.
Published in London in 1737. My namesake contributed much of the
information for Ames's *Typographical Antiquities*.

WESTMONASTERIENSIS
Ecclesiæ, quondã Con
ventualis, facies occi
dentalis.

P. S.
Ne memoria Pe
tri, Pauli modo
cum mole ruat.

P
Wenceslaus Hollar
Eq: Bohem,

compares a Caxton page with a contemporary Jenson page set in roman types, the Jenson looks like a piece of modern printing, the Caxton belongs to a different world. In appearance and in spirit his books belong to the Age of Chivalry and to the closing years of the Middle Ages. Cologne, where he learned his craft, Bruges, where he first practised it, and Westminster where he set up his press, were all medieval cities. As far as England went, books were still a Gothic production. After fifteen years of printing, editing and publishing, Caxton died in 1491, the year before Columbus discovered the New World.

Yet even in England changes were in the wind. John Colet the Oxford Scholar, later to be Dean of St Pauls, went to Italy to study Greek in 1496. He returned to Oxford fired not with Italian humanism but with the certainty that his knowledge of Greek would reveal the scriptures to him anew. In 1496-7 Colet delivered his famous lectures on the Pauline Epistles, casting a brilliant new light on the New Testament. His rational interpretation of the real sense of the words of the epistles seen against an historically understood background was a revelation to his listeners. In 1499 Erasmus, a young and penniless author and tutor in Paris, was just as anxious to learn Greek. Failing to raise the fare to Florence, Erasmus, at the suggestion of his pupil, William Blount, Lord Mountjoy, came to Oxford as the one northern centre of learning where he might stand a chance of learning the Greek language. He was entranced with the university and its teachers. 'I have found in Oxford' he writes, 'so much polish and learning that now I hardly care about going to Italy at all, save for the sake of having been there. When I listen to my friend Colet it seems like listening to Plato himself.' And much more in the same vein.

In England, as in Germany, France and the Low Countries, there was a prolonged period of transition from the Middle Ages to the Renaissance. The breadth of vision of the Renaissance was still limited by medieval ways of thinking. The Gothic spirit was still the dominant factor in art and in architecture. Printing was cast in a Gothic mould yet was the first of the modern mass production industries. Northern Europe continued to use the textura, bâtarde and the rotunda faces. Even France reverted to gothic letters. Only in Italy, the home of the 'New Thought', was the roman typeface firmly established.

The Italian Renaissance and its Effects on Printing

As a result of the interest of Italian scholars in antiquity, the appearance of a large part of the print production of Western Europe was soon to differ most dramatically from the productions of Mainz, Cologne and Westminster. Printers have never been visual trend-setters. They follow the tastes and fashions of their surroundings. It is only in *what* they print, not *how* they print, that they have influenced events, sometimes to a world-shaking degree.

The most potent influence on the first Italian presses in Rome and Venice was the exciting feeling of freedom that was in the air. A little mild antiquarianism with a few enthusiasts armed with pick, shovel and measuring tapes digging up Roman ruins, or scholars poring over half-understood Greek texts, would hardly have generated this feeling. There was more behind it than this.

In the Middle Ages, the power of the Church put the fear of God, not only into the peasantry who were already frightened enough by their feudal lords, but into their masters and the growing middle classes as well. With the decay of both Church and feudalism, the way was opened for free thought. Long before the first presses were in action, writers such as Petrarch, Boccaccio and Dante had shown the light of humanism in the way they wrote about humanity. Petrarch showed particularly in his copious letters ' . . . the vital element, the revival of learning (which was) a just perception of the dignity of man as a rational, volitional and sentient being.'[1]

Petrarch's *Canzoniere*, Boccaccio's *Decameron* and Dante's *La Divina Commedia* were all written in Italian, yet all three authors professed to despise the vernacular and to see virtue only in Greek and Latin. More by what they actually wrote rather than what they imagined they were saying, did they herald the new age. Soon the humanist authors were disdaining their own language and writing only in Latin and Greek. The classical education followed by all educated Europeans until so very recently is the direct result of this attitude.

This belief in the study of antiquity was coupled with a feeling of modernity. Antiquity was to provide the impetus for new thought, new art and new architecture. Much of the inspiration came from Constantinople, the city chosen in A.D. 330 as capital of the Roman Empire by Constantine the Great (its first Christian emperor).

After being besieged, Constantinople fell to the Turks in 1453, but scholars had for some time been filtering through to Italy, bringing libraries of books with them. Not only Italian scholars, but scholars from all over Europe flocked to the centres of learning that these teachers from Constantinople had established.[2] As soon as these scholars had learned the ancient language, they set about transcribing the Greek manuscripts and establishing libraries to house them. The years between the fall of Constantinople and the end of the century saw the

Decorative engraved initial letter S printed by Jodocus Badius in Paris c. 1520 after a Venetian design used by Bernardus de Vitalibus in Venice in 1498

1 *The Renaissance in Italy*, 1875–86. John Addington Symonds. See also *The Italian Renaissance in its historical background*, Denys Hay, Cambridge: 1961.
2. *The Fifteenth Century*: Margaret Aston. Thames and Hudson. London, 1968. 'The arrival of Manuel Chrysoloras in Florence in 1397 marked the real beginning of the continuous study of Greek in Italy.'

full flowering of the Renaissance. During this time, the inventions of the Mariners' Compass, firearms and the printing press were perfected. The printing press was ready to meet the massive demand for books. Some of these printers were not mere tradesmen, but editors, translators and scholars. The greatest practitioners at this time, of this now international craft, were Aldo Manuccio in Venice, Froben in Basel and the Estiennes in Paris.

In architecture, the ruins of ancient Rome were carefully worked over by architects and sculptors, such as Filippo Brunelleschi (1377–1446) and Donatello (1380–1466). Brunelleschi did a great deal of measuring and as a direct result of his studies, designed and built the huge dome on the cathedral in Florence. His design for the *Duomo* incorporated classical elements, yet was technically a great step forward.

Of the writings of the architects of the ancient world, only Vitruvius's work had survived. According to Leone Battista Alberti, it had become so corrupt as to be barely understandable. In his *Ten Books on Architecture* Alberti tried to interpret Vitruvius to his contemporaries by defining certain principles of harmony. In 1435, Alberti published his treatise on perspective. This was the first theoretical exposition on the subject though the painters Masaccio, Fra Angelico and Uccello were all practising what Alberti preached at least a dozen years before his book appeared. 'The rule book was beginning to replace the rule of thumb.' The master mason, whose skills were passed down to him by previous generations of master masons, was supplanted by what he may well have regarded as an intellectual amateur – the architect, whose head was filled with new-old theories and a completely new architectural grammar. In painting, the same rules of perspective were being hotly debated and were evolving into something more than a trick of representation. Three-dimensional space was to become one of the essentials of painting for the next few hundred years, until the second decade of the twentieth century, when the Cubists finally exploded that particular viewpoint.

And as in architecture, so in painting. Where the master mason was replaced by the architect, so the craftsman-painter was replaced by the artist. Michelangelo's idea was to restore art to the status of a profession – to the same level as he fondly imagined the Greek artists had enjoyed. Leonardo da Vinci's change of status was the beginning of the separation of art from craft. The artist was raised from the humble sphere of craft guild, for painting was no longer a matter of craftsmanship, it was now an intellectual science. Until Michelangelo's time, the medieval methods had prevailed. At twelve years old, a boy would be apprenticed to a painter's workshop. In the next half dozen years he would learn the whole craft of painting, from colour grinding to drawing and from preparing grounds to actually painting on them. At the end of his time, he

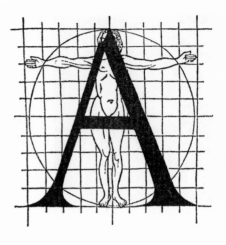

would become a journeyman and finally would be awarded by the local guild of painters his certificate as a master painter.[3]

His art, like all the art of the Middle Ages, was an applied art. Leonardo, in an attempt to break away from this system, proposed an academic syllabus with the artist first learning the *theoretical* rule book. In this he studied perspective and proportion and when he had absorbed these theories he would be set to copying his master's drawings, to drawing from the antique and then from nature. Finally he would practise his art.[4] The artist began to paint to please himself. His patron had to like it or leave it, unlike the medieval patron who commissioned the painting and expected the artist to follow his precise instructions. Leonardo had laid the foundations of future art education at least until the second quarter of the twentieth century. 'The painter (had) lost in social security what he gained in status.'[5]

Leonardo's genius embraced even the design of a new form of printing press. His design for a lever-operated printing press was, as far as is known, never actually built in his lifetime. The ingenuity of the design was in the fact that the bed of the press was linked to the lever movement so that when the lever was pulled the imposed forme was drawn under the press and at the same moment received the impression. Like so many of Leonardo's ideas, it came many years before its time.

Michelangelo under the patronage of Lorenzo de Medici and Raphael at the court of Leo X both lived like lords and were treated like royalty. The painter was now on a par not only with scholars and poets but also with his patrons. Art and literature, from the time of the *Quattrocento*, were to break down class barriers. A painter or a poet could be treated by the aristocracy as equals. A printer or a book seller (later to be called a publisher), with rare exceptions of scholars like Aldus, were to be regarded as tradesmen for many a day.

The passion for producing rule books was not confined to architecture and painting, but covered technical and scientific works as well. The first of these to be published and printed in Italy was *De Re Militari* by Robert Valturius. This work was illustrated with open line designs, cut on the wood. The book covered such subjects as siege ladders, gun turrets and a diver's suit. Mathematics and the graphic and typographic arts had come together. Inevitably there had to be treatises on the study of letter forms. The revived interest in the content of early medieval manuscripts spread to the Carolingian scripts in which they were written. Petrarch based his handwriting on these scripts and Niccolo Niccoli (1363–1447), following the same precedent, exercised some influence on the humanists. A further development of this book hand through speed, slope and compression lead to the so-called italic hand, which was also used by scholars and diplomats for their correspondence. This style of writing

3. *Academies of Art Past and Present*. Nikolaus Pevsner, Cambridge University Press, 1940.
4. Ibid.
5. Ibid.

Glos appellatur mariti foror: atq; idem fratris uxor.
Leuir dicitur frater mariti:quafi leuus uir.
Fratriæ appellantur quafi fratrum inter fe uxores.
Amitini fratrum & matris & fœminæ filii.
Patrueles matrum fratrum filii.
Cõfobrini ex duabus editi fororibus:de quibus exempla mul/
ta funt in antiquis auctoribus:& maxime in Affranio:& ui/
ris uetutiffimis fcriptoribus.

Jenson's roman typeface cut in 1470

Et cufi dunque la facra Antiftite intrando el Templo cum la inge-
nua & præftáte Nympha,& io pertinace fequétila, & cũ tutte le altre fa-
cre Damicelle,cum le uberrime capillature p gli lactei colli ornatiffime
cadéte, Veftite di electiffima purpura, Et di fopra riportate le tenuiffime
Gofapine piu breue, o ueramente curte del primo indumento. Al fata-
le orificio nella myfteriofa cifterna diuote & feftiue ne condufferon-

Griffo's roman typeface cut in 1499

Λυφί, καθά περ' τινω' φασι, Εν αταχασμω κδῦ τὰμ̄. μεταβάλ
λτ̀ἰω χόαν. τὰ ἢ μὴ. απεέκλυ τώ τερα θιειλόμὴ τερα μονέ τερα
ίνεθαι· κỳ ῇ ρου ρο λέγοιτιν,ὐθἐν ά ρορον ἤτι ῇ πεείσασκ οκ λη
ρότηρ∞κỳ τῇ ξ Εαδρωσῑ, ὐ θἐ νὴ τούτωναγό ζ̇ ρῖς ά τε ρά μο
σι. ρ,τε μὴ αγ οιδ̄∞ κα παπνεό μϵνα, σημαίỳ οκ ληρότητά τι

Griffo's Greek typeface cut in 1501

6. *The Fifteenth Century*, Margaret Aston. Thames and Hudson, 1968.
7. This is Stanley Morison's title for the 1928 edition. The original had no title.
8. See *Renaissance Handwriting*, Alfred Fairbank and Berthold Wolpe, Faber and Faber, London: 1960.
9. *Five Hundred Years of Printing*, S. H. Steinberg. Penguin Books, 1955.
10. Aldo Manuccio latinised his name to Aldus Manutius. Many scholars and printers followed suit.

was given official recognition by the Papal Chancery and was adopted for Papal Briefs, etc. Treatises on the construction of capital letters, based on both human proportions and geometrical principles, appeared in the later part of the fifteenth century. The first of these was written in the 1460's by Felice Feliciano of Verona.

The Paduan painter Andrea Mantegna (1431–1506) showed his obsessive interest in antiquity by the use of inscriptional letter forms in his paintings of what he imagined ancient Rome must have looked like.[6] Leonardo da Vinci, whose sketch books show the great number of studies he made of human proportions, may have illustrated one of these treatises – Luca de Pacioli's *De Divina Proportione*, which was completed in 1497, but not published until some years later. Leonardo, however, did not draw the actual letters in this book. The first lettering book to be printed that actually related the form of capital letters to human proportions was Damianus Moyllus's *A Newly Discovered Treatise on Classical Letter Design* published in Parma in 1480.[7]

It seems an odd notion to base a capital letter O on the form of a naked man standing with his arms stretched out and his legs apart. To the humanists it was the most natural thing to do. In his *De Divina Proportione* Pacioli says: 'From the human body are all measures and their names derived . . . to this end (architectural inscriptions) I have placed at the end of our book the manner and form and all the proportions of a fine ancient alphabet.' In this manner he reduced the roman alphabet to a geometrical formula based on a combination of squares and circles, bisected diagonally and diametrically. The thickness of the strokes of the letters were arrived at by divisions of the height.[8] Similar formulae were put forward by numerous writing masters, mostly in hearty disagreement with each other as to what the exact proportions of inscriptional capitals really should be. Renaissance logic was in danger of becoming illogical.

In this atmosphere of humanism, it was natural enough that the first German and French printers to settle in Italy should adapt themselves to the fashions of the humanist scribes. They had every inducement to meet their customers' requirements, for here was a ready-made market of infinite potential. As S. H. Steinberg says: 'The mother-land of new learning, . . . offered opportunities to adventurous publishers and printers for which there was little room in the still predominently medieval structure of German society.'[9]

The widespread success of the roman typeface was largely due to the publishing flair of Aldus, and not to any intrinsic excellence that his types may have had. The bulk of his texts were either in Latin or Greek, and the rich dark gothic letters must have seemed inappropriate for the one and impossible for the other. Aldus,[10] whose publishing career lasted from 1494 until

31 A page from the manuscript copy of Livy's *Ab Urbe Condita* which belonged to Petrarch and shows annotations in his own handwriting. c. 1350. *British Museum*

32 Leonardo's sketch plan for a printing press. When the lever was pulled the bed of the press was drawn under the platen and then received the impression. *Biblioteca Ambrosiana, Milan*

33 Perspective drawing in the study for the background of *The Adoration of the Kings* by Leonardo. c. 1481. *Uffizi Gallery, Florence*

34 An initial letter S drawn by Felice Feliciano for the Vatican *Codex*, 1460

35 Drawing of a geometrical construction by Leonardo. An illustration from Luca Pacioli's *De Divina Proportione*, 1497

36 Leonardo's drawing of the proportions of the human figure after Vitruvius, c. 1492

37 Ludovico Arrighi's handwritten script on a page from the manuscript copy of Aristotle's *Ethica. University Library, Amsterdam*

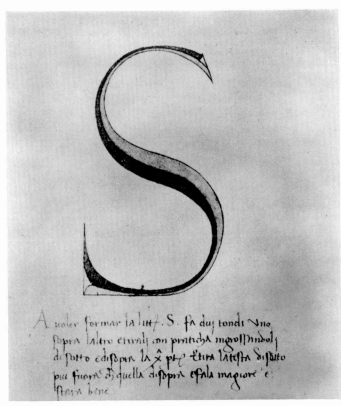

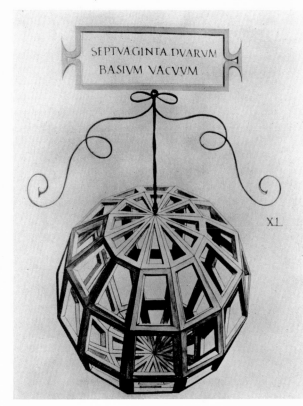

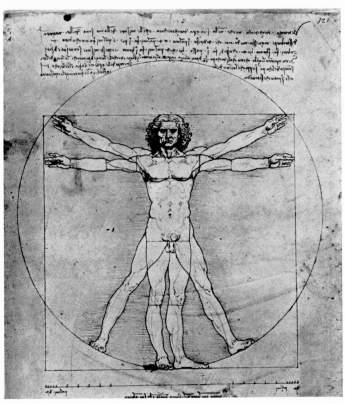

38 The dome of the cathedral in Florence designed by Filippo Brunelleschi and built 1420–34. *Mansell Collection*

Woodcut illustration showing the author's idea of a fighting ship from *De Re Militari* by Robert Valturius, printed at Verona by Johannes Nicolai in 1472. The first book to be printed with technical illustrations. *British Museum*

S E l'honorata fronde che prescriue
Lira del ciel, quandol gran ioue tona,
Non mhauesse disdecta la corona,
Che suole ornar chi poetando scriue
Io era amico a queste uostre diue,
Le qual uilmente il secolo abbandona:
Ma quella iniuria gia lungi mi sprona,
Da linuentrice de le prime oliue:
he non bolle la poluer dethiopia
Sottol piu ardente sol: comio sfauillo
Perdendo tanto amata cosa propia.
Cerchate dunque fonte piu tranquillo,
Chel mio dogni liquor sostien inopia:
Saluo di quel che lacrymando stillo

A Mor piangeua & io con lui tal uolta:
Dal qual mie passi non fur mai lontani:
Mirando per quleffecti acerbi e strani
Lanima nostra de suo nodi sciolta.
Hor dal dritto camin lha idio riuolta
Col cor leuando al cielo ambe le mani:
Ringratio lui che iusti prieghi humani
Benignamente suo mercede ascolta.
t se tornando a lamorosa uita,
Per farui al bel desio uolger le spale
Trouasti per la uia fossati o poggi:
Fu per mostrar quante spinoso cale:
Et quante alpestra & dura la saluta,
Onde al uero ualor conuien chuom poggi.

PROPER.

Et datur inculto tramite dura quies,
E t quodcunq; meæ possunt narrare querelæ,
Cogor ad argutas dicere solus aues,
S ed qualiscunq; es, resonent tibi Cynthia syluæ,
Nec deserta tuo nomine saxa uacent.

AD CYNTHIAM.

n On ego nunc tristes uereor mea Cynthia manes,
Nec moror extremo debita fata rogo,
S ed ne forte tuo careat mihi funus amore,
Hic timor est ipsis durior exequijs,
N on adeo leuiter noster puer hæsit ocellis,
Vt meus oblito puluis amore uacet,
I llic phylacides iucundæ coniugis heros
Non potuit cæcis immemor esse locis,
S ed cupidus falsis attingere gaudia palmis,
Thessalis antiquam uenerat umbra domum,
I llic quicquid ero semper tua dicar imago,
Traicit & fati littora magnus amor,
I llic formosæ ueniant chorus heroinæ,
Quas dedit arguis dardana præda uiris,
Quarum nulla tua fuerit mihi Cynthia forma
Gratior, & tellus hoc ita iusta sinat.
Quamuis te longæ remorentur fata senectæ,
Cara tamen lachrymis ossa futura meis,
Quæ tu uiua mea possis sentire fauilla,
Tum mihi non ullo mors sit amara loco,
Quam uereor ne te contempto Cynthia busto,
Abstrahat e nostro puluere iniquus amor,
C ogat, & inuitam lachrymas siccare cadentes.
Flectitur assiduis certa puella minis.

his death in 1515, was blessed with a very skilful type-cutter in Francesco Griffo of Bologna. Griffo, the first independent type-cutter, cut some of the most effective of all roman typefaces. Griffo's types were still being copied over a hundred years later. He also, as a method of saving space, produced a cursive letter – the italic. This was for use in small octavo editions intended

Top: Woodcut illustration of Savonarola preaching from the
Compendio de Revelatione printed in Florence in 1495. *British Museum*

Below: Woodcut to Savonarola's *Operetta della Oratione Mentale*,
Florence, c. 1495

for carrying in the pocket. Griffo's first cutting of a roman letter
was seen in a book called *De Aetna*, written by Cardinal Pietro
Bembo (hence the name of the modern revival). The italics were
used for a series of octavo books by Greek and Latin authors.
These cursive letters were not particularly elegant and the
Greek faces that Aldus used were none too legible. However,
his roman founts provided models for practically every type-
founder in Europe for the next two hundred and fifty years.
The Jenson letter, in some ways more handsome than Griffo's
roman, was never copied, until one or two ineffectual efforts
were made to re-draw it at the end of the nineteenth and the
beginning of the twentieth centuries.

The best of Italian printing was Venetian, with Aldus and his
successors in the lead. Their printed texts were beautifully
placed on the page and remained competently printed at least
until towards the end of the sixteenth century. Aldus never
used a gothic type, though twenty years after his death, one of
his rivals, Lucantonio Giunta, printed in Venice in 1536 an
edition of the *Opera* of Boethius in a fine black letter. Aldus's
name and his dolphin-and-anchor device[11] were known all over
Europe. His printing house was a home for scholars and in
1507–8 Erasmus stayed with him, working on a new edition of
his *Adagia*. Aldus's books were pirated, sometimes acknowledged, sometimes with faked imprints. The Florentine printing
house of Giunta was among the Aldine imitators. The printers
of Florence were remarkable for mass production rather than
quality. The most interesting of their productions were Chap-
book (pamphlet) editions of miracle plays and Savonarola
tracts with naïve little woodcuts set within decorative borders.
Vasari's *Lives of the Painters* was first printed in Florence in
1550. The edition was well printed by Torrentino.[12]

The most interesting sixteenth-century Italian painter, apart
from the Venetians, was the writing master Ludovico degli
Arrighi. In 1522, before he had become a printer, Arrighi had
published what was to be the first *printed* handwriting manual,
to instruct the layman in the writing of Papal Briefs. This was
La Operina da impare de scrivere lettera Cancellarescha. The book
is superbly engraved on the wood. The Papal script that Arrighi
showed was a cursive form of the more static writing first used
in Florence by Niccolo Niccoli, which in turn was based on the
Carolingian miniscule.

Arrighi, who had been born at Vicenza, taught writing first in
Venice then moved to Rome where he had a job in the college
of writers of Apostolic Briefs in the Roman Curia. In 1524,
whilst still in Rome, Arrighi went into partnership as a printer
with Lautizio Perugia, a skilled engraver of seals. Arrighi shows
a typeface, cut by Lautizio, based on his calligraphic italic in
the preface to *Il Modo de Temperare le Penne*, which he printed
in 1522. On this italic type rather than on that cut by Griffo for
Aldus, the future form of italic types was to depend.

11. Aldus's device was derived from a decoration in *Hypneromachia
Poliphili*; the original of this device was on a coin which, according
to Erasmus, was sent to Aldus by Cardinal Bembo.
12. *Printing Types.* D. B. Updike, Harvard University Press,
Cambridge Mass., 1922.

One of Arrighi's founts of type was bought by Antonio Blado, who was a relation of Aldus, and later became Papal printer.[13] In spite of the fact that printing was three-quarters of a century old, copyists were still at work and their works still prized. Arrighi wrote on vellum a magnificent edition of Aristotle's *Ethica*,[14] in 1517. His writing reveals a superbly competent cursive, the obvious forerunner of that cut for *La Operina*. The italic hand taught by Arrighi and other contemporary Italian writing masters, such as G. A. Tagliente and Giovanbattista Palatino, became formal and increasingly narrow. This aspect of the typeface appealed to the map-makers of the period and established a lasting precedent for the cartographic use of italics. The use of the humanistic script in Italy led to the use of the roman typeface by the first Italian printers in Rome and Venice.

13. *Renaissance Handwriting*, Alfred Fairbank and Berthold Wolpe, Faber and Faber, London: 1960.
14. This, one of the few known manuscripts written by Arrighi, came to light a few years ago. It is in the University Library at Amsterdam.

60

Marci Hieronymi Vidae, Rome 1527. This poem about the game of chess was the last book printed by Arrighi. Rome was sacked a week or so after the book was completed. This was the version of italic typeface that Blado acquired

MARCI HIERONYMI VIDAE
CREMONENSIS
SCACCHIA
LVDVS.

1

V dimus effigiem belli, simulataque ueris
P rælia, buxo acies fiEtas, et ludicra regna.
V t gemini inter se reges albusque, nigerque
P ro laude oppositi certent bicoloribus armis.
D icite Seriades Nymphæ certamina tanta
C arminibus prorsus uatum illibata priorum.
N ulla uia est. tamen ire iuuat, quo me rapit ardor,
I nuiaque audaci propero tentare iuuenta.
V os per inaccessas rupes, et inhospita euntem
S axa Deæ regite, ac secretum ostendite callem.
V os huius ludi imprimis meminisse necesse est.
V os primæ Studia hæc Italis monStraStis in oris
K

It was somewhat strange that Florence, the home of humanism, should have shown so little interest in printing that it was not until 1471 that the first press was established there – and even then the Florentine printed books were of little interest, except for their rustic chap-book style of illustration.

Venice alone was the one great centre of fifteenth- and sixteenth-century Italian printing. If Jenson was the founding father of the roman typeface (with due respect to his predecessors Sweynheim, Pannartz and Rusch), Griffo established its permanent character and Aldus was certainly the prototype of the modern publisher. The Venetians between them established the form that the printed book was to take for the next four or five hundred years. And it was a form that carried the authentic imprint of Italian humanism.

Printer's mark used by Aldus, 1502

Page from the *Nuremberg Chronicle,* printed by Koberger in 1493,
with illustrations by Michael Wolgemut and others

Quarta etas mūdi

Lycurgus

Lycurgus scdm Eusebiu insignis est habitus. q̃ et iura lacedemonijs com
posuit. et licet gētilis fuerit leges tamē iustissimas nāli diuioq̃ iuri cōsol
nas dedit. Nec quicqd censuit. c̃ nõ ipe exēplū pꝛi̇ daret. Auri argētiꝗ
q̃ vsuz et oim sceleru materiā nõ sustulit. Fundos oim equaliter inter oēs diuisit
vt equata patrimonia neminē potētioꝛe altero redderēt. cōuiuari publice iussit.
ne alicuꝰ diuitie vel luxurie in occulto essent. Iuuenib⁹ nõ ampl⁹ quã vna veste
vti toto anno: nec aliq̃ culti⁹ q̃ aliū ꝑgredi voluit. nec opulēti⁹ epulari. Emi sin
gula nõ pecunia sed cōpatiõe mercaū iussit. Pueros puberes nõ in foꝛum sed in
agrū deduci iussit. vt primos ãnos nõ in luxuria:ß in oĩ ope ac laboꝛe agerēt. Ni
hil eos sõnnij causa substernere. ꝛ vitā sine pulmēto degere. nec pꝛi̇ in vrbē redi
re q̃ viri facti essent. Constituit virgines sine dote nubere: vt vxoꝛes nõ pecunie
causa eligerēt. seueriusq̃ matrimonia sua viri coercerēt cū nullis dotis freñis te
nerēt. Maximū honoꝛe nõ diuitiꝰ ꝛ potētuz ß senū esse cēsuit. Hec ꝛ alia si̇lia q̃
solutis antea moꝛib⁹ dura videbanꝛ auctoꝛe eoꝛ appolline delphicū finxit ꝛ in
de se ea detulisse. Deinde vt eternitatē suis legib⁹ daret iureiurado eos astrinxit.
ne quid de tam diuis legib⁹ mutarēt donec reuerteret in patriā. ꝛ simulãs se ite
rum cōsulere appolline. vt qd addendū ꝗcq̃ diminuēdum his legib⁹ videretur.
Profect⁹ ē aūt Cretā̃bi voluntariū exiliū ꝑpetuo egit. sed ꝛ moꝛies ossa sua in lo
culo plūbeoꝛ i mari abijci iussit. ne si ad patriā deferꝛ
ꝗtigeret. lacedemões se a iuramēto solutos eē putarēt.

Heu filius Iosaphat regis iuda decim⁹ rex israel
vnct⁹ a puero belizei pcussit Ioꝛã cū omni dõmo
achab. ꝛ destruxit domū baal ꝛ eo⁹ ꝓphas occidit. Sz
heu vitulos aureos in bethel ꝛ dan nõ dereliq̃t. Ideo
Asael rex syrie missus a dño mltos occidit in israel vbi ꝛ
moꝛitur postq̃ regnauit. 28. annis.

Sayas ꝓpha nobilis: magl euãgelista a bõ hie
ronimo diciꝛ q̃ ꝓpha. vn⁹ de q̃ttuoꝛ ꝓncipalioꝛ
bus circa ß tpa clar⁹ habet ꝓpter euidētiā ꝓphie sue.

Iste Ioachas valde attꝛit⁹ est cū tota gēte ab aza
hele rege Syrie. et ideo deprecabaꝛ dominum et
pauxillum releuatus est.

Osee ꝓpha primus de. xij. mittiꝛ contra decem tri
bus. Hic fuit fili⁹ Beeri q̃uis ꝓphia beeri nõ
habeaꝛ apud nos. ꝓphauit aūt Osee tempe ieroboã
regis israel filij Ioas qui ioas simul regnauit cuz osia
rege iuda. 14. annis. ꝛ in iuda fuerunt quatuoꝛ reges
sub quibus Osee ꝓphauit vt diciꝛ osee. 1. scz osias.
Ioathas. Achaz ꝛ ezechias.

Iste Ioas pcussit syros tribus vicibus iuxta ver
bum belizei. ꝛ tulit vrbes de manu Azaelis ꝛ be
nadab filij Asaelis. restituitq̃ regno suo. Ipse etiã af
flixit amasiam non volés sed compulsus. supbiam eꝰ
humiliauit incipiés regnare. 37. anno ioas regl Iude.

Iohel scdus ꝓpheta de. xij. de iuda. et futurã eꝰ
tribulationem ꝓphetizat.

Ieroboam satis bellicosus et victoriosus fuit. con
triuitq̃ regem syrie et restituit regnum israel sicut
prius insuper et damascum iuxta verbum. Ione ꝓphe
te. Attende q̃ sit instabilis status regnoꝛum israel. cõ
tritus vsq̃ ab nouissimum humiliatus est valde. Sy
ri eleuati iam ad infirmis mirabiliter deprimunꝛ. sic
qui fuit supꝛa fiet infra. et econtra. qui fuit infra ascen
dit supꝛa vt post descendat infra. Hec est rota volubi
lis huius tempoꝛis. et ideo non est mirum q̃ pau
ci electi ad hoc assumuntur a domino et q̃ viri sensati
buiusmodi instabilitatis negociū totis viribus fugere
contēdunt. Uide augustinum de ciuitate dei in multis
locis Si boni regnãt mltis ꝓsunt. ecõtra. si mali ꝛc.

Ysaias

Osee

Jobel

Linea Regum israel Hieu

Joachas

Joas

Jeroboam

The Reformation and the Printing Press:
Artists take an interest in the Printed Illustration

In Italy in the late fifteenth century the fine book was still considered to be the hand-written and not the printed volume. Vespasiano da Bisticci, the Florentine bookseller, writing about the Duke of Urbino's library, said: 'In this library all the books . . . are written with the pen; and were there a single printed book it would have been ashamed in such company'.[1] This, of course, may have been a loaded comment, for Vespasiano, as well as being a bookseller, employed more scribes than anyone in Italy. At one time he had forty-five writers working for him. Certainly most of the illustrating talent went into manuscript books, which was not the case in Germany and Flanders, where printed books with woodcut illustrations were being produced before the sack of Mainz. Block books, that is books where illustration and text were all cut on the wood, date at least from the 1420's. This somewhat crude and inflexible method continued in use in Germany for broadsheets until the end of the eighteenth century.

The obvious advantage of the woodcut, unlike the individually drawn illumination, was that not only could a whole edition be printed from it, but it could be used in other books, possibly for quite different purposes than those for which it had originally been intended. The *Nuremberg Chronicle*, printed by Koberger in 1493, illustrated by Michael Wolgemut and others, had 1809 illustrations, but these were printed from only 645 separate woodblocks.[2] This was a practice that was to be repeated by early nineteenth-century broadside printers such as James Catnach at the Seven Dials Press in London, whose 'Last Dying Confessions' always carried a portrait of the latest murderer, indistinguishable from the previous ones, except perhaps for the addition of a moustache or a patch over the eye.

The early Italian printed books that carried illustrations were quite unlike such northern productions as the *Nuremberg Chronicle*. These were light and airy designs, to match the light grey pages of the roman type. The difference in Renaissance and Gothic illustration was as marked as the differences in the typefaces. In fact a comparison between the typical book illustration of Italy or France with that of Germany or the Netherlands, reveals even more than the typographic differences of those countries, for on occasions the Italians still used the Gothic types and Germany the roman letters.

In Germany, from the time Gutenberg had started his printing experiments, Latin and Greek were being studied widely. A number of universities had been founded by the end of the fourteenth century. Nuremberg, Strasbourg, Augsburg and Basel became centres of learning not only for humanist scholars, but also for artists such as Dürer, the Holbeins and Altdorfer. Germany was waking up, but her awakening bore little resemblance to that of the Italian Renaissance. Germany's awakening was as spiritual as it was intellectual and was soon to develop into rebellion against ecclesiastical corruption.

Wood engraving attributed to Mantegna; illustration to Pliny. 1513

1. *Four Centuries of Fine Printing*, Stanley Morison. Benn, 2nd. Edition, 1949. See also *Renaissance Handwriting*, Alfred Fairbank and Berthold Wolpe, Faber and Faber: 1960.
2. *Five Hundred Years of Printing*. S. H. Steinberg. Penguin Books, 1955. See also *A History of Book Illustration*. David Bland, Faber and Faber, 1958.

The printing press accelerated this awakening, not only by the dissemination of words and ideas, but by means of printed pictures as well. Engravings clarified ideas for the literate and were the source of ideas for those who could not read. The artist in Germany who played the biggest part in this was Albrecht Dürer, for not only was he one of the greatest German painters of his time, but his engravings had an influence that was felt from one end of Europe to the other.

Dürer was born at Nuremberg, the son of a goldsmith. At fifteen, he was apprenticed to Michael Wolgemut's studio, having already learned the goldsmith's trade. Wolgemut, like many painters in that part of Germany, was practising as an illustrator, as a designer and as a painter of religious subjects. The latter were commissioned by wealthy burghers or by business houses. Wolgemut's clients seemed to have had a marked liking for scenes of martyrdom and torture, yet the paintings show great skill in the treatment of costume and landscape. Dürer found himself not only learning his trade as a painter, but assisting in the production of woodcuts for book illustrations, which Wolgemut's studio turned out in great quantity.

In 1490 Dürer's apprenticeship was over. In order to learn the craft of intaglio engraving, in 1492 he stayed for a while at Colmar, attaching himself to the surviving brothers of the artist Martin Schongauer. The Schongauers worked in the German-Flemish tradition that Dürer was later to make so much his own. It would seem that as soon as Dürer started drawing on a woodblock, or when he took a burin in his hand, the mantle of this Gothic tradition would settle heavily on his shoulders, whereas the drawings in his sketch books show little evidence of it. Two years later he was in Italy, where the work of Mantegna and Giovanni Bellini made a deep and very lasting impression on him.

In 1495 he was back in Nuremberg, where he made his home for the rest of his life, practising his art of painting, but with frequent excursions into illustration, either drawing on the woodblock for book illustration, for other hands to engrave, or engraving with his own hand on copper, for plates that would be sold individually or in sets.

In 1498 he illustrated, printed and published an edition of the *Apocalypse*. He produced sixteen designs which were based on traditional concepts. Sidney Colvin, former Keeper of Prints and Drawings at the British Museum, wrote of these engravings some half century ago: 'The northern mind had long dwelt with eagerness on these phantasmagoric mysteries of things to come ... Dürer conceived a set of designs in which the qualities of the German late Gothic style, its rugged strength and restless vehemence, its love of gnarled forms, writhing action and agitated lines, are fused into something of the power he had seen in Mantegna's works.'[3]

3. Sidney Colvin writing on Dürer in the *Encyclopaedia Britannica*, 11th Edition, 1911.

These splendid engravings contained the essence of the Gothic culture that was to endure in Germany long after the classical spirit of the Renaissance had dominated the art of illustration elsewhere. Only a year after Dürer had completed his work on the *Apocalypse* engravings, Aldus published *Hypneromachia Poliphili*. The contrast between the clotted technique of the Dürer engravings and the ethereal quality of *Poliphili* is indicative of the two cultures, yet the gnarled strength of the Dürer engravings was to have incomparably more impact and far greater staying power than the Italian illustrations. Dürer was drawing from the very depths of his feeling, the Italian illustrator was performing nothing more than a somewhat airy mental exercise.

In the autumn of 1505, Dürer made a prolonged visit to Venice, staying there for eighteen months. There was some kind of epidemic at Nuremberg and maybe this set him on his travels. He went in search of new markets for his paintings and engravings and also to carry out a commission for the German community in Venice. This was to decorate the church of St Bartholomew and resulted in the painting 'The Madonna of the Rose Garlands'. It is probable that Titian and certain that Giorgione were working on frescoes for this church whilst Dürer was painting his altarpiece for it. In his letters written from Venice to his closest friend, the Nuremberg humanist Willibald Pirckheimer, Dürer describes some of the petty jealousies that he had to cope with from lesser artists, because of the high position the Venetians accorded him and the friendliness he received from the Bellinis. All his reverence is for Giovanni, the younger of the two Bellini brothers. And he bemoans the fact that he was too late to pay homage to Mantegna, to whose art he owed so much, for Mantegna had died just before he arrived in Italy.

From 1507 to 1520, Dürer, now with a European reputation, lived a happy, successful life (even if he did have a shrewish wife) in the medieval atmosphere of Nuremberg. Nuremberg was a city of much activity. It was also the home of Anton Koberger (1445–1513), the founder of the greatest European publishing house of the fifteenth and sixteenth centuries.[4]

In 1520 Dürer and his wife journeyed to the Low Countries to attend the coronation of the Emperor Charles V. The object of this journey was for Dürer to seek further patronage from Maximilian's successor. He travelled down the Rhine to Cologne and then by road to Antwerp. His reception matched his fame. He moved in the highest society and spent much time with Erasmus and also with artists, including Lucas van Leiden. His diary records the details of his many encounters and of the places he visited, such as Aachen for the coronation, and Bruges, Brussels and 's Hertogenbosch. The latter place had been the home of Hieronymus Bosch who had died in 1516. Dürer may have seen his work. If so, he kept his thoughts

---

4. 'At the height of his activities, Koberger ran 24 presses served by over 100 compositors, proof-readers, pressmen, illuminators, and binders. The catalogue for his firm over the years 1473–1513 enumerates more than 200 titles'. S. H. Steinberg in *Five Hundred Years of Printing*. Penguin Books, 1955.

Ecco fencia præftolatióe fue patefacta, & ítromeffi, Se fece ad nui una
Matrona chryfaora cum gliochii atroci & nellafpecto prompta, uibran-
te cú la leuata fua fpatha in mano & prælucéte. In medio della quale, una
corolla doro, & uno ramo di palmula ítrauerfato fufpefa pendeua, Cum
brachii Herculei & da fatica, cùm acto magnanimo, Cum il uétre tenue,
bucca picola, humeri robufti, Nel uolto cum demonftratione di non ter
rirfe di qualunqua factione ardua & difficile, ma di feroce & giganteo ani
mo. Et il fuo nomíatiuo era Euclelia, Et dixene nobile giouenette & obfe
quiofe uenerabilmente comitata. Il nome della prima Merimnafia, Della fecunda, Epitide. Dellaltra, Ergafilea. La quarta era chiamata, Anectea.
Et Statia nominauafi laquinta. La ultima era uocata Oliftea. Il loco & fi-
to mi parea effere molto laboriofo. Per quefto auidutafi Logiftica prompta ícomícioe cú Dorio mó, & tono di cátare tolta la lyra di mano di The
lemia, & fonando fuauemente a dire. O Poliphile nó ti rencrefca in quefto loco uirilmente agonizare. Perche fublata & ammota la fatica, rimane
il bene. Tanto fue uehemente il fuo canto, che gia confentiua cum quefte
adolefcentule cohabitare, quantunque lo habituato di fatica appariffe,
Subito Thelemia politula & blandiuola, & cum dolce fembiante mi di-
xe. Cofa ragioneuola ad me pare, che ante che qui Poliphiletto mio ocu-
liffimo te affermi, debbi per omni modo & la tertia porta uidere. Confen

i

1520 Antwerp

5. *Albert Dürer*. T. Sturge Moore. Duckworth, 1905.

about Bosch's horror-fantasy paintings to himself. He write
however with indignation of the supposed man-handling and
kidnapping of Martin Luther, at the time of the Diet of Worms
By mid-summer of 1521, his objective of obtaining Charles'
patronage achieved, Dürer was back in Nuremberg, his mind
full of ideas for religious paintings he wanted to paint and o
books he wanted to write. As a result of his visit to Antwerp
he was anxious to get his theories on geometry, perspective
human proportions, letterforms and even fortifications onto
paper. His book *Geometry and Proportion* appeared in 1525 and
was published in Nuremberg. The perspective book appeared
in 1527. The *Human Proportions* was not published until after
his death.

Dürer died on 6th April 1528. Martin Luther, writing to a
mutual friend said: 'As for Dürer, assuredly affection bids us
mourn for one who was the best of men, yet you may well hold
him happy that he has made so good an end, and that Christ
has taken him from the midst of this time of trouble and from
greater troubles in store, lest he, that deserved to behold
nothing but the best, should be compelled to behold the worst
Therefore may he rest in peace with his fathers. Amen.'[5]

ürer's fame in his lifetime was largely owing to the wide stribution of his engravings and woodcuts. The pen is ightier than the sword, and sometimes the burin is more otent than the pen. When the two were allied to the printing ress, a formidable weapon was forged. Dürer's amalgam of hat Germain Bazin has described as 'The conflict between ermanic Pantheism and Renaissance Idealism', resulted in ork that showed that German artists had horizons and objec- ves quite different to those of the Florentine humanists. The erman printed books of the fifteenth and sixteenth centuries e full of engraved illustrations, whereas very few early alian books were illustrated. The Renaissance humanists may ave regarded printed dialogue as sufficient. To the Germans, e Gothic imagery revealed by such artists as Dürer and olbein, was as important as the printed word, for the Gothic orld lived on, not only in the medieval city of Nuremberg and ot only in Dürer's paintings and engravings, but in the work f such artists as Grünewald at Mainz, Altdorfer at Regensburg, urgkmair at Augsburg and Lucas Cranach at Wittenberg. The olbeins, Burgkmair and Cranach spent a large proportion of eir time engraving and illustrating books and Hans Burgk- air and Dürer actually worked together on engravings for the mperor Maximilian I, which Johann Schönsperger the Elder rinted at Augsburg. Hans Holbein the Younger was born at ugsburg in 1497. Because of money troubles, the Holbein mily moved from Augsburg to Basel in 1514. Hans and his rother Ambrosius soon obtained work from the various Basel rinting houses, including those of Petrus, Wolff and Froben. ook illustrators were in some demand and the Holbeins are redited with a very large body of work. Hans Holbein's first ommission was to illustrate Erasmus's *Moriae Encomium*. Soon e was engaged on designs for title-pages and for decorative itials for Froben and other publishers. His illustrations in- luded woodcuts of Gospel incidents from Luther's Bible, atiric cartoons on the sale of indulgences and his renowned et of forty-one cuts for *The Dance of Death*. This macabre ision of death originated in France in 1485, with Guyot Marchant's *Danse Macabre*, in turn perhaps copied from some aintings that once decorated the cloisters of the Innocents in aris. The theme is of three putrifying dead men dancing with heir living images; Holbein replaced the putrifying corpses ith skeletons and subsequent versions of *The Dance of Death* ollowed this lead.

he preoccupations of the Middle Ages were by no means layed out – and of these, fear of death was the strongest, and as reinforced by the recurrent outbreaks of the plague. It not nly pervaded everyday life but provided unlimited subjects or the printing press – and continued to do so until the end of he eighteenth century.

Wood engraving continued to be the medium for illustration

The family of Sir Thomas More, pen drawing by Hans Holbein
the Younger, 1528. *The Kunst Museum, Basel*

in Germany, though metal engraving for book work was in us
in both the Low Countries and Italy well before the end of th
sixteenth century. Over a thousand title-pages produced i
this century had wood-engraved borders. Professional engra
vers such as Hans Weiditz were fully employed on such work
as well as designing and engraving decorative initials. Weidit
also illustrated herbals.

The Reformation brought an economic depression to Souther
Germany. Holbein found himself out of work, so, in 1526 wit
the help of Erasmus, whom he had first met in 1515, and wit
letters of introduction from him to Sir Thomas More, h
departed for England. Here he spent most of the rest of hi
life, apart from one short visit to Basel, doing those meticulou
portraits of Henry VIII and his various wives as well as
courtiers and rich merchants. Holbein lived in the City
London amongst the German Hanseatic League colony in th

teelyard, where Cannon Street Station now stands. It is said
hat for a while he lodged at one of the houses on old London
ridge. In addition to his portraits and his work for printers,
Holbein also worked as a designer for jewellers, armourers and
ookbinders. One of his last designs was for a clock, which was
resented to Henry VIII.

Of Dürer's other contemporaries, Lucas Cranach (1472–1543)
s of interest, for he bridges more than one gap as painter,
ngraver and printer. In 1508, the Elector of Saxony had granted
Cranach exclusive privileges in the printing and copyright of
ibles and also, as an odd counterpart, in the monopoly of the
ale of drugs and medicines in Wittenberg. Cranach was a
lose friend of Martin Luther and designed propaganda wood-
uts for him. His press also printed various Lutheran tracts.
Cranach's paintings of seductive nudes make odd bed-fellows
o his Protestant pamphlets, but Luther was no Puritan.
Cranach's part in the history of printing, or Dürer's for that
matter, is of course insignificant in comparison with Luther's,
or Martin Luther's Protestant Reformation was the first oc-
asion when the printing press made an overwhelming impact
on Western civilization.

THE REFORMATION AND THE PRINTING PRESS

The groundwork for the Reformation lay in various religious
movements and social changes. The main pre-Reformation
movements were those of the Lollards in England and the
Hussites in Moravia and Bohemia. The Hussites, whose
doctrine largely derived from the teachings of Wyclif, had by
he beginning of the sixteenth century achieved some domi-
ance; the Lollards, on the other hand, after much persecution
had had to go to ground. The printing press played an ever increasing part in these religious upheavals.

The doctrine of personal, as opposed to institutional, Christi-
nity outlined by Thomas à Kempis in his *Imitation of Christ*,
hanks to the printing press, was being read all over Europe in
he early years of the sixteenth century. It was first printed by
Gunther Zainer of Augsburg in 1473, two years after the death
of the author. By 1500, ninety-nine editions of the work had
een published. It was the first best-seller,[6] but its popularity
was slight in comparison with the world-wide fame that the
printing press had bestowed on the works of Erasmus.

Desiderius Erasmus, the greatest of Christian humanists, was
he bastard child of a doctor's daughter and a monk from
Gouda. He was born in 1469 in Rotterdam. His parents having
died from the plague, his guardians pushed him into a
monastery. Somewhat reluctantly, he was ordained in 1492, the
year Columbus was to make so memorable. Though Erasmus
remained a priest within the Roman Catholic church for the
rest of his life, he was more at home reading proofs in a print
shop than working in a monastery. Printing houses, such as

6. *Five Hundred Years of Printing*, S. H. Steinberg,
Penguin Books, 1955.

Top: Basel. Detail from an engraving by Hartmann Schedel, 1493

Below: The device used by Joh. Froben of Basel from 1521.
Probably drawn by Hans Holbein

hose of Badius, Aldus or Froben, that Erasmus knew so well,
were centres of intellectual activity as well as being book
production factories. Erasmus's peripatetic life seemed to lead
him not only from country to country but from city to city,
to wherever the printing trade flourished. He was constantly
travelling to Venice, Basel, Paris, Strasbourg and Antwerp.
Renaissance Florence or Papal Rome meant little to him, but
he spent over eight years in Basel, finally ending his days there
in the house of Froben's son.

By 1496, the year Erasmus published his *Adagia*, Italian
humanism and scholarship had begun to penetrate theological
study. Erasmus saw the Christian doctrine as a way of living,
rather than as a collection of superstitious beliefs. This was not
at all the same thing as Protestantism. Erasmus was above all
things a pacifist. He also questioned the infallibility of the Pope.
He was in favour of priests marrying, of liberal divorce laws
and of the use of the vernacular in the Mass.

In 1516, Johannes Froben printed and published Erasmus's
New Testament in Latin and Greek. Froben, one of the finest of
European scholar-printers, had been associated with Erasmus
since he had left England two years before. Whilst his books
were going through the press, Erasmus lived in Froben's
house, as he had done a dozen or so years before with Aldus.
He was an inveterate visitor and apparently a most welcome
guest. As well as seeing his own books through the press, he
also acted as a literary editor for Froben. The *New Testament*
was in a smallish quarto format with fine decorations. Erasmus's
Antibarbari is another production of Froben's printed in 1520
and illustrated with woodcuts by Holbein. Erasmus applied an
historical approach to his biblical texts. He and his followers
'Stood opposed to Protestantism . . . represented a cultural
trend, not a school of thought, still less a Reformation.'[7]

Yet Erasmus, by his brilliant satires about ecclesiastical corruption, most successfully sapped the authority of the Roman
Church. That he was not burned at the stake must have been
due not only to his personal charm, but also to his great
popularity with High Society and even with High Churchmen.
The Sorbonne censured him but it was not until 1559, long
after his death, that the *Index Expurgatorius* banned the reading
of all his books.

In Germany it was an age of inquiry and unrest, with the class
struggle only just beneath the surface, and it was also an age of
great trade expansion. The dominant characters in public life at
least in the free cities, were no longer the great landowners, but
the urban businessmen, bankers and printers. There had been a
fast growth of literacy amongst all classes, including the
craftsmen, the artisans and the shop assistants. Nuremberg, at
the centre of European commerce, was to retain its medieval
atmosphere yet absorb a large measure of Italian humanism.
Its once narrow horizons were growing wider, encompassing

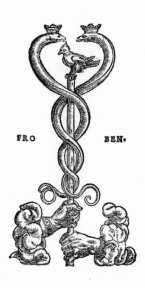

FRO   BEN.

7. *Reformation and Society in Sixteenth Century Europe*, A. G. Dickens,
Thames and Hudson, London: 1966.

new thought. To comprehend the age and the difference between Germany and, say, France, one has only to compare Dürer's engravings for *The Apocalypse* with the tapestry of 'The Lady with the Unicorn', where life seems to be a gentle promenade through wild-flower-strewn paths, amongst fearless birds and beasts. *The Apocalypse* offers no such earthy paradise and has fear in every engraved line.

The practice by the Church of selling indulgences for the remission of part of the feared consequences of sins was very common at the beginning of the sixteenth century. It was a well established practice with over a thousand years of precedence. With the coming of the printing press, it was possible to run off copies of these indulgences in great numbers. It proved an easy method of raising money. The earliest surviving copy of a printed indulgence is one printed at Mainz in 1454. It is set in two founts of black letter, a large textura and a rounded small letter, with something of the bâtarde about it.

On the 1st November 1517, as an act of protest against the misuse of these indulgences, Martin Luther nailed his famous ninety-five theses on the church door at the new university town of Wittenberg. This action was in reply to an indulgence instigated by Pope Leo X, to raise money in part for the rebuilding of St Peter's at Rome, but half of it was to go to the Archbishop of Mainz, whose agents, the House of Fugger, were the collectors, taking a commission for their trouble.

These theses completely undermined the validity of indulgences by bluntly stating that an indulgence could only be a remission of an ecclesiastical penalty, it could not remit what God had imposed. Luther went on to say that an indulgence could never remit guilt – nor for that matter could the Pope; it could not remit the divine punishment of sin, only God could do that; it could not do anything for souls in Purgatory; and finally any Christian who has true repentance has already received pardon from God, so he certainly does not need to buy an indulgence. The ninety-five theses 'were ninety-five sledgehammer blows directed against the most flagrant ecclesiastical abuse of the age'.[8]

Everybody wanted to read the theses and the university press could not keep up with the demand. Other presses were soon printing them, and within four weeks they had been heard of all over Europe. Controversy flared up and the sale of Luther's pamphlets soared and that of the indulgences rapidly slumped. The Pope's reaction was prompt; he branded Luther as a heretic (the Church has always been touchy about its pocket). Luther was unabashed, for he had the fervent support of the common people and also of the Elector Frederick of Saxony. In 1520 Luther published his three most important works, his 'three primary treatises'. The Pope replied with a Papal Bull 'Against the errors of Martin Luther and his followers,' which Luther publicly burned. If this had happened in Spain, Luther

8. *Luther*. Thomas Martin Lindsay LLD.DD. *Encyclopaedia Britannica*, 11th Edition, 1911

Title-page of the *New Testament*, printed by Hans Lufft, 1546. This
was the last edition that Luther corrected

Title-page of the *New Testament*, printed by Hans Lufft, 1546. This
was the last edition that Luther corrected

would have been burned at the stake as a heretic. Things began
to look a little ugly at Wittenberg after the death of the
Emperor Maximilian. His grandson and successor, Charles V,
more Spanish than German and perhaps more Flemish than
either, was crowned at Aachen on 23rd November 1520 and
opened his first parliament (the Diet) at Worms on 22nd
January 1521. Luther was summoned to Worms, but popular
support was so great for him and he so confounded his critics
that after some alarm for his safety (the rumour that had so
disturbed Dürer), and backed by his Elector, Luther returned
to Wittenburg in an unassailable position.

From that time Luther became the spiritual leader of the
German people. The lightning spread of his fame was due to
one thing only – the printing press. But if he had not had
something to say that every one wanted to hear, all the presses
in the world would not have helped him. Literally hundreds of
thousands of Luther's pamphlets were printed and published in
his lifetime. Incidentally, he never received a penny for any of
them, and never expected to. His writings were not limited to
pamphlets, for he had undertaken the complete translation of
the Bible into German.

Melchior Lotter printed and published Luther's translation of
the *New Testament* in 1522. It was illustrated with woodcuts by
Lucas Cranach. It took Luther a further twelve years to complete his translations of the *Old Testament* and the *Apocrypha*.
The popularity of Luther's *Bible* was enormous and its effect on
the unification of the German language as great as Caxton's
more wordly productions had been on the English vernacular.
Luther's translation of the Bible ran through something like
four hundred editions before his death. His was not the first
translation into German, but it was the first one to sell in
thousands. To the Germans, as later to the English, the Bible
in the native tongue came as a revelation, for humanism had
opened their eyes, stimulated their powers of reasoning. The
Reformation was indeed a Gothic Renaissance. The new spirit
of rational enquiry and learning which in Italy had inspired art,
architecture and literature, in Germany rejuvenated (if in a
sombre mould) Christianity and helped to free the earth-bound
spirit. A. G. Dickens in his book *Reformation and Society in
Sixteenth-Century Europe* writes: 'For the first time in human
history, a great reading public judged the validity of revolutionary ideas through a mass medium which used the
vernacular language together with the arts of the journalist
and the cartoonist.' Professor Dickens goes on to summarize
Luther's creative theology as the heard word of teaching, the
visual word of the two gospel sacraments, the written word of
the scriptures, seen and interpreted as a whole.

Protestantism developed fastest against an urban background.
France with its mainly agricultural economy and feudal pattern
of life was not a promising field for Protestant missionaries.

76

However Lutheranism did make inroads and hundreds of Lutheran books were imported from cities such as Antwerp and Basel. Luther's successor in the fight against Rome was the Frenchman John Calvin, who, though born in Picardy, spent most of his life in Geneva. Trained as a lawyer, he brought a brilliant mind to the study of biblical theology. He wrote fluently and lucidly in both French and Latin. His first book was a commentary on Seneca's *De Clementia*, whose stoic morality clearly appealed to him. In 1536, when he was only twenty-six, he published from Basel his *Institutes of the Christian Religion.* Much that he wrote was based on Luther's teaching. When he finally settled in Geneva, he set about the reformation of that restless and restive city. Under his inspiration, the *Church Ordinances* laid down a code of conduct that forbade attendance at public entertainments, dancing or the singing of lewd songs, and stated that adulterers were to be hanged. 'Yet Geneva became a clean and orderly town in which poor, aged and sick were well tended and where educational opportunity became excellent . . . and where, through Calvin's efforts, a new university was founded in 1559.'[9]

With the closing of taverns, and the banning of frivolous or bawdy talk the pattern for much sober Puritanism was being established, yet Calvin's influence on the 'recognition of the liberal democratic rights of the individual' was far-reaching.[10] The Lutherans in France were branded with the name of Huguenots, because, so the printer Henri Estienne says in the preface to his *Apologie d'Herodote*, the Protestants at Tours used to gather at night near the gate of King Hugo who was regarded as a spirit, who like them, only walked at night.

Henri Estienne, one of the greatest of French printers, was to some extent the mouthpiece of the French Protestant movement. He was a confirmed Calvinist and a personal friend of François I. After François's death in 1550, the hostility of the Sorbonne theologians was so marked, that Estienne thought it best to retire to Geneva.

In spite of persecution, the movement spread, mainly to the maritime provinces and Channel ports, aided by the Estiennes' printing presses. In 1562, religious liberty was granted to the Huguenots, but this proved a hollow promise and civil war broke out between Catholic and Protestant – a war that was to last until well into the seventeenth century.

By 1572, it looked as though a *modus vivendi* could be found and peace established. But on the night of the twenty-fourth of August, the treacherous massacre of St Bartholomew took place. All the leading Huguenots were killed. The murderings spread through France and thousands more Protestants were slain. The strife continued. Henry III was assassinated by the monk Jacques Clement. His successor Henri of Navarre was for a while the leader of the Protestants although he had promised to maintain the Roman Church. In 1610, he was, in his turn,

9. *Reformation and Society in Sixteenth-Century Europe.* A. G. Dickens, Thames and Hudson, 1966.
10. *Printing and the Mind o Man.* John Carter & P. H. Muir. Cassell, 1967.

CALVINUS
VESPEREN.

NSen Vader Calvinus, grooten vyandt der Papen,
 Is gekomen als eenen dief in onse Koeyen der Schapen,
 Om te verslinden ende oock te verscheuren,
  Is ghekomen als eenen dief, niet door de rechte deuren:
Waer-in hy brenghen wilt alle sijn 't Consistorialisten,
 Om persecutie te doen aen alle goede Papistien.
Ghy noemt u den ouden wegh, en dat wy volghen uw' weghen,
 Ende al dat uw' Ouders u leeren, ghy seght daer teghen:
Volght ghy den ouden wegh? ba gy moet droomen:
 Hoe komt dat ghy niet en kent den Paus van Roomen?
Als CHRISTUS heeft gheseydt, *Kont ghy my met logenen betrapen?*
 Als hy tot Petrus seyde, *voeght ghy myn' Schapen.*
Oft hout ghy den Paus voor Antechrist, soo ghy hebt ghesworen
 Soo zynder veel Antechristen als Pausen gheboren.
Ick lese wel van eenen Antechrist 'die daer sal wesen,
 Dat den Paus Antechrist sou wesen en heb' ick nergens gelesen.
Ghy behoord' u te schamen de waerheydt te willen verkonden,
 Om dat ghy niet kond' bethoonen wie u heeft ghesonden.
Volght ghy den Ouden wegh, en thoont u niet als de plomste,
 Wilt my bethoonen van waer dat is uwe af komste.
Doen ons Catholyck Gheloof ghepredickt wirdt in alle hoecken,
 Doen was Calvinus Gheloof noch al verre te soecken.
Alle andere Leeraers verworpt ghy, ô maghere schooven,
 Den ouden quidam, die niet en deught, wilt ghy ghelooven.
Den ouden wegh leert my myn' sonden voor den Priester belyden,
 En al dat Godt bevolen heeft wil ick totter doodt voor stryden.
Segghende, *Soo mijn' Vader my heeft ghesonden in dit leven,*
 Soo sende ick u (seyde CHRISTUS) *om de sonden te vergheven:*
VViens sonden ghy vergheeft hier op-der aerden,
 Zyn vergheven in den Hemel, en ghehouden voor waerden.
Den ouden wegh leert my te stichten Cloosters ende Kercken,
 Maer gy breecktse en scheurtse, en thoont soo u goede wercken.
Ghy meynt Godt te doen een' Sacrificie ende Offerhande,
 Als ghy ons' Priesters mocht dooden met groote schande.

Als CHRISTUS syn' Apostels Priesters maeckte, ô gy schalcke spruytē,
 En maeckte geen' Priesters om's Sondaghs te spelen Paep-uyten.
Oock heeft hy Misse ghecelebreert, om ons te gheven een lesse,
 Wel dat CHRISTUS selver inne-ghestelt heeft de Messe.
CHRISTUS seydt, *Gaet by den Priester en wilt dan keeren,*
 Waerom en wilt ghy dan den Priester Godts niet eeren?
Leest Joannes in 't seste, oft en wildy om hem niet buyghen;
 Neemt Paulus, Marcus, Mattheus, die sullen 't u betuyghen,
Het Broodt dat ick u gheve (seyde Paulus) *ick my niet en schame,*
 Het is de ghemeynschap van CHRISTUS *Lichame.*
Soo en is 't gheenen gebacken Godt: dat had' Paulus wel gespeten,
 Leerende wier onweerdigh af at sou d'eeuwighe doot aen eten.
Al quamer eenen Enghel uyt den Hemel en laet u niet verdooyē,
 Die u anders leeren en wiltse niet ghelooven.
Is u Gheloof beter als d'onse, en doet dan gheen obstakel,
 Confirmeert ons gelyck d'Apostels hebbē gedaen met mirakel.
Calvinus soude een mirakel gaen doen voor all syn Calvinisten,
 Maer voor d'eerste reys hy seer schandelycken misten.
Den levenden man heeft hy in de doodt-kist gheleydt met listen,
 Wetende dat hy sou verrysen als hy sou kloppen op de kiste.
Godt wist dat door dit mirakel veel menschen souden bedorven,
 Soo Calvinus klopte is den levenden Man in de kiste gestorven.
Dat is 't mirakel dat Calvinus kan doen in steden en hoven,
 Sou hy syn'Calvers soo in de kiste leggen, soudē hun niet beloven.
O Vader Calvin ghy hebt menich' mensch verleydt en bedorven,
 Die buyten het oudt Rooms Catholyck geloof zyn ghestorven.
Pausen, Keysers, Koninghen menigh'duysent' van alle Staten,
 Zyn in 't Catholijck Gheloof gestorven, en Calvinus verlaten:
Dees' hebben 't wel ondersocht, ghelijck het is ghebleken,
 Zyn in 't Catholyck Gheloof ghebleven, en niet af-gheweken,
Blyft in 't oudt Gheloof, ghelyck dees' hebben gheweten,
 Soo en wordt ghy van Calvinus leere niet bescheten,
Gloria Patri by wiēn alle Catholycken sullen komen te-samen,
 En alle verdoolde Calvinisten ter hell', *in saeclua saeculorum. Amen.*

78

The gospell of S. Mathew.
The fyrst Chapter.

Hys ys the boke of
the generaciõ of Jesus Christ the so=
ñe of David/The sonne also of Abra
¶Abraham begatt Isaac: chã.
Isaac begatt Jacob:
Jacob begatt Judas and hys bre=
Judasbegat Phares: (thren:
     and Zaram of thamar:
Phares l egatt Esrom:
Esrom begatt Aram:
Aram beg att Aminadab:

* Abraham and
David are fyrst re
hearsid/ because
that christe was
chefly promysed
vnto them.

Aminadab begatt naassan:
Naasson begatt Salmon:
Salmon begatt boos of rahab:
Boos begatt obed of ruth:
Obed begatt Jesse:
Jesse begatt david the kynge:
¶David the kynge begatt Solomon/of her that was the
Solomon begat roboam: (wyfe of vry:
Roboam begatt Abia:
Abia begatt asa:
Asa begatt iosaphat:
Josaphat begatt Joram:
Joram begatt Osias:
Osias begatt Joatham:
Joatham begatt Achas:
Achas begatt Ezechias:
Ezechias begatt Manasses:
Manasses begatt Amon:
Amon begatt Josias:
Josias begatt Jechonias and his brethren about the tyme of
     the captivite of babilon
¶ After they were led captive to babilon/ Jechonias begatt

Saynct mathew
leveth out certe=
yne generacions/
z describeth Ch=
ristes linage from
solomõ/after the
lawe of Moses/
but Lucas descri=
beth it accordyng
to nature/frõ na=
than solomõs br=
other. For the la=
we calleth them
a mannes childrẽ
which his broder
begatt of his wy=
fe lefte behynde
hym after his de=
the. deu. xxv. c.

THE FIRST
BLAST OF THE
TRVMPET AGAINST
THE MONSTRVOVS
regiment of
women.

✽

Veritas temporis
filia.

M· D· LVIII·

¶ A proclamacion, ordeyned by the Kynges maiestie, with the aduice of his honourable counsayle for the Byble of the largest and greatest volume, to be had in euery churche. Deuised the .vi. day of May the. XXXIII. yeare of the kynges moste gracious reygne.

Here, by Iniunctions heretofore set forth by the auctoritie of the kynges royall maiestie, Supreme head of the churche of this his realme of Englande. It was ordeyned and commaunded amongest other thynges, that in al and synguler paryshe churches, there shuld be prouyded by a certen day nowe expyred, at the costes of the Curates and paryshioners, Bybles conteynynge the olde and newe Testament, in the Englyshe tounge, to be fyxed and set vp openlye in euery of the sayd parysshe churches. The whiche Godlye commaundement and iniunction was to the onlye intent that euery of the kynges maiesties louynge subiectes, myndynge to reade therin, myght by occasyon therof, not only consyder and perceyue the great and ineffable omnipotent power, promyse, iustice, mercy and goodnes of Almyghtie God. But also to learne thereby to obserue Gods commaundementes, and to obeye theyr soueraygne Lorde and hyghe powers, and to exercyse Godlye charitie, and to vse them selues, accordynge to theyr vocations: in a pure and synecere chrysten lyfe without murmure or grudgynges. By the whiche Iniunctiõs the kynges royall maiestie intended, that his louynge subiectes shulde haue and vse the commoditie of the readyng of the sayde Bybles, for the purpose aboue rehersed, humbly, mekely, reuerently and obedientlye: and not that any of them shulde reade the sayde Bybles, wyth lowde and hyghe voyces, in tyme of the celebracion of the

assassinated by Ravaillac. And so the civil war continued until finally in 1629 the power of Cardinal Richelieu finally brought the destruction of the Huguenots to a bloody conclusion. As a social force the Huguenots were not finally eradicated until the revocation of the Edict of Nantes, under Louis XIV.

Protestantism spread to the Netherlands, with William of Orange as one of the converts. The first Calvinist strongholds were in Antwerp and Ghent, but with the Spanish conquests in the south the Protestants either had to recant or to fall back on the estuary towns of Zeeland and the ports of north Holland. Pieter Bruegel, working at this time in Antwerp, had to destroy some of his paintings for fear of Spanish persecution. The Sea Beggars, a militant Dutch Protestant group, captured and held a string of almost impregnable island or maritime bases, stretching from Veere in the south to the Texel in the north.

By 1600, nearly half the population of the Netherlands were Calvinists. The memory of the Catholic Spanish invaders is with the Dutch to this day.

In Scotland, John Knox (c.1505–1572) established a militant Calvinism which took a formidable and lasting hold. In England Henry VIII unconsciously had prepared the way for Protestantism, first by his matrimonial disputes with the Pope, and then on the instigation of Thomas Cromwell by permitting the publication of translations of the Bible into English by Tyndale and Coverdale. William Tyndale's bible was actually printed in Germany, at Worms by Peter Schoeffer in 1525–6. Tyndale had found his reforming zeal had met with so little sympathy in England, that he felt it prudent to move to Germany. He based his translation on both Erasmus's Greek text, and on Martin Luther's German version of the New Testament. Miles Coverdale's translation was largely based on Tyndale's bible and was actually the first to be printed in England in 1536, the same year in which Tyndale was strangled and burnt at the stake.

In England, in 1584, the power of the press was savagely curtailed by the Court of Star Chamber. The religious wars of the sixteenth century were largely due to the productions of the printing press, which at the same time was consolidating national languages and nationalism itself. Luther more than anyone else, by the vast circulation of his writings, helped to establish the power of the press as well as to fashion the modern German language, at the same time locking the vernacular into the gothic mould of black letter typography. The use in Germany of Schwabacher and Fraktur until the twentieth century is the strongest reflection of their enduring Gothic culture. Elsewhere the gothic typefaces were replaced by the roman letter, less quickly in the far north. Even when the roman face was well established, the use of black letter lingered on in legal documents and proclamations.

39 Portrait of Michael Wolgemut by Albrecht Dürer, 1516

40 Copper engraving *The Annunciation* by Martin Schongauer, c. 1475 – 85

41 Johann Froben: detail from a copy of the portrait of the Basel printer by Hans Holbein the Younger. *Oeffentliche Kunstsammlung, Basel*

42 Charcoal drawing by Albrecht Dürer of Willibald Pirckheimer, 1503. *Dumesnil Collection, Paris*

STVLTICIAE LAVS.

rerum humanarum fortunatrix, mecū
adeo consentiat, ut sapiētibus istis semper fuerit inimicissima. Contra stultis
etiam dormientibus, omnia commo-
da adduxerit. Agnoscitis Timotheum
illum, cui hinc etiam cognomen, & pro-
uerbium ἡ εὔδοντῷ κύρῷ αἴρει. Rursum
aliud γλαὺξ ἵπταη. Contra insapientes q̄-
drant illa, ὧ πτ̔ρ̄άδι γεννηθέντες, & equū habet Seianum, & aurum Tolosanū. Sed
desino παροιμιάζεσθ̄, ne uidear Erasmi
mei cōmentaria, suppilasse. Ergo ut ad
rem

nes, triste i fere habui-
isse exitū, idignatus
scripsit, Σωκράτλω ὁ
κόσμῷ πεποίηκε σο
φὸμ εἶναι κҩὶ κακῶς
ἀνεῖλε τῇ μ σοκεάτλω ὁ
κόσμῷ Εμ τῇ φυλα
κῇ, κώνειομ ὅτι πιὼμ τέ
θνηκεμ πελύποδα φα
γὼμ ὁ διογλύκης ὡμὸμ
τέθνηκεμ Αἰχύλω γρά,
φοντι ἐπιπέπωκε Χε
λώνη Σοφοκλῆς ρᾶσα
φαγὼμ σαφυλῆς πνι-
γεις τέθνηκε κωες ὁ-
κατὰ ρ̄ράκλω, εὑριπῖ-
δημ ἔξωγομ τὸμ θεῖομ

Dum ad hunc lorum pue-
niebat Erasmus, sepius
sic uidens exclamauit, Oh-
ohe, Si Erasmus adhuc ra-
lis esset, duraret profecto
uxorem.

ἐμ κρομ, λιμὸς κατεδαπάνησεμ .i. Socratem mundus fecit sapientem esse. Et
male sustulit Socratem mundus. In carcere cicutā, quoniā bibens mortuus
est. Polypedē comedens Diogenes crudum mortuus est. Aeschylo scriben-
ti incidit testudo. Sophocles acinū comedens uuæ, suffocatus perijt. Canes
Thracij Euripidem uorauerunt. Diuinum Homerū fames confecit. Timotheum.) Hic dux erat Atheniesiū, longe omniū fortunatissimus, de q̄ Sui-
das sic scripsit, Επ οίουμ πτ αὐτὸμ ἐμ εἰκόσιμ οἱ ζωγράφοι κοιμώμεμορ, κҩὶ τὰς τύ
χας φορόσας αὐτῶ εἰς δίκτυα πόλҩς, ἡ πορθῶμ Τα αὐ Τὰς, αἰνιττόμμιοι πὴμ εὐδαι
μομίαμ αὐτῶ, ἀλαζομ δυόμ μμιος ἢ ἐπι εὐτυχία ὁ τίμ οθεος, ἔφη αὐτ̄ εἶναι μᾶλλομ, ἢ
τ̄ τύχης, Τα κατορθώματα. διὸ ἡ ἡ τύχη μσεμ ὕσ̄ρομ, νεμεσμσάσης, αὐτῶ τ̄ τύχης .i.
Finxerūt ipsum in imaginibus pictores dormientē, & fortunas ferentes ipsi
in retia ciuitates, & populantē eas inuentes felicitatē ipsius, surpiens aūt pr-
pter bonā fortunā Timotheus, dixit ipsius magis q̄ fortunæ esse, egregie fa-
cta. Quocirca infelicior euasit postea, indignātē ipsi fortuna. ἡ εὔδοντος κύρ
Τος αἴρει) .i. dormietes rete capit. Hoc puerbiū q̄drat in eos, qbus citra labo-
rē & conatū, oiaq̄ cupiūt, eueniūt. Natū ab ipso Timotheo, q uulgo εὐτυχὴς
.i. felix cognominat° est, qd fortunatior q̄ prudētior haberet. γλαὺξ ἵπταη)
.i. noctua uolat. Noctua sacra est Mineruæ. Ea dicta est Atheniēsiū male cō
sulta, in bonū uertere exitū, unde puerbiū, Noctua uolat. Εμ πτ̔ρ̄άδι γεννηθέμ
τ̄ς) .i. q̄rta luna nati, puerbiū est in eos, q ex durissimis laboribus, qb° alijs
prosunt, ipsi nihil fructus capiunt. Quod Hercules hac luna natus ferat.
  Equū habet Seianū) Vtruq̄ puerbiū dicebat de extremo infortunio, unī
de natū sit, explicat Au. Gellius. παροιμιάζεσθ̄) .i. puerbiari, siue puer-
brijs uti. Suppilasse) .i. furtim usurpasse. Neminē nominatim taxauit, præ-

49 *Januarius* from a set of the months, engraved by Hendrik Hondius the younger after J. Wildens. c. 1640. Hondius belonged to a family of map engravers, associated with the great geographer Gerardus Mercator (Gerhard Kremer)

50 Map of Antwerp showing the West Scheldt. Tinted engraving. 1567. As many as 500 ships passed through the port in one day and there were over 60 printers when Plantin arrived there in 1549. *Guildhall Library*

of the Elzevier 'Little Republic'
d in the hand to show how very
se books were. Printed in 1634.
Printing Library

52 Engraved title-page by Pieter van der Borcht from Plantin's
Polyglot Bible. 1572

The Renaissance in France,
and the 'Golden Ages' of French, Dutch and Flemish Printing

The expedition of Charles VIII to Italy in the last decade of the fifteenth century opened the eyes of Frenchmen to the new world of the Renaissance. The succeeding and singularly futile campaigns in Italy at least had the value of increasing French interest in contemporary Italian thought.

François I (he reigned from 1515 to 1547) was obsessed with everything Italian. He made his great new place at Fontainebleau, designed by Gilles le Breton, a treasury of Italian art and invited Italian artists to decorate it with wall paintings and sculpture. Fontainebleau and the other châteaux were overloaded with all the decorative features of northern Italian art, including plaster *putti*, medallions and floral arabesques. The painted stucco figures of Del Rosso and Primaticcio are the first indications of the Baroque movement that was to sweep across Europe in the next century. The mixture of these features with the sub-structure of Gothic building was a curious amalgam. It was not until 1541 with the arrival of Italian architects in France, that at last a building vernacular was established that had absolutely nothing to do with the Gothic.

François I, as well as being a supporter of all the arts, also included printing in his patronage. His reign covered what Daniel Berkeley Updike has appropriately described as 'The Golden Age of French Printing'.[1]

The first great French contribution to the art of printing was made by a former reader at the printing offices of the Estiennes. His name was Geofroy Tory. Updike called him 'a divine jack-of-all-trades'. He was France's answer, at least in the typographic fields, to the 'complete man' of the Italian Renaissance. Tory was a poet, a translator, an orthographer, an artist and a type designer. He was also an extremely competent and logical layout man, one of the first to follow, at least on occasions, the only absolute rule of typography, that is, he allowed the sense of the words to govern the typographic form they should take. Tory, the Renaissance man, came from the medieval background of the cathedral town of Bourges. As a young man, he spent some time travelling in Italy, where the revival of classicism made a deep impression on him. On his return to France he started his typographic experiments, combining the semantic and the visual elements, and also putting into words the thoughts he was formulating about both language and letter design. This link places Tory firmly at the beginning of a line of literary typographers, that is, of men concerned fundamentally with more than tasteful arrangements of prettily designed typefaces, concerned in fact with methods of communication.

In 1525 Simon de Colines published a *Book of Hours* with decorations by Tory, which showed a very nice balance between borders and types. In 1529 Tory published from his own press 'at the Sign of the Broken Pot' another *Book of Hours* and in the same year he issued his most important book,

Le fu Roy francois premier

François I of France: after a chalk drawing by François Clouet. *Mansell Collection*

1. *Printing Types*, D. B. Updike. Harvard University Press, Cambridge, Mass., 1922.

Champ Fleury (*The Field of Flowers*). This book, begun in 1523,
was largely concerned with the form of the French language.
Tory actually introduced the cedilla, the apostrophe and the
accent into French printing. In *Champ Fleury* he discussed the
Florentine doctrine of humanism and followed the precedent of
Leonardo in relating the proportion of roman capital letters to
the proportions of an ideal man. He demonstrated, as Pacioli
and Dürer had done, the geometrical construction of letters.
He also showed methods of drawing letters for purposes as
varied as stained glass and weaving.

In *Champ Fleury*, Tory had some fairly tart observations to
make about both Pacioli and Dürer. He complained that
Pacioli in *De Divina Proportione* gave no explanation how his
capital letters were constructed. He also said: 'I have heard from
some Italians that he purloined the said letters from the late
Messire Leonardo da Vinci, who died recently at Amboise (2nd
May 1519), and who was a most excellent philosopher and
admirable painter, and, as it were, another Archimedes. That
Frère Lucas (*Pacioli*) *has had Leonardo's Attic Letters printed as
his own*. In truth, they may well be his, for he has not drawn
them in the proper proportions.' He then gave Dürer a rap by
saying that he also 'has gone astray in the proper proportion
of the design of many letters in his book on perspective.'
However he softened the blow with, 'We can forgive the said
Albert Dürer, inasmuch as his vocation was painting, and it
rarely happens that painters are good grammarians in the
matter of understanding the qualities and proportions of well
formed letters.'

As a result of the publication of *Champ Fleury*, François
awarded him the title of the first official printer to the King of
France. As well as his type- and letter-design, Tory produced a
number of floral decorations, based on designs he had seen in
Italy, which were forerunners of those used by Robert Adam
for door surrounds and overmantles. Adam claimed his
decorations were based on those discovered in the eighteenth
century at Pompeii and Herculaneum. There is, however, a
marked similarity to Tory's engravings, which the architect may
never have seen.

Four years after the publication of *Champ Fleury* Tory died.
But his influence on book design lived on long after his death.
In a flowery epitaph where tribute is paid to his many qualities
there is also a statement that he had the great type designer
Claude Garamond as his pupil.

In spite of the fact that his *Champ Fleury* was solidly set in a
rather clumsy roman fount, Tory's influence led to the introduction of lighter typefaces (such as Garamond's) and more
open line illustrations. He also effected the change in French
printing, from the use of gothic typefaces to roman, and in
about a tenth of the time that it took to bring about the same
change in England. With Tory's death, royal interest in

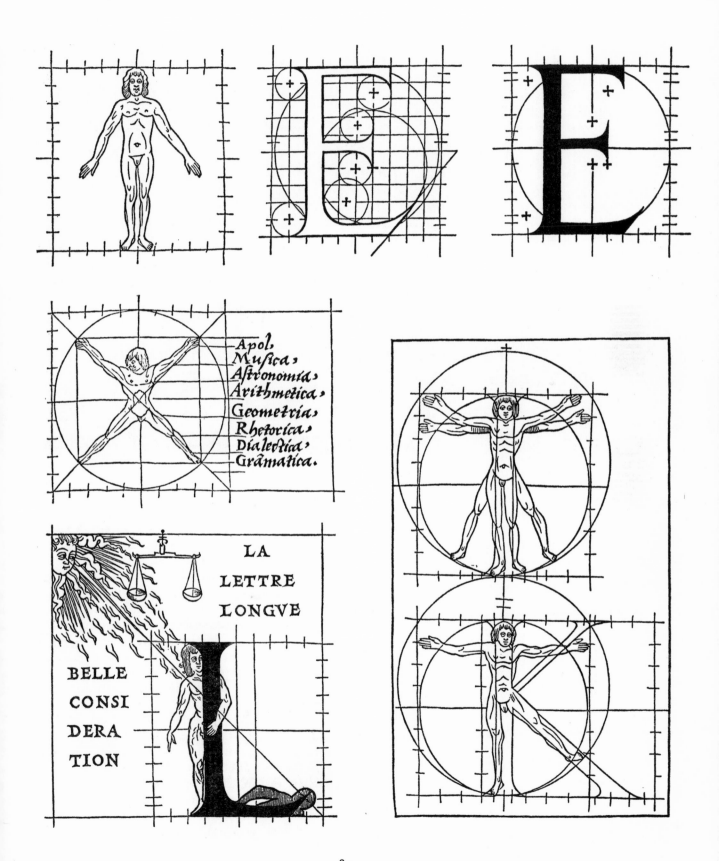

printing showed no signs of waning. It was this same roya interest that induced Garamond to cut his Greek founts o type, appropriately called the *Grecs du Roi*.

In 1547 the first French edition of Vitruvius was published b Jean Martin. This helped to establish even more firmly Italia Renaissance building styles in France. A Fountainebleau lyrica school of painting came into being at the same time, led by De Rosso and Primaticcio. In portraiture, the leading figures wer the Clouets. Jean Clouet, who had been born in Antwerp, cam to France in 1521 and settled in Tours. He and his son Françoi were both expert in portraits drawn in coloured chalks, as wel as precisely detailed oil paintings.

Jean Clouet was given the title of 'Varlet (sic) de Chambre d sa Majesté'; on his father's death in 1540. François succeede to the same appointment. François Clouet was an acute obser ver of character and both his painting and chalk drawings ar reminiscent of Holbein's work. His style was much mor Flemish or German than French and positively astringent i comparison with that of the numerous rather sentimenta Italian painters working at Fontainebleau and elsewhere i

84

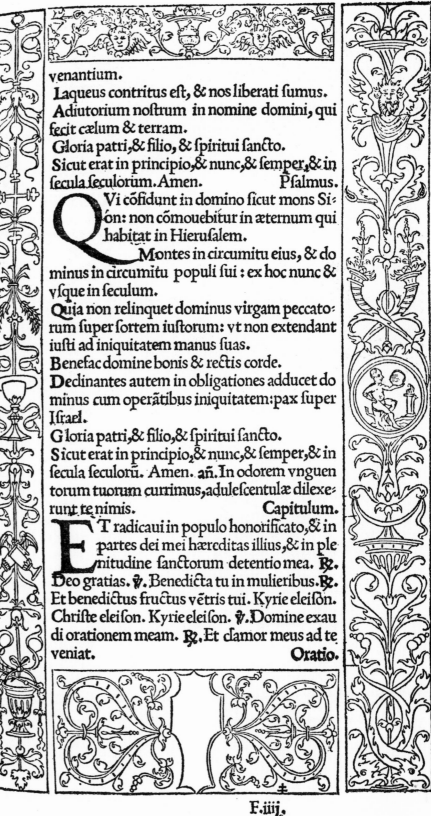

venantium.
Laqueus contritus est, & nos liberati sumus.
Adiutorium nostrum in nomine domini, qui
fecit cælum & terram.
Gloria patri,& filio, & spiritui sancto.
Sicut erat in principio,& nunc,& semper,& in
secula seculorum. Amen.   Psalmus.
Qvi côfidunt in domino sicut mons Si-
ón: non cômouebitur in æternum qui
habitat in Hierusalem.
            Montes in circumitu eius, & do
minus in circumitu populi sui : ex hoc nunc &
vsque in seculum.
Quia non relinquet dominus virgam peccato-
rum super sortem iustorum: vt non extendant
iusti ad iniquitatem manus suas.
Benefac domine bonis & rectis corde.
Declinantes autem in obligationes adducet do
minus cum operãtibus iniquitatem:pax super
Israel.
Gloria patri,& filio,& spiritui sancto.
Sicut erat in principio,& nunc,& semper,& in
secula seculorū. Amen. añ. In odorem vnguen
torum tuorum currimus,adulescentulæ dilexe-
runt te nimis.   Capitulum.
Et radicaui in populo honorificato,& in
partes dei mei hæreditas illius,& in ple-
nitudine sanctorum detentio mea. R̷.
Deo gratias. ꝟ. Benedicta tu in mulieribus.R̷.
Et benedictus fructus vētris tui. Kyrie eleisón.
Christe eleison. Kyrie eleison. ꝟ.Domine exau
di orationem meam. R̷.Et clamor meus ad te
veniat.   Oratio.

ΤΗΝ Ρωμαϊκὴν ἱστορίαν ἐρχόμενος συγγράφειν, ἀναγκαῖον ἡγησάμην προτάξαι τοὺς ὅρους ὅσων ἐθνῶν ἄρχουσι Ρωμαῖοι. εἰσὶ ὃ οἶδε· ἐν μὲν τῷ ὠκεανῷ, Βρετανῶν τῆς πλείονος μέρους· διὰ ὃ τῶ Ἡρακλείων στηλῶν ἐς τήνδε τὴ θάλασσαν ἐσπλεόντες, καὶ ὅπι τὰς αὐτὰς στήλας περιπλέονται, τῶν ἄρχουσι πασῶν, καὶ ἤπειρον ὅσαι καθήκουσιν ὅπι τῆ θάλασσαν ὧν εἰσὶν ἐν δεξιᾷ πρῶτοι Μαυρούσιοι ὅσοι περὶ τ θα—

France. At Chantilly, there are eighty-eight of François Clouet crayon portraits, which provide a revealing insight into the kind of people that thronged the French Court of François I.

The great French printing presses that distinguished the reign of François I, were those of the Estiennes (assisted by Tory, Badius, de Colines and Vascosan, all in Paris; and Trechsel and Gryphius (with Rabelais as an editor) in Lyons. In the early years of the century, the Lyons presses benefited by their distance from the Sorbonne, whose professors exercised a cramping censorship on the Paris printers.

The first printer in Lyons was a Walloon, Guillaume le Roy by name, who had learned his trade in Venice from the de Speier brothers. Le Roy was succeeded by Johann Trechsel, whose daughter married Jodocus Badius. The intermarriage amongst printers' daughters, widows or sons continued with remarkable persistence, helping to maintain a 'closed shop' principle. The Badius's child Perette in turn married Robert Estienne and so it went on!

The privileged position of Lyons as a centre of the book trade (Anton Koberger the Nuremberg printer-publisher had a flourishing branch there) cannot hide its provincialism or its dichotomy of Renaissance and medieval cultures. This dichotomy is certainly reflected in the life and work of François Rabelais, whose books if he had lived under the shadow of the Sorbonne might never have been printed. At the same time as he was editing an edition of Hypocrates, he was working on his medieval fantasies *Pantagruel* and *Gargantua*.

Rabelais was born in Touraine about the year 1490. When he was nearly eighteen, he entered the Franciscan monastery of Fontenay-le-Comte. During his years in this monastery and from 1524 when he changed to the more liberal Benedictine order at Maillezais, Rabelais not only lived the devout life of the Cloister, but also acquired a great store of scholarship. He slowly developed a distaste for the monastic life. Even the hospitable Benedictines were too confining for his far-ranging intelligence. In 1530 he left the monastic life for secular parish work. He had already become interested in medicine when two years later he moved to Lyons, to be appointed physician to the Hôtel Dieu. Here he lectured on anatomy. In the same year he edited for Sebastian Gryphius the medical *Epistles* of Giovanni Manardi and the *Aphorisms* of Hypocrates with the *Ars Parva* of Galen. He is also believed to have edited *Les Grandes et Inestimables Chroniques du Grand et Énorme Géant Gargantua*, which was published in Lyons in 1532. The book was based on the romances of the Round Table and included amongst its characters Arthur, Merlin and the giant Gargantua. Gargantua and Pantagruel were recurring names for giants in the fables of the Middle Ages. In 1533, Rabelais's own *Pantagruel* appeared and his *Gargantua* in 1535. These works, the first part of a four or five volume edition, were full of lively

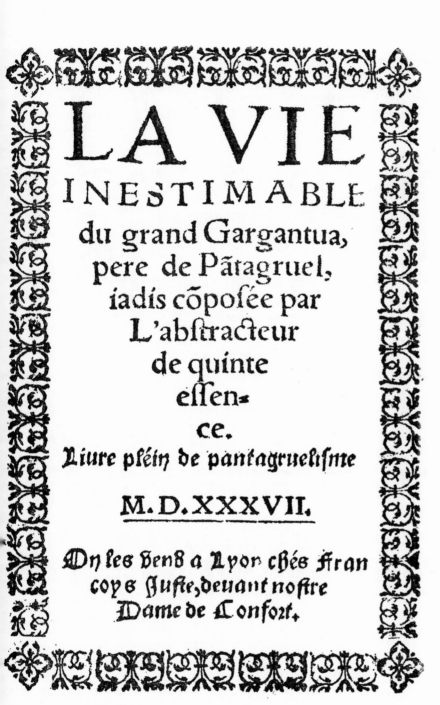

LA VIE
INESTIMABLE
du grand Gargantua,
pere de Pātagruel,
iadis cōpoſee par
L'abſtracteur
de quinte
eſſen-
ce.
Liure plein de pantagruelisme

M.D.XXXVII.

On les uenꝺ a Lyon chés Fran
coys Iuſte, deuant noſtre
Dame de Confort.

satire and much humorous incident, but there was an underlying and serious purpose in his writing, which showed a
concern for the plight of man, for the improvement of education and above all for the chance for everybody to lead a full
and joyous life. In many ways he was like Erasmus, in that he
attacked the worst abuses of the Church. Yet, like Erasmus, he

An engraving of Paris in 1533, showing the River Seine and the Ile de la Cité

was certainly no Protestant. The broad earthy coarseness of his writings was of little concern to his contemporaries, for popular French literature of his time was every bit as bawdy. (This was not true of the contemporary courtly literature, which was surprisingly pure and high-minded.) The Sorbonne disapproved but more on the grounds of his dangerously liberal sentiments than for his obscenity. Yet, because of the liberal atmosphere at Lyons and of his wide connections and powerful friends, Rabelais suffered no persecution. The year *Pantagruel* was published, he was appointed as physician to Jean du Bellay, whose family had provided him with board and lodging after he had left the Benedictines.

With du Bellay, he made two visits to Rome and there was granted a bull of absolution giving him the right to practise medicine and also to return to the Benedictine Order again, if he so wished. In 1537, he took his Doctor of Medicine degree at Montpelier. He held various appointments and for a while lived in Rome. Geofroy Tory describes a quarrel he is supposed to have had with Pierre de Ronsard the French poet, when Ronsard was attached to Jean du Bellay's suite (du Bellay was now a Cardinal). There seems to be no reason for the quarrel, or foundation for this story. Rabelais added two further books to his *Pantagruel* and *Gargantua*, the last appearing in 1552, the same year as Ronsard's *Amours de Cassandre*. Ronsard's support of the vernacular, strongly backed up by du Bellay, started up a fierce literary argument with classicist opponents. Rabelais's fourth book achieved more – it was banned! The Sorbonne censored it and Parliament suspended its sale. However the ban was soon revoked but Rabelais died within the year. Ten years after his death, a fifth book of his saga was published, its authenticity at the time somewhat doubted. Rabelais's books had been repeatedly reissued during his lifetime. A first complete edition was published by Jean Martin at Lyons in 1567 and sixty editions appeared before the end of the century. François Rabelais, in spite of his learning and the width of his knowledge, was a man of the late Middle Ages rather than of the Renaissance. In his writing, the often irreverent way in which he used sacred words and sacred images was to the educated man of the late Middle Ages a perfectly normal thing to do. This was because those sacred words and images were such a familiar and natural part of their life. A Renaissance writer could not have written in this way, because he would not have felt this complete normality of spiritual matters. John Addington Symonds in an expansive moment once said of Rabelais 'What Shakespeare is for England, Rabelais is for France.' Certainly his immense erudition, his wit, his humanity and his superb satire, place him above all his contemporaries. To return to Paris and the printers. Robert Estienne (1503–59) entered his father's firm in 1525. When his father-in-law died, he took over the Badius press, so combining the two firms. The King's patronage was bestowed just as willingly on Robert Estienne as it had been on Geofroy Tory. François I had no doubts about the power of the printed word.

The Estiennes printed and published various royal and government publications, explaining the motives and actions of the King and his parliament to the French people. In 1538, François established a precedent by ordering the Estiennes to deposit a copy of every Greek book that they printed in the Royal Library. In 1539, François produced a code of rules for printers including one covering the copyright of their trade marks and devices, to obviate confusion and plagiarism.[2] Neither Badius nor the Estiennes made use of gothic typefaces.

ΑΙ ΤΟΥ ΑΓΙΟΥ ΓΑΥΛΟΥ ΕΠΙΣΤΟΛΑΙ.

Αἱ καθολικαὶ ἐπιστολαί.
Ἀποκάλυψις τοῦ ἁγίου ἰωάννου τοῦ θεολόγου.

Βασιλεῖ τ' ἀγαθῷ κρατερῷ τ' αἰχμητῇ.

LVTETIAE,
Ex officina Roberti Stephani typographi. Regii, typis Regiis.

M. D. LXVIII.

2. See *Five Hundred Years of Printing*, S. H. Steinberg. Penguin Books, 1955.

ᴅDIVI AVRE=

LII AVGVSTINI HIPPONEN-
fis Epifcopi, in Euangelium Ioan-
nis Expofitio.

Ab eo quod fcriptum eft, In principio erat uerbum
er uerbum erat apud deum, er deus erat uerbum:
ufque ad id quod ait, Et tenebræ eam non compre-
henderunt.   *Tráctatus*   I.

INTVENTES quodmodo au-
diuimus ex lectione Apoftoli-
ca, quòd animalis homo non
percipit ea quę funt fpiritus dei,
& cogitãtes in hac ipfa præfen-
ti turba charitatis veftrę, neceffe
effe, vt multi fint animales, qui
adhuc fecundũ carnem fápiant.

Robert Estienne employed Claude Garamond to cut both roman and italic founts for his press. Garamond's roman was based on one of the typefaces that Griffo cut for Aldus. His italic was copied from that of Arrighi. As Morison says: 'Thus was produced the modern prototype of our old faces; the design that comes down to us by the medium of Voskens, Van Dyck and Caslon.'[3]

Estienne's great Bible published in 1532 gives an early showing of Claude Garamond's *Gros Canon* typeface. The influence of Garamond was immense and not only in France, the Netherlands and ultimately England, but even in Venice. The compliment was repaid to the shades of Jenson, de Speier and Aldus. In 1547, François I died. The protection the Calvinist Estienne had enjoyed had come to an end. With Robert Estienne in Geneva, the firm in Paris passed into the control of various members of the family and suffered varying fortunes, until Antoine Estienne was made *Imprimeur du Roi*. Antoine's death in 1574 brought to an end, after two centuries, 'the most brilliant family of scholar-printers that ever existed'.[4] The great age of Parisian printing had reached and passed its zenith. From now on there was to be a slow decline.

In Lyons, however, great things were still to be done. In 1557 Robert Granjon the Parisian printer and type-founder moved to the south and set up shop in Lyons. In the following year he introduced to the Lyonnais his *civilité* typeface, which certainly had nothing to do with the Renaissance roman letter. It was something like a bâtarde and was based on a cursive gothic handwriting apparently in quite wide use at that time. The model of the *civilité* was generally known as the *lettre courante*. It was a slightly more cursive hand than the bâtarde. The English equivalent is the Secretary Hand, which was often, though not exclusively, used for letters written in the vernacular, while an *Italian* or *Italic* hand was used for Latin. One theory has it that it was named *civilité* because it had been used in a translation from Erasmus of *La Civilité Puérile distribuée par petitz chapitres et sommaires*.[5] The wayward charm of the *caractères de civilité* should not blind us to either their illegibility or to the skill of their punch-cutting.

Ten years earlier Granjon had supplied an italic fount to the Lyons printer Jean de Tournes I. This was for a book called *Paraphrases de l'Astrolabe* by Jacques Focard, most beautifully illustrated by Bernard Salomon. The same combination of italic type and Salomon engravings was to appear in *La Vita et Metamorfoseo d'Ovidio*, reprinted from the edition of 1557 by the younger Jean de Tournes in 1584. Granjon was married to Salomon's daughter. As well as supplying printers such as Jean de Tournes with typefaces, Granjon set up his own print shop and printed and published on his own account. The de Tournes father and son, Robert Granjon and Bernard Salomon were a remarkably talented, if short-lived, quartet of which Lyons

3. *On Type Designs,* Stanley Morison, Benn, 1962.
4 S H. Steinberg.
5. *Printing Types,* D. B. Updike. Harvard University Press, 1922.
   (S. H. Steinberg disagreed with this attribution.)

Double spread from *Paraphrase de l'Astrolabe* by Jacques Focard, illustrated by Bernard Salomon and printed by Jean de Tournes at Lyons in 1535. *British Museum*

Pour trouuer la longueur d'vne circonference.

CHAP.   IX.

 PRES auoir declairé la façõ de trouuer les hauteurs, lõgueurs, largeurs, & profonditez des choses, ne sera inutile de donner à entẽdre ici le moyen pour trouuer la lõgueur de la circõference d'vne figure ronde, estãt tãt en lieu accessible, que inaccessible. Auise (comme par le troisieme chapitre de ce traité est dit) la hauteur de ta figure: ou bien, prens le diametre d'icelle, si tu en peux approcher, car l'extreme hauteur est tousiours le diametre du rond : icelui diametre triple auec vn settieme, font la longueur de la circonference. Presuppose donq qu'il Exemple. y eust vn rond en quelque lieu, duquel tu ne sceusses approc

approcher. Auise par le cinquieme chapitre, la hauteur d'icelui, laquelle as trouuee de sept piez. Multiplie iceux sept piez, qui est le diametre, par trois, & auras vint & vn : aioutez y la settieme partie du diametre, qui est vn pié, & auras en tout vint & deux piez. Par ainsi pourras dire, & conclure, que la longueur de la circonference de ta figure est de vint & deux piez. Et pour plus facile intelligence de ce, tu as ici la figure pourtraite au vif.

ET note, que pour sauoir, que tient toute la fi- Notable. gure, multiplie la moitié des piez de la circonference, qui sont onze, par la moitié des piez du diametre, qui sont trois & demi, & trouueras qu'il viendra 38 piez & demi.

could be justifiably proud. Granjon moved to Antwerp to work for Plantin and their association came to an end when Granjon was invited in 1578 by Pope Gregory XIII to go to Rome. He died a year later. In 1585, the younger de Tournes, because of his Calvinist beliefs, followed Robert Estienne's lead and retired to Switzerland.

By this time, not only had the standards of Parisian printing slumped – largely owing to the reactionary theologians of the Sorbonne having such a dampening effect on free thought, but Lyons also was past the time of its greatest glories.

The Netherlands had by now taken the place of France as the most important centre for the book trade and the printing industry.

Printing as a service industry flourishes wherever industry prospers. It needs conditions of stability, where governments are sufficiently sure of themselves to have no fear of the press. The religious tensions in sixteenth-century France had made conditions difficult, if not impossible, for printers and publishers with Protestant sympathies. Even for others less religiously biased, opportunities were not good. Christopher Plantin was one whose religious sympathies were extremely flexible.

Born in Touraine, he had spent his youth in Lyons and Orléans. At the age of fifteen, he was apprenticed to a bookbinder at Caen. As well as learning a trade, he fell in love with his master's serving wench and married her. In 1545 they settled in Paris, just off the Rue St Jacques, in a house owned by a printer named Jacques Bogard, from whom Plantin learned how to print. The Rue St Jacques is in the middle of both the bookselling trade and the university quarter. Students and lecturers thronged the shops and the cafés, and here Plantin must have made many friends, some of whom were to be of use to him in later life. Many of these friends came from the Netherlands, and maybe as a result of their suggestions and also because of the religious tensions, after only three years in Paris, he moved to Antwerp. One had to be a brave man to print in France in the mid-sixteenth century. Robert Estienne and the younger Jean de Tournes had both become refugees in Switzerland and another unfortunate Lyons printer, Étienne Dolet, had been burned at the stake in Paris, with his entire stock of books helping to feed the flames.

Bruges, for so long the most prosperous city in the Netherlands, had had to give place to Antwerp. Bruges's decline must have been due in part to the silting up of the river Zwyn, whereas Antwerp was superbly placed at the head of the West Scheldt, with deep water right up to her quays. As many as five hundred ships passed through the port in one day. When Plantin arrived at Antwerp it was a city with a population of 100,000. It was the most important banking centre in northern Europe, with the House of Fugger, other financial houses and over a thousand merchants resident in the city. Antwerp was also the centre for Flemish painting and sculpture. 'Between 1491 and 1520, the Guild of St Luke received 358 new members, 150 painters, 30 sculptors and 50 engravers. Quentin Matsys and the Bruegels resided there . . . Joachim Patinir of Dinant, Lucas van Leiden and Jan Sanders of Hemissen all lived there for a time.'[6]

There were over sixty printers in Antwerp when Plantin arrived in 1549. It did not take him long to realise the trading opportunities the city offered. He started with a small bookbinding and print-selling business. He was soon doing well, but one night when delivering a piece of work for a customer, he was set upon by a party of drunken louts and wounded in the right arm. As a result of this accident, he had to give up his

6. *Christopher Plantin*, Colin Clair. Cassell & Co. London, 1960.

Engraving by J. van Velde after P. Saenredam of the interior of
a printing office from S. Ampzing's *Beschryvinge ende lof der stad
Haarlem*. Haarlem, 1628. *St Bride Printing Library*

bookbinding work and in 1555, to replace this lost trade, he set up as a printer and publisher. He still continued in the retail trade, subsidizing his printing and publishing by the sale of maps and engravings, as well as lace and drapery, much of this exported to his contacts in Paris.

His business prospered and he moved to a large house in the Kammerstraat. Soon after this, he took on a boy called Jan Moerentorf, who was later to marry Plantin's second daughter, Martine and, as was fashionable amongst sixteenth-century printers, to Latinize his name to Jan Moretus.

Even in prosperous Antwerp it was not all plain sailing. Whilst Plantin was away on a visit to Paris in 1562, he was charged (probably unjustly) with heresy. His backers and creditors foreclosed and his goods were sold up. In fact, this may well have been a put-up job, for his creditors were his closest friends, who may have taken this drastic action to save his press and his books from confiscation by the authorities. Anyhow, within two years, he had bought it all back!

Plantin remained in Paris for eighteen months, possibly in fear of his life, remembering that between the years 1542 and 1545 three Antwerp printers had been executed for heresy. Whilst Plantin was in Paris, Claude Garamond died. To augment his stock of Garamond founts, Plantin bought from the executors, punches, matrices and moulds for a Hebrew type.

In 1563 he returned to Antwerp and a year later moved to much larger premises in the same street and called the house *De Gulden Passer* (the Golden Compasses). By this time though his resources were still limited he had 32 different sets of punches and matrices (7 of them cut by Claude Garamond and 10 by Granjon). He certainly made a good choice of type-founders. His press flourished but years of fear and worry lay ahead. In 1567 the Duke of Alva began his fearful campaign. The Netherlands was becoming the battlefield between the Reformation and the Counter-Reformation.

Christopher Plantin took considerable trouble to clear himself of any connection with Calvinism. 'In religion and in politics Plantin was evidently something of a trimmer.'[7] To square the ecclesiastical authorities and to consolidate his reputation as a printer Plantin started work on what was to be his greatest achievement, the eight folio volumes of the *Polyglot Bible*. This bible was to be printed in the original languages and with learned commentaries by the most eminent theologians that could be found.

Plantin found a patron in Philip II of Spain, and how he must have regretted it. It would seem that as far as Plantin was concerned, the only good thing that came out of the operation, apart from the Bible itself, was the friendship he formed with Arias Montano, the King's personal chaplain, who came to Antwerp to supervise and proof-read. Montano was a humane man, utterly opposed to Alva's repression. Poor Plantin, the

7. Colin Clair.

Pressmen at work: from an engraving by J. van Velde after P. Saenredam, also from S. Ampzing's book. Saenredam is better known for his paintings of church interiors than for his drawings of print shops. *St Bride Printing Library*

st of the enterprise nearly bankrupted him. *Labore et
nstantia* was the appropriate motto in his device. In spite
being an immensely hard worker, he was constantly short
cash. His press produced a huge output of all kinds of
oks, and he had a monopoly for the sale of Breviaries in the
panish dominions. At his busiest, Plantin employed about
o men and had sixteen presses working at the Golden
ompasses.

antin's books were well printed and immaculately set in
aramond, Granjon, Tavernier and Van der Keere founts of
pe. He made wide use of the copper-engraved title-page,
hich had first been seen in London in a book published in
45. These engravings soon came to serve a double purpose.
the bound book, they provided an elegant preface, a way
to the book. The designs were often in the form of an arch-
ay, with classical and later Baroque pillars and details. It is
so likely that they might have served in the manner of a book
cket. They would have been placed at the top of a tied-up
ndle of collated but unsewn sections, for books were often
ld in this form, so that the customer could choose his own
yle of binding.

antin had close connections with a number of artists and
gravers. His early books had woodcut illustrations but from
e 1560's he used copper engravings. Arnold Nicolai was the
ost prolific of the engravers who worked for Plantin. His
nest engravings were made from eighty botanical illustrations
rawn by Pieter van der Borcht of Malines,[8] a most talented
tist and the son of a painter. When Malines was sacked by the
panish in 1572, the Van der Borchts fled to the Plantins' house
the Kammerstraat. Plantin gladly gave Van der Borcht full
mployment. Pieter van der Borcht was as versatile as he was
lented, as happy drawing people or landscapes as he was
ching or engraving botanical and other illustrations. He
esigned several of Plantin's 'Golden Compasses' devices.

spite of the times, Plantin's publishing, printing and retail
sinesses continued to thrive. He had close connections with
e great geographer, Gerard Mercator, who provided him
ith globes and maps for sale, and he kept Paris and Frankfurt
int sellers supplied with engravings after the works of Pieter
ruegel, Hieronymus Bosch and other Flemish painters. As
ng as he was fit to travel, he went to the annual Frankfurt
air, which was attended by booksellers from every country in
urope. Plantin used to make the journey by horse-drawn
agon to Cologne and then up the Rhine by boat to Frankfurt.
or the Lenten Fair in 1579, he took six barrels of books con-
ining 5,212 copies of 67 different titles.[9]

1576 Plantin moved to the site where the present Plantin-
oretus Museum stands.[10] This was between Vrijdagmarkt and
oogstraat. Four months later the 'Spanish Fury' hit the town.
he unpaid mutinying Spanish mercenaries raped, murdered,

8. *Florum et Coronarum Historia* by Dodoens. Plantin, Antwerp, 1568.
9. Colin Clair.
10. The Plantin-Moretus Museum in Friday Market has been a
museum since 1876, when the Moretus family transferred the house
and its contents, including all the printing materials and library, to
the City of Antwerp.

ransomed and pillaged. Over 6,000 people died and 800 house were gutted in those three days of horror. Three times the ne Plantin press was nearly burned down and nine times th wretched Plantin paid ransoms for his wife and family, good and chattels.

The city was nearing starvation. A loaf of bread cost a sma fortune and business came to a standstill. It would seem tha Plantin was ruined, yet his friends, some of them Spaniard came to his rescue and within a couple of years his press was i production once again. In 1583, he moved to the quiete atmosphere of Leiden to open what amounted to a Universit Press for the new university. The Antwerp house he left i charge of his two sons-in-law. In the congenial surrounding of Leiden, Plantin made many friends. One of these was th son of a pressman who had once worked for him. His name wa Louis Elzevier; he was a bookbinder who was later to becom the founder of the famous Elzevier publishing and printin house.

In 1585, yet another blow fell on the prosperity of Antwerp when the Duke of Parma captured the city after a long sieg and promptly exiled all its Protestant inhabitants. Plantin wa now an old man, yet once again he set about restoring th fortunes of his printing house. Four years later he died, an Jan Moretus became the sole proprietor. In his lifetime Planti had printed nearly two thousand books, mostly in editions o between 1,000 and 4,000. After Plantin's death the pres prospered but it was never again to reach the heights to whic he had taken it. Jan Moretus's son Balthazar, who in tur succeeded his father at the press, was a close friend of the grea Baroque painter Pieter Paul Rubens, who as well as coverin acres of walls and ceilings with allegorical paintings of flesh Flemish females, designed illustration and title-pages for th Plantin press.

Rubens illustrated the *Breviarum Romanum* and Seneca's *Oper* for the Plantin press. The latter book was engraved by Corneli and Theodore Galle, as were many of the elaborate Baroqu title-pages that Rubens designed for the press.

This use of the engraved title-page was continued by th Elzeviers who shared the Netherlands trade with the Planti house. The Plantins had the whole of the Catholic market o the southern Netherlands to themselves, the Elzeviers ha almost a clear field in the Protestant north.

We are now approaching 'the golden age' of Holland and of th Dutch book trade. The Elzeviers were the great popula printers of their time. Their books were comparable in man ways to the modern 'serious' paperback. Dutch classica scholarship was at its peak and the Elzeviers had little difficult in recruiting editors competent to edit the great series o classical texts that they printed.

Louis Elzevier, Plantin's friend, who had settled in Leiden as

Title-page designed by Pieter Paul Rubens and engraved by
Marinus for *Le Voyage du Prince Fernande Infant d'Espagne*.
Antwerp, 1635

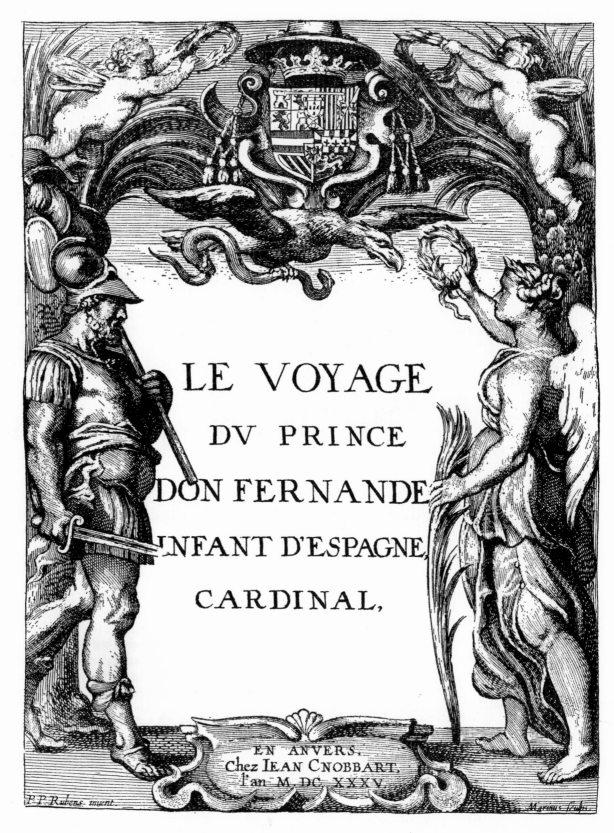

LE VOYAGE
DV PRINCE
DON FERNANDE
INFANT D'ESPAGNE,
CARDINAL,

EN ANVERS,
Chez IEAN CNOBBART,
l'an M. DC. XXXV

P.P. Rubens. invent.

Marinus sculp.

'A small water-logged country . . .' The port of Veere in Zeeland.
An engraving showing the sixteenth-century tower of the
Stadhuis and the massive bulk of the Grote Kerk. 1753

'A small water-logged country . . .' The port of Veere in Zeeland.
An engraving showing the sixteenth-century tower of the
Stadhuis and the massive bulk of the Grote Kerk. 1753

bookseller, turned his attention to printing and established hi
press in 1583. His books consisted mostly of reprints of classica
texts. The first contemporary author that Elzevier published
was a typical Hollander, the lawyer and don Hugo Grotius
whose *Mare Liberum* appeared in the founder's lifetime in 1609
Louis Elzevier died in 1617 and three years later the press wa
appointed as official printers to the University of Leiden, which
had a high proportion of foreign students. In 1626, Louis's son
Bonaventura who had succeeded his father in the managemen
of the press went into partnership with one of his nephews
The firm prospered and its fame spread to the farthest corner o
Europe. In 1629 they launched their series of little book
(12 mo) of classical texts which sold for a florin. Not a student lef
Leiden University without taking one or more Elzevier book

back home with him. The next series the Elzeviers published, was under the title of 'Little Republics'. These tiny (16mo) books covered history, politics and economics and were edited by a director of the Dutch East India Company,[11] (see plate 51). One of the most illustrious of the Elzevier employees was Christoffel van Dyck who ran their type foundry and cut many of their typefaces. The firm spread its activities to bookselling, both antiquarian and contemporary, and opened branches in Utrecht and The Hague, and another printing office in Amsterdam. Their once greatly prized little books are rather run-of-the-mill productions. Many of them were close set in Van Dyck's version of Garamond, a solid looking typeface with a good ink bearing surface.

After one hundred years of successful printing and publishing

11. S. H. Steinberg.

AMSTELODAMI.
Apud Ioannem à Ravesteyn. A°. 1669.

the firm's fortunes began to decline, coming to a full stop in the year 1712.

In writing about the Netherlands, J. H. Huizinga in his essay *Dutch Civilization in the 17th Century*, said: 'We can see why Athens and Florence, Rome and Paris should, in their time, have all been centres of culture, but it seems incredible that their mantle should have fallen, for however brief a time, on a small water-logged country between the Ems and Vlie and the Maas and Scheldt.'

There were a number of reasons for the economic growth of the Netherlands in the seventeenth century. Long before they became an independent state, events were shaping the future of this 'water-logged country'. In a country bordered by the sea, with the Zuider Zee and the Wadden Zee within its boundaries, and threaded with a network of rivers and canals, it had communications that were far more economic than roads, methods of transport far more capacious than packhorses and wagons. With sheltered ports like Harlingen, Hoorn and Enkhuizen there were opportunities for seafaring, fishing, and sea-warfare, let alone piracy. From the Middle Ages the Dutch seamen traded in the Baltic and to Norway in rivalry with the ships of the Hanseatic League. By the beginning of the seventeenth century, the Dutch were making trading voyages to India and to the East Indies. In 1609 the Dutch East India Company wishing to extend its interests even more, commissioned Henry Hudson, an Englishman, to find a northern route to China for them. With maps from the cartographer Hondius, he at least found the site of what is now New York and in time reached Hudson Bay, even if he found no North-West Passage. In spite of war and unrest, trade went on expanding and by the beginning of the seventeenth century Dutch seaborne trade was larger than that of England and France together. With the decline of Antwerp after 1585 and with the closure by the Duke of Alva of the Scheldt, Amsterdam came to the fore as the most prosperous trading port in Northern Europe, but, as Huizinga says, 'the absence of competitors was a prime cause of the vast commercial expansion of the republic.'

All the Netherlands' potential rivals in trade were so enfeebled by their prolonged wars, or so concerned with their domestic problems, that they left the field clear for this mainly Calvinistic, quiet, staunch, little country to gain immense riches in an unbelievably short time, and in spite of the Spanish domination. The Calvinistic principles of the Dutch Reform Church were laid down at the Synod of Dort in 1608, but the spirit of Erasmus was too much a part of their life for Calvinism to have it all its own way.

There were factors other than religion that led to their prosperity. Commerce benefited not only from a lack of competitors, but also from a lack of a centralised government, and the kind of bureaucratic restrictions that usually flow from such

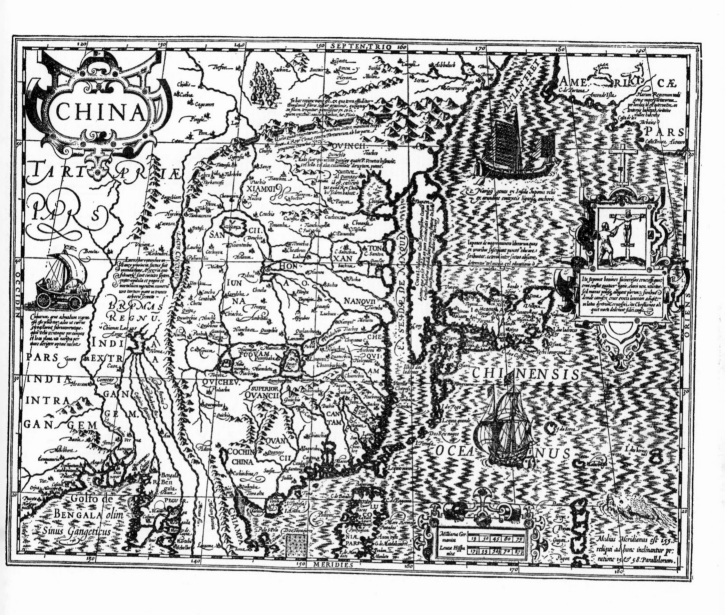

controls. In the towns – the Netherlands is a country of towns, often small, always self-sufficient – the old guild systems still operated. When Christopher Plantin went to Antwerp, the first thing he did was to join the Guild of St Luke, the Guild that in the Low Countries governed the activities of all printers, as well as engravers, painters and sculptors. Industry developed quite satisfactorily under this medieval system and industries concerned with such commodities as spirits, salt, soap, sugar, tobacco or herring-curing, were little affected by guild rules. By the middle of the seventeenth century, Amsterdam, with a population of 150,000, had far outstripped Antwerp. Instead of building vast palaces, the democratic aldermen and burgomasters of Amsterdam followed their watery bent and built

canals. Three new concentric canals were built within half a
century. The Herengracht, the Keizersgracht and the Prinsen-
gracht, with their superbly graceful houses were the Dutch-
man's democratic answer to the flamboyance of Versailles or
the Hôtel des Invalides in Paris. There was little scope in this
small country for architecture on the grand scale.

It was a conservative, relatively democratic country, where the
shopkeeper could rub shoulders with rich industrialists or
learned professors in such cultural associations as the Chambers
of Rhetoric, or in the meetings of the Civic Guard. And all this
middle-class prosperity produced the first great demand in
Europe by *ordinary* people for pictures to decorate their homes
or to portray their wives in the midst of their brightly burnished
interiors. This was no renaissance attitude to artists, where
Michelangelo was treated as a prince and Rubens and Van
Dyck from neighbouring Flanders were given knighthoods by
gratified English royalty. The Dutch painters, as painters have
often been, were of the lower middle classes, and were regarded
as tradesmen, in much the same way as if they had been shoe-
makers or bookbinders. It was of little concern to the upper
classes if sometimes they starved.

Rembrandt alone, as much by his eccentric Bohemianism as for
the quality of his work, did arouse some attention. Franz Hals
died penniless in a Haarlem almshouse, Vermeer was thought
of no account and little is heard of the lives of masters such as
Pieter de Hooch, the genre painter, or Jacob van Ruisdael, the
greatest of Dutch landscape painters. Their pictures could be
bought for a few florins, not only in shops but from street

HET HOF VAN HOLLANDT

Copye.

T Erſame/wijſe/voorſienighe ſeer diſcrete Heeren.

NAdemael het Godt den Heere Almachtich/ door ſyne Majeſteyts grontlooſe barmherticheyt ghelieft heeft/ naer eene ſoo langhduyrighe gheſtadighe bloedighe Inlantſche Oorloghe van ontrent veertich jaren/ buy ten alle apparentie/ ende ghenouch teghens de alghemeyne opinie der menſchen/de ghemoederen van beyde trpghende deelen te diſponeren ende capabel te maken / tot het aennemen / ende eyntelijck beſluyten van een Beſtant van alle acten van vyantſchap/ſo ter Zee/ andere Wateren/ als te Lande/ voor den tijt van twaelf jaren/ daer upt dat door de ghenade des Heeren Almachtich te verhopen ſtaet/ te ſullen volgen eenen God lijcken/eerlicken/ ende verſekerde Peys/ mette behoudeniſſe vanden Vrydom/ Gerechticheyden/ ende Pri vilegien vanden Lande/ (weſende de eenighe upcompſte diemen vande voorſz. langhduyrighe Oorloghe met groot ghedult verwacht heeft) by ſoo verre als wy ons daer toe bequaem maecken/ ende met behoor lijcke danckbaerheyt/deſe grootſte ende hoochſte weldaet/ende ghenade van Godt teghen hem erkennende/ ſyne Godlicke Majeſtept daerom bidden/ ende hem daer voren eeren/ loven/ pryſen ende dancken/ſyn hey lich woort aen te nemen/ende ons daer naer rechten/ende dat beleven.

SOo iſt/ dat de Hooge Moghende Heeren Stat Generael der Vereenichde Nederlanden/t'ſelve naer hunne groote wijſheyt eñ ervarentheyt met aendacht/naer behooren bedenckende/noodigh geacht hebbē te ordonneren tot eenen alghemeynen danckſegghinghe ende Bededach in alle de vereenighde Provintien/ woenſdach/den vj. dagh der Maendt van May/ toecomende. Omme ten ſelven daghe Godt den Heere Almachtich voor de voorſz. ſyne weldaet/ende beweſen over groote ghenade by het Beſlupt van het voorſz. Beſtant/van gantſcher herten te loven/pryſen/ende dancken/ende ſyne Godlicke Majeſteyt vierichlicken te bidden/ſyne milde ghenade deſe Landen voorder noch te willen continueren/ ende ende ſelve zijn heplich woordt hoe langher ſoo meer verbreyden/ ende ſynen rijcken ſeghen in neeringhe ende welvaren oock ver meerderen/ende ten ſelven effecte den ghewenſchten Godtſalighen/ eerlicken/ ende verſekerden Peys verlee nen: Mitſgaders de vereenichde Provintien in vaſte eenicheydt/ vryndtſchap ende correſpondentie by mal deren/onder eenen wel gheauthoriſeerde Regieringhe handthouden ende conſerveren/ oock afwerpen ende te niete maecken alle liſtighe raedtſlaghen ende practijcken/ die daer teghen/ by yemanden int heymelijc of te openbaer voorghenomen ende beleydt ſoude moghen worden: Verſoecken daerom / ende begeeren Wy/ ende des niet te min/inden naem als boven/ordonneren ende bevelen/den voorſz. danckſegginge ende Bede dagh/binnen uwe Stede ende Juriſdictie van dien/ter plaetſe daer dat gebruyckelick is/ te doen tijſtelijcken publiceren/ ende vercondighen/ende eenen ygelijck te ordonneren/ ende laſten hen daer naer te reguleren/ ende ten ſelven daghe hen te onthouden van alle Handtwerck/Kaetſen/kloot-ſchieten/Bal-ſlaen/ Tappen/ Drincken of dierghelijcken/daermede de voorſz. Vaſten/ Danckſegginghe/ ende Bededach ſoude moghen ontheplicht worden/by ſekere groote penen daer toe te ſtatueren: Daer op wy ons ſullen verlaten.

Hier mede

Eerſame/wijſe/voorſienighe/ſeer diſcrete Heeren/uwer in ſchuts des Almogende bevelende. Gheſchreven inden Haghe/ den xxij. Aprilis 1609. Onder ſtondt/ Ter Ordonnantie vande Ghecommitteerde Raden vande Staten.Onderteeckent/ A. Duyc.

De Superſcriptie:

Eerſamen/wijſen/ſeer Diſcreten Heeren/ den Burghermeeſteren ende Regierders van Amſtelredam.

Interior of a printing office engraved by Abraham von Werdt, Nuremberg 1678. This well-known engraving shows compositors at work, a warehouseman packing sheets into a tub and two pressmen, one inking a forme and the other lifting off a printed sheet. Unlike many earlier presses, there appears to be no bracing from the ceiling. Possibly the gryphon on the top of the press was of cast iron and acted as a counterbalance. *St Bride Printing Library*

markets and booths in travelling fairs. This essentially bourgeois attitude to art might have resulted in a flood of mediocrity just as it did in England in the 19th century. Yet the traditions of Van Eyck and of the last years of the Middle Ages were still alive. The faithful portrayals of domestic scenes, architecture or landscape were the result of much thoughtful analysis. The work of such painters as Gerhard Ter Borch or Heyman Dullaert bore no relation to the banal pot-boilers of Victorian England.

This middle-class prosperity also brought an unprecedented demand for books. This demand was largely met by the Elzeviers, both with their own publications and their large trade in bookselling. The jobbing printer and the engraving shops were even busier, serving every kind of trader.

The most popular authors in the Netherlands were the Catholic poet Joost van den Vondel, the lawyer Hugo von Grotius, whose *De Jure Pacis et Belli* was the first book to deal in full with international law, and the Amsterdam shoemaker's

on, Gerbrand Adriaanszoon Bredero, made famous by his picar-
sque *Spanish Brabanter*. Bredero had been trained as a painter.
His book *Moortje*, based on a French translation of Terence's
Eunuch, was written only as a painter could write, the narrative
enriched by the visual sense and the trained eye of the artist.
Apart from Plantin and Elzevier, the most interesting side of
Dutch printing, perhaps naturally enough for this seafaring
nation, was the production of maps and charts. Hondius and
Jansson published in 1638 a three-volume folio atlas entitled
Atlas Novus sive Descriptio geographica Totius Orbis Terrarum,
compiled by Mercator and Hondius and printed by Hondius.
Soon after, the rival firm of Blaeu published their *Novus Atlas*
in six large folio volumes. The diarist John Evelyn records
visiting both Blaeu's and Hondius's workshops in 1641. Updike
quotes a contemporary account of Blaeu's establishment: 'On
the Blumengracht . . . may be found the printing house of John
Blaeu furnished with nine type presses, named after the nine
muses, six presses for copper-plate printing and a type foundry'.
This anonymous account continues with a detailed description
of the building, beginning with the ground floor, where were
the copper-plate pressroom, the book-printing pressroom and
the composing room. Upstairs were the proof-readers, the
warehouse and the foundry.[12] The layout of this seventeenth-
century printing house was not so different from that of one
today.

Gothic typefaces were still in daily use in seventeenth-century
Holland; in character they were robust, fat and square (*lettres
de forme*). The French type-founder Pierre Simon Fournier
writing in his *Manuel Typographique* about Dutch type-founders
records that Dirk Voskens had established a new foundry in
Amsterdam at the end of the seventeenth century and that
another foundry in Amsterdam was started by Christoffel van
Dyck and a third by Izaak van de Putte. An Amsterdam printer
called Hendrik Floris Wetstein also had a small foundry and
used type-punches cut by the German letter-cutter J. M.
Fleischmann. This foundry was bought up by Izaak Enschedé
and his son Johannes in 1743 and moved to Haarlem. Though
Fournier called Fleischmann a very skilful type-cutter, he went
on to berate him for the narrowness of his typefaces. He wrote
'The descendants of the Elzeviers are more shopkeepers than
artists. They judge books by the profits they make. . . . Their
desire to economise the space which a well-made letter has a
right to occupy has led them deliberately to acquire types of a
cramped starved look, so that they may get in more words to
the line and more lines to the page.'[13]

The typographic battlefield had switched from gothic versus
roman, to narrow, short-descendered roman letters versus
wide, rounded, roman letters with long ascenders and descenders. It was to be a prolonged series of skirmishes that
continued for the next two hundred years.

ACTUS IV. SCENA I.

DEMIPHO, CHREMES.

QUID? qua profectus causa hinc es Lemnum,
  Chremes,
Adduxtin' tecum filiam? c. non. D. quid ita non?
c. postquam vidit me ejus mater esse hic diutius,
Simul autem non manebat ætas virginis
Meam neglegentiam; ipsam cum omni familia
Ad me profectam esse aiebant. D. quid illic tam diu,
Quæso, igitur commorabare, ubi id audiveras?

           c. Pol

12. *Printing Types*, D. B. Updike. Harvard University Press, Cambridge, Mass., 1922.
13. *Fournier on Typefounding* translated by Harry Carter, Soncino Press,
London, 1930.

Title-page from R. Higden's *Polycronycon* (*sic*), 1527 edition.
Printed by Peter Treveris at the 'Sign of the Woodwose' for
John Reynes whose mark appears at the foot of the design

Caxton died in 1491 and was succeeded at the Westminster press by his chief workman, an Alsatian called Wynkyn de Worde. The following year Richard Pynson, a Norman Frenchman from Rouen, set up in opposition to de Worde. Both printers continued to use gothic typefaces, though in 1509, to meet the demands of the New Learning, Pynson imported from Paris some roman founts for occasional use. There were no type-founders as such in England, nor in France for that matter. Printers still had to cut their own punches, or buy type or matrices from the larger printing houses, such as Froben's in Basel. They then had to employ itinerant casters, to cast the type. This state of affairs was to last until type-founding and type-cutting became established as a separate trade in the 17th century. One of the first 'modern' type-foundries was the Luther Foundry, which was operating in Frankfurt in the late 16th century.

In 1509, Erasmus published *The Praise of Folly*. The New Learning that Erasmus inspired was supported by John Colet, the Dean of St Pauls, and by the King, Henry VIII, who was then eighteen years old. Colet was the founder of St Paul's School and virtually of the system of middle-class education in England. Oxford and Cambridge were lifted from a state of academic stagnation and students turned eagerly to the study of Greek literature and to new grammars produced by Erasmus and others. At Cambridge they actually had Erasmus as Greek Professor and how he complained of the weather and the beer! The influence of the Renaissance was belatedly making an impact, an impact that was accelerated by the printing press. Erasmus remained at Cambridge until 1514, when disappointed by the war-like antics of King Henry VIII, he left for Basel to stay with his printer-friend, Johann Froben. Here he spent most of the next few years, acting as general editor and literary adviser to the Froben press. It is interesting to speculate what might have happened to the course of English printing if he had devoted his time to one of the English presses. It is doubtful if he even contemplated such a thing, for the English printers must have seemed to this man of letters very primitive establishments in comparison with the great Basel press.

In a time of complicated theological dogma, Erasmus's plea was for a return to a simple Christian belief. His edition of the Greek testament was in part the result of the encouragement he received from English scholars, though it was not printed in England but printed and published in Basel by Froben in 1516, two years after Erasmus had left England. In its turn, it provided the basis for Luther's German and Tyndale's English translations.

Erasmus's closest friend in England was Thomas More, in whose house, during the winter of 1509–10, he had written *The Praise of Folly*. (Its Latin title was *Moriae Encomium*, a compliment to his host.) Erasmus says of England: '. . .where-

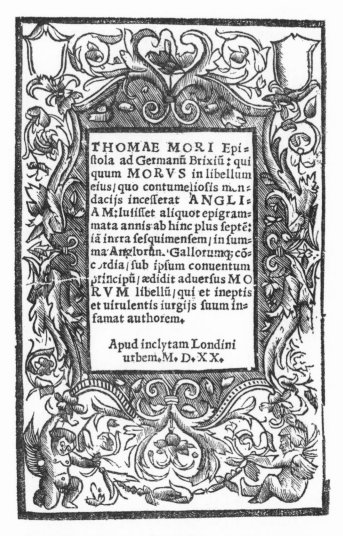

Thomas More's *Epistola ad Germanu Brixiu*, printed by Richard Pynson in London, 1520. The spirited engraving was based on one cut by Urs Graf at Basel for Froben

ARISE·FOR — IT IS DAY.

ever you go, you get your share of kisses. No country was so
much to my liking, a most agreeable and healthy climate and
such an abundance of civilization and learning.' And of Thomas
More: 'What has nature ever produced that was milder, gentler
and happier than the mind of Thomas More?'[1]
More's *Utopia* was published in 1516 by Theodoric Martin at
Louvain for lack of a competent English printer or for a
printer brave enough to publish this tract. *Utopia* came out only
a few months after Erasmus's *New Testament* had been printed
by Froben. In *Utopia*, More pleads against autocracy and for
justice between rich and poor. His plea was occasioned by the
enclosures of common land by wealthy landowners, who thus
deprived the peasants of much independence. He also calls for
education for all and for freedom to worship as people wished.
'In *Utopia*, More is concerned to show that the old, medieval
institutes, if freed from abuse, are the best';[2] a little reactionary
he was yet foreshadowing a new political doctrine.
With Henry VIII firmly established on the throne, Erasmus
showed some wisdom in leaving the country he loved so well.
A reign of terror began with Wolsey's death in 1531 and all
Thomas More's charm, virtue and learning could not save him
from the consequences of refusing the Oath of Allegiance,
which had to be coupled with the acknowledgement that
Henry's marriage to Katharine of Aragon was invalid. The
King had knighted him in 1521. Fourteen years later he had
him executed. Thomas More's friend Erasmus died in the
following year.
Henry, served first by Wolsey and then by Thomas Cromwell,
had made himself head of the English Church. The monasteries
opposed him, so with this as a partial excuse and with Cromwell's support, he set about annexing their lands. Revolt broke
out in Lincolnshire and Yorkshire, both in support of the
monasteries and because of the land enclosures. In 1539, the
great abbeys of Jervaulx and Fountains were suppressed after
over four hundred years of existence and their Abbots were
hanged at Tyburn.
Thomas Cromwell, former commercial agent in Venice and
wool merchant in Middelburg, met the fate common to those
who serve a despot, and in his turn had his head chopped off.
Such a climate was not one in which either art or printing
would thrive. The only notable artist in England was the
German Hans Holbein, who recorded with great precision the
likenesses of the King and of his wives, Jane Seymour and Anne
of Cleves (an over-flattering portrait so Henry thought). It was
whilst he was painting his picture *Henry VIII Confirming the
Privileges of the Barber Surgeons*, that Holbein was taken ill with
the plague and died. If anyone had any doubts about what kind
of man Henry was, a close look at one of Holbein's drawings
of the king should put the matter beyond doubt.
The City of London, in spite of the vagaries of her monarch,

1. *Man not Citizen: Erasmus in our time*, Hans Redeker, Trs. H. Romeijn,
Boymans-van Beuningen Museum, Rotterdam, 1969.
2. *Printing and the Mind of Man*, John Carter and Percy H. Muir, Cassell
and Co. Ltd, 1967.

...as already one of the main centres of European trade. The most important English trade had been with Flanders, where the value of the annual export of wool was over £2,000,000 a year. After the siege of Antwerp by the Duke of Parma, the power of this great port waned and many of its bankers and merchants fled to London. In spite of such commercial opportunities, when Elizabeth came to the throne in 1558, England was in a state of penury.

Printing, like art, thrives when there is both the prosperity of commerce and the intellectual curiosity of scholars and laymen to establish a demand for books and pamphlets. But printing can only thrive if the press is free. Nothing was free under Henry VIII, nor under his elder daughter, least of all the press, yet more people could read then than two hundred years later. In the last year of Queen Mary's reign the Stationers' Company was formed with a Royal Charter to control seditious or heretical books. No book might be printed unless it was licensed. Presses were closed down and printing shops were finally restricted to a few in London and one in each of the two main university towns. Editions were limited to not more than 1,500 copies from one setting. Yet the demand for books was greater than ever. The presses met this demand somehow, but with a standard of printing worse than anything Caxton had printed a hundred years before. The presswork was wretched, the typefaces battered and the imposition inaccurate. The glories of Elizabeth's reign, the defeat of the Spaniards or Drake's epic voyages, were not matched by any glorious printing. There was only one printer-publisher-type-founder of any note, and that was John Day.

Day was a Suffolk man, who had been born at Dunwich in 1522. He was working in London in 1544 and through the friendship of another Suffolk man, Archbishop Parker, who had once been Warden of the College of Stoke-by-Clare, Day was enabled to install himself in a little flat-roofed shop in St Paul's Churchyard, an area that housed a number of booksellers. Day soon became one of the foremost printers of his time, though during Mary's reign he had been both imprisoned and exiled. By the time Elizabeth had ascended the throne, he was back in England and was one of the first printers to be listed by the re-formed Stationers' Company. One of Day's proofreaders was John Foxe, and three editions of Foxe's *Book of Martyrs* were issued from Day's press.

Day's device is of interest for it shows a sleeper being awakened. The caption reads: 'Arise, for it is Day', both a pun on the printer's name and a reference to the dawn of religious emancipation. The only other contemporary English printers of any consequence were the Barkers, father and son. Christopher Barker was appointed Queen's printer in 1577 and was succeeded by his son Robert in 1582. In 1611, Robert Barker printed the first edition of the Authorized Version of the

Much adoe about Nothing

As it hath been *sundrie times publikely*
acted by the right honourable, the Lord
Chamberlaine his seruants.

Written by William Shakespeare·

LONDON
Printed by V.S.for Andrew Wise,and
William Aspley.
1600.

Bible, which he set in black letter. To a public conditioned to
reading imported bibles in English, but set in roman type, it
proved unacceptable. Cutting his losses, a year later he reprinted it, having entirely re-set it in a roman fount.

It was Robert Barker who, as King's Printer, reprinted the
Star Chamber Decree in 1637, which had limited the number of
presses and type-founders to those then in operation in London
and in Oxford and Cambridge. Four years later the Court of
Star Chamber was abolished but the Licensing Act was not
finally dropped until 1695. Yet during this time such presses
as there were published amongst much ephemeral printing

A
DECREE
OF
Starre-Chamber,
CONCERNING
PRINTING,
*Made the eleuenth day of July
laſt paſt.* 1 6 3 7.

❧ Imprinted at London by *Robert Barker,*
Printer to the Kings moſt Excellent
Maieſtie: And by the Aſſignes
of *Iohn Bill.* 1 6 3 7.

penser's *Shepheard's Calendar* and his *Faerie Queene*, Marlow's
Tambourlaine and *Jew of Malta*, all Shakespeare's works, begin-
ing with *Venus and Adonis* in 1593 and ending with the
omplete plays (the 'first folio') in 1623. Within a few years of
hakespeare's death, Ben Jonson's plays, Herrick's poems,
Hakluyt's *Voyages* and the English Bible were all printed and
miserably printed in great quantities. The influence of these
ibles, ill-printed though they were, was universal. The Bible
became the one book of the literate working man.[3] It formed
is thought and his language. Its literal interpretation was the
asis of Puritanism.

3. The price of Coverdale's Bible was ten shillings if in sheets, or
twelve shillings if bound. *The English Common Reader*. Richard D.
Altick, University of Chicago Press, 1957.

AREOPAGITICA;

A

SPEECH

OF

M^r. *JOHN MILTON*

For the Liberty of V N L I C E N C'D PRINTING,

To the PARLAMENT of ENGLAND.

Τὸ λίθερον δ' ἐκεῖνο, εἴ τις θέλει πόλι
Χρηστόν τι βέλδμ' εἰς μέσον φέρειν, ἔχων.
Καὶ ταῦθ' ὁ χρήζων, λαμπρός ἐσθ', ὁ μὴ θέλων,
Σιγᾷ, τί τέτων ἐστὶν ἰσαίτερον πόλι;
                                    Euripid. Hicetid.

This is true Liberty when free born men
Having to advise the public may speak free,
Which he who can, and will, deserv's high praise,
Who neither can nor will, may hold his peace;
What can be juster in a State then this?
                                    Euripid. Hicetid.

LONDON,
Printed in the Yeare, 1644.

In 1620, the most notable emigration of Puritans took pla[ce] when the Mayflower sailed for Massachusetts. Five years lat[er] Charles I came to the throne and a new set of troubles bes[et] the English people. In 1629, the king's dissolution of parli[a]ment reduced the Puritans to despair. Many of them follow[ed] the Pilgrim Fathers to the New World. In the next ten year[s] over twenty thousand Englishmen landed on the coast of Ne[w] England. They went in search of freedom of speech and fre[e]dom to worship as they wished. In 1639, the first America[n] printing press was established by Stephen Daye at Harva[rd] College, in Cambridge, Massachusetts. The first piece [of] printing was, perversely enough, an 'Oath of Allegiance to th[e] King'. The trade developed slowly and there was still n[o] American type-founder in Benjamin Franklin's day. To produ[ce] new sorts, Franklin was put to the expedient of using suc[h] types as he had bought from Europe as if they were punche[s]. These he struck in to both clay and lead. From these very im[-]perfect matrices, he cast his type.

In 1644, John Milton published his *Areopagitica: A Speech f[or] The Liberty of Unlicenc'd Printing, to the Parlament of Englan[d]* (The printer wisely remained anonymous.) However, with th[e] end of the Court of Star Chamber in 1641, the worst days [of] censorship were over, even though the Government had r[e]established the Licensing Laws by the Ordinance of 1643. Th[e] cry for freedom of the press is as relevant today as it was thre[e] hundred years ago.

Milton's *Comus*, which had appeared ten years earlier, was i[n] itself a protest against the bigotry of many of the Puritans wh[o] regarded playgoing as a deadly sin and dancing round a may[-]pole or wearing a wig as acts beyond redemption. It certainl[y] was not a propitious age for artists, and from the time [of] Holbein native artists had not prospered. The Protestant ha[d] too deep an aversion to religious painting and the only job le[ft] for the painter was to portray the Court, the nobility and th[e] rich merchants. England had no native painter of genius an[d] had to import her talent, at first from Flanders and later fro[m] Germany. Charles I knighted Sir Pieter Paul Rubens in 162[9] when he was on a diplomatic visit to England and presumabl[y] to encourage him to work there. Six years later Rubens com[-]pleted his decorations for the ceiling of Inigo Jones's Ban[-]queting House in Whitehall. At the same time Rubens's mos[t] gifted pupil, Anthony van Dyck, settled in England and ha[d] an instant success as a Court painter. He was in his tur[n] knighted by an approving monarch.

In the seventeenth century, the only native-born artists of not[e] were the miniaturists Nicholas Hilliard (who had died in 1619[)] Samuel Cooper and William Dobson, portrayer of the Cava[-]liers at war, and the animal painter Francis Barlow (1626[-]1702) who was a painter, an illustrator and an engraver. In 166[6] Francis Barlow illustrated an edition of Aesop's *Fables* wit[h]

The Whole Booke of Psalmes title-page, printed by Stephen Daye at
Cambridge, Mass. in 1640. This was the first book to be printed
in North America

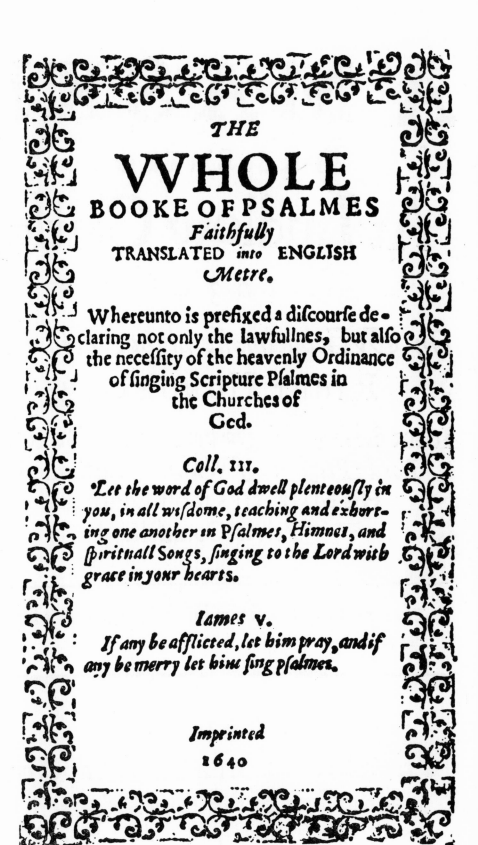

THE

VVHOLE

BOOKE OF PSALMES

Faithfully

TRANSLATED *into* ENGLISH

Metre.

Whereunto is prefixed a discourse declaring not only the lawfullnes, but also
the necessity of the heavenly Ordinance
of singing Scripture Psalmes in
the Churches of
God.

Coll. III.

*Let the word of God dwell plenteously in
you, in all wisdome, teaching and exhort-
ing one another in Psalmes, Himnes, and
spirituall Songs, singing to the Lord with
grace in your hearts.*

Iames v.

*If any be afflicted, let him pray, and if
any be merry let him sing psalmes.*

Imprinted
1640

A MASKE

PRESENTED

At Ludlow Castle,

1 6 3 4:

On *Michaelmaſſe night*, *before the*

RIGHT HONORABLE,

IOHN *Earle of Bridgewater*, *Vicount* BRACKLY,
Lord Præſident *of* WALES, And one of
HIS MAIESTIES moſt honorable
Privie Counſell.

Eheu quid volui miſero mihi! floribus auſtrum.
Perditus ————

LONDON,

Printed for HVMPHREY ROBINSON,
at the ſigne of the *Three Pidgeons* in
Pauls Church-yard. 1 6 3 7.

Syrus

Hebræus

Arabs

Chaldæus

Ægiptius

Græcus

Romanus Antiquus

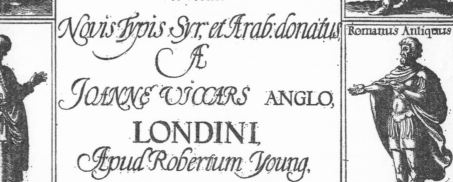

DECAPLA IN
PSALMOS
siue
COMMENTARIVS EX
decem Linguis, antiquis
Patribus, Rab: Historicis
et Poetis.

Novis Typis Syr: et Arab: donatus
A
JOANNE VICCARS ANGLO,

LONDINI,
Apud Robertum Young,
CIƆ. IƆ. C XXXIX.

W. Hollar fecit.

Gallus

Hispanus

Romanus recentior.

one hundred and ten plates, etching these plates himself, but many of his illustrations for other books were reproduced by his friend, the prolific Bohemian engraver Wenceslaus Hollar. If we had no painter of genius in the seventeenth century we had in Inigo Jones, Wren and Vanbrugh architects who were a match for those of any country. Certainly these architects had far more effect in England than any painter of their time on the general culture of their age as well as on the design of books and the appearance of printing. This was reflected in the engraved title-pages which were often architectural in character with arches, pillars, niches, etc. as essential parts of the design. These architects were certainly 'rounded' characters, who quite apart from their building achievements were respectively famous as stage designer, astronomer and scientist, and playwright.

Inigo Jones was the first great English Renaissance architect. He was born in Smithfield and when quite young went to Italy to study art, stage design and architecture. His first patron was King Christian IV of Denmark who in turn passed Jones on to his brother-in-law, the English King, James I. He collaborated with the playwright Ben Jonson in *The Masque of Blackness* then returned to Italy for further study. His particular interest in architecture was growing and his constant companion was a copy of Palladio's *I Quattro Libri dell' Architettura*. He filled the margins of this book with his own notes.[4] After a couple of years in Italy, Inigo Jones returned to England and was given the post of Surveyor-General to the King. The bulk of his work was still designing sets and costumes for the theatre, for masques and plays.

In 1619 work was started on his great scheme for the Whitehall Palace, but only the Banqueting House (with its Rubens ceiling) was completed. As usual, the Stuarts were short of money. The doric-porticoed St Paul's Church, Covent Garden, 'the handsomest barn in England' (which Hogarth painted and in front of which Bernard Shaw set Eliza Doolittle selling violets), parts of Wilton House and the Queen's House at Greenwich are the most notable Inigo Jones buildings still standing. But in literally hundreds of sets for masques and plays, Jones was able to experiment with his ideas of Renaissance architecture, as well as with more exotic styles, without the problems of actual building construction.

Inigo Jones changed the vernacular. The white and gold double cube room at Wilton, with its superb proportions, its panelled walls with gilded and be-ribboned swags of flowers and fruit, its magnificent fireplace and Van Dyck's portraits set in frames designed by the architect, is something unique in English architecture. In 1631, while Queen Henrietta Maria was still waiting for Inigo Jones to complete her little house at Greenwich, Christopher Wren was born in Wiltshire. His father was a parson, later to become Dean of Windsor, his

4. Inigo Jones's annotated copy of Palladio's book provided the basis for the first English translation of *Architettura* in 1715–16.

118

Palladio's *I Quattro Libri dell' Architettura*, printed and published in Venice in 1570. *Victoria and Albert Museum*

IN VICENZA sopra la piazza, che uolgarmête si dice l'Isola; ha fabricato secondo la inuentione, che segue, il Conte Valerio Chiericato, cauallier & gentil'huomo honorato di quella città. Hà questa fabrica nella parte di sotto una loggia dauanti, che piglia tutta la facciata : il pauimento del primo ordine s'alza da terra cinque piedi: il che è stato fatto si per ponerui sotto le cantine, & altri luochi appartenenti al commodo della casa, iquali non sariano riusciti se fossero stati fatti del tutto sotterra ; percioche il fiume non è molto discosto ; si ancho accioche gli ordini di sopra meglio godessero del bel sito dinanzi. Le stanze maggiori hanno i uolti loro alti secondo il primo modo dell'altezze de' uolti: le mediocri sono inuoltate à lunette; & hanno i uolti tanto alti quanto sono quelli delle maggiori. I camerini sono ancor essi in uolto, e sono amezati. Sono tutti questi uolti ornati di compartimenti di stucco eccellentissimi di mano di Messer Bartolameo Ridolfi Scultore Veronese; & di pitture di mano di Messer Domenico Rizzo, & di Messer Battista Venetiano, huomini singolari in queste professioni. La sala è di sopra nel mezo della facciata : & occupa della loggia di sotto la parte di mezo. La sua altezza è fin sotto il tetto : e perche esce alquanto in fuori ; ha sotto gli Angoli le colonne doppie, dall'una e l'altra parte di questa sala ui sono due loggie, cioè una per banda; le quali hanno i soffitti loro, ouer lacunari ornati di bellissimi quadri di pittura, e fanno bellissima uista. Il primo ordine della facciata è Dorico, & il secondo è Ionico.

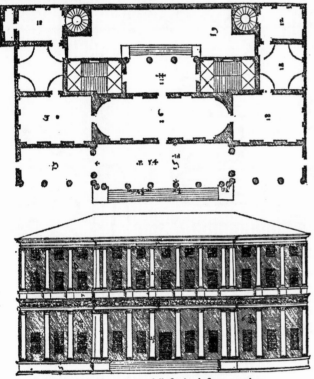

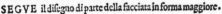

SEGVE il disegno di parte della facciata in forma maggiore.

uncle was the Bishop of Ely. In 1649, the year Charles I stepped to his execution from a first-floor window of Inigo Jones's Banqueting House, Wren left Westminster school for Wadham College, Oxford. Three years later he was a Fellow of All Souls and in 1657 became Professor of Astronomy at Gresham College (the forerunner of the Royal Society). By this time, whilst not yet thirty years of age, Wren had a European-wide reputation as a scientist and astronomer. Wren had no sympathy with the Commonwealth, for he was a staunch Royalist. On Charles II's Restoration, he was commanded to make a 'lunar globe' and in 1662 he became assistant in His Majesty's Office

of Works. His architectural career began in the same year with
a commission from his uncle the bishop. This was to build a
new chapel for Pembroke College, Cambridge. In 1663, he
began work on the Sheldonian Theatre, Oxford. Whilst this
was being built he spent six months in Paris, completing his
architectural studies. He talked with Bernini, looked at
Mansard's buildings and paid visits to Louis XIV's court and
to a number of châteaux. These experiences were to provide
the essential design factors in his work. Unlike Inigo Jones,
Palladio meant nothing to him and he never visited Italy,
though he may have studied the plans of Italian architecture
whilst he was in France. All his influences were French. As the
tastes of Charles II had been formed during his exile in France,
the King and the architect were very much of one mind.

After the Civil War, the execution of Charles I and the gloomy
days of the Protectorate, the Restoration of Charles II in 1660
brought an inevitable reaction against the austerities of
Puritanism, even though people still flocked to churches to
hear sermons. Every other page of Pepys's diary seems to have

A pamphlet printed in 1624 describing the proceedings against the English at Amboyna by the Dutch. Issued by the English East India Company

reference to these sermons, some tedious and some not. Pepys seemed to spend as much time at the playhouse as he did in church and admitted to getting roaring drunk on the night of the King's coronation. Of Charles's court Pepys says: 'Things are in a very ill condition, there being so much emulacion (*sic*), poverty, and the vices of drinking, swearing and loose amours.' Yet it was not all bawdy plays and loose living. In many ways the Restoration marked the beginning of modern England. The young Pepys talks like a modern man, Wren with his analytical and scientific attitudes would make many a modern architect seem old fashioned.

In English printing, pamphlets and tracts proliferated. The one noteworthy production was the London *Polyglot Bible*, where 'the learning of the scholar, the enterprise of the publisher, the industry of the editor Dr. Walton, the ability of the printer combined . . . to an extra-ordinary degree'.[5] It was printed by Thomas Roycroft in six folio volumes. A double-spread would show ten or more versions of the same text, set in parallel columns in Hebrew, Samaritan, Syriac, Arabic, Ethiopic, Greek, roman and italic typefaces. Cromwell encouraged its production, which was duly acknowledged in the preface of the first volume. As soon as Charles II came to the throne Brian Walton cancelled the last three leaves of the preface and substituted a fulsome dedication to the King. For his timely loyalty he was later made Bishop of Chester, and Roycroft the printer was granted the title of *Orientalium Typographus Regius*.

In 1665, the plague carried off nearly 100,000 Londoners, and a year later, the Great Fire destroyed 90 churches and over 1,200 houses. There was hardly a building standing between the Tower and the Temple, and Old St Paul's was a ruin. All the print shops and booksellers in Paul's Churchyard, including Roycroft's, must have gone up in smoke. On 7th September Pepys writes: 'Up by five o'clock . . . and by water to Paul's wharf. Walked thence and saw all the town burned and a miserable sight of Paul's church, with all the roofs fallen and the body of the quire fallen into St Fayth's'.

Great occasions sometimes produce great men, but for once a man already great was waiting for such an occasion. Wren seized the opportunity. His superb plan for the re-building of the City of London was never put into effect, but he was able to rebuild 54 city churches, with fascinating variations of spire from the chunky, squat St James's, Garlickhithe to the many-tiered wedding-cake tower of the printer's church of St. Bride, Fleet Street. But these charming fantasies were a minor prelude to his great cathedral which was started in 1674 and finished in 1710, still under the guidance of its architect and one master mason.

It was in Wren's Sheldonian Theatre that the revival of good printing began. Here Dr John Fell, Dean of Christ Church and Bishop of Oxford, conducted a press from 1672 to 1686.

A TRUE **RELATION** OF THE VNIVST, CRVELL, AND BARBA- ROVS PROCEEDINGS against the ENGLISH at **AMBOYNA** *In the* EAST-INDIES, *by the* Nea- therlandish GOVERNOVR and COVNCEL *there*

Also the copie of a Pamphlet, set forth first in Dutch and then in English, by some Neatherlander, falsly entituled, A TRVE DECLARATION OF THE Newes that came out of the EAST-INDIES, with the Pinace called the HARE, which ar- riued at TEXEL in *June*, 1624.

Together with an Answer to the same PAMPHLET.

By the English EAST-INDIA Companie.

Published by Authoritie.

LONDON, Printed by *H.Lownes* for *Nathanael Newberry.* 1624.

5. *A History of the Old English Letter-Foundries*. T. B. Reed, first published 1886. New and revised edition edited by A. F. Johnson. Faber and Faber, 1952.

.... My son, be admonished: of making many books there is no end; and much study is a weariness of the flesh.

Bishop John Fell,

Interred in Christ Church, Oxford, 1689.

In 1667 Dr Fell, on the advice of Thomas Marshall, a Fellow of Lincoln College, had bought matrices for typefaces from Holland and engaged Harman Harmanszoon to come to Oxford to run a foundry.

Marshall had been a Royalist exile in Holland and acted as Fell's agent in the purchase of typefaces. After a couple of years, Harmanszoon was succeeded by a German of Huguenot extraction called Peter de Walpergen, who was both type-founder and, more important, a punch-cutter as well. Walpergen had worked at his trade for the Dutch East India Company in Batavia. He was a versatile craftsman and cut some very beautiful music types.

Fell's typefaces, based as they were on rather clumsy Dutch and German models, have a curiously old-world feeling. They went out of use by the 1800's, but were revived by the Rev. C. H. O. Daniel, the Bursar of Worcester College, for his private press in the 1860's. The Fell types were not at all in harmony with what Christopher Wren called 'the gust of the age'. Wren would probably have had much more sympathy with the crisply cut Garamond or Granjon characters.

In the year that Dr Fell bought his first Dutch typefaces, John Milton's *Paradise Lost* was published by Samuel Simmons, printer of Aldersgate Street. This sublime if somewhat humourless Puritan epic dealt with sin and redemption and the struggle of good against evil. Unlike Chaucer or Shakespeare, Milton had little sympathy for human weaknesses, yet *Paradise Lost* remained for generations the most widely read poem in the English language. The agreement between Milton and his publisher-printer, which is illustrated in plate 59, is in the British Museum. Milton agreed to dispose of his copyright for £5 down with a further £5 to come after the first edition of 1,300 was sold out, and two more payments of £5 if two further editions of the same size were sold. A modest return for his work. Milton had lived on, out of his time. He was the last of the great Elizabethans, he probably saw Shakespeare act and may have talked with Ben Jonson and Herrick. In his old age he was blind and poor, yet his house in Artillery Row in Bunhill Fields became a place of homage for the wits and notabilities of the Restoration; 'Much more than he did desire', so a contemporary said.

The first quarto edition of Milton's *Paradise Lost* was a very slovenly piece of printing. In spite of Dr Fell, the general standard of English printing continued to remain as low as ever. An even worse production, technically speaking, was the first edition of Bunyan's *The Pilgrim's Progress*, printed in 1678 in an edition of 2,000 by Nathaniel Ponder at the Sign of the Peacocke in the Poultry, a street near where the Bank of England now stands. This allegorical best-seller had been written in Bedford Gaol where Bunyan had been shut up for twelve years on a charge of unlicensed preaching. This simple, stirring tale

THE
Pilgrims Progreſs:
In the ſimilitude of a
DREAM.

AS I walk'd through the wilderneſs of this world, I lighted on a certain place, where was a Denn; And I laid me down in that place to ſleep: And as I ſlept I dreamed a Dream. I dreamed, and behold *I ſaw a Man * cloathed with Raggs, ſtanding in a certain place, with his face from his own Houſe, a Book in his hand, and a great burden upon his back.* I looked, and ſaw him open the Book, and Read therein; and as he Read, he wept and trembled: and not being able longer to contain,

* Iſa. 64. 6.

Lu. 14. 33
Pſ. 38. 4.
Hab. 2. 2.
Act. 16: 31.

Engraved title-page from Joseph Moxon's *Ductor ad Astronomiam & Geographiam* translated from the text by W. Blaeu. Published by Moxon, London: 1659

DUCTOR ad
ASTRONOMIAM
&
GEOGRAPHIAM.
vel ufus
GLOBI,
Cœleſtis quam *Terreſtris.*

In Libris ſex,
Aſtrón. & Geogr. Rudim.
Aſtró. & Geogr.
Nautica.
viz. Aſtrologica. Probl.
Gnomonica.
Sphæric. Triang.

Per *Joſephum Moxon.*

LONDINI, *Sumptibus* Joſephi Móxon.

in its homely language provided 'one of the two foundation texts of the English working-class movement'.[6] It also provides a piece of printing which the earliest 'Donatus' printers would have been ashamed to have allowed out of their print-shops.[7] At least one other man had some concern about the shoddy standards of English printing in the latter years of the seven-

6. *Printing and the Mind of Man.* Ed. John Carter and Percy H. Muir, Cassell and Company, 1957. The other 'foundation text' referred to was Thomas Paine's *The Rights of Man.*
7. A 'Donatus' was a clumsily printed Latin grammar, contemporary with Gutenberg.

Plate 30.

teenth century and that was a mathematical instrument- and globe-maker called Joseph Moxon. In 1683–4 Moxon published *Mechanical Exercises on the Whole Art of Printing*. Moxon, who had been born at Wakefield in Yorkshire, had lived in Delft and Rotterdam, where his father was a printer. In 1646 the Moxons, father and son, were in partnership as printers in Houndsditch but Joseph soon foresook the trade and established himself in business making globes, maps, etc. He spoke Dutch fluently and returned to Holland in 1652, possibly for instruction in his new trade. Whilst in Amsterdam, he met the type designer, Christoffel van Dyck, who confided in him, no doubt with some pride, that he had been offered £80 for laying out an inscription for the new City Hall. In 1654, Moxon translated Willem Blaeu's Latin text of *A Tutor in Astronomy and Geography* and published it from his shop at the Sign of the Atlas in Cornhill. Because of the Licensing Act he could not have set up as a printer (or type-founder) even if he had wanted to. In 1662 Moxon was sworn in as Hydrographer to the King and on 8th September of the same year, Pepys bought two globes from him for £3.10.0d. 'For which', Pepys wrote, 'I am well pleased'. Moxon's shop and all his belongings were destroyed in the Great Fire, but he once again set up the Sign of the Atlas, this time in Russell Street, Westminster. In 1674 he dedicated a new edition of his *A Tutor in Astronomy and Geography* to Pepys, who was frequently in and out of his shop. In 1676 he published a book on lettering for sign painters and letter-cutters and when elected a Fellow of the Royal Society, he said 'I find all the accomplishments and some more of an architect necessary in a typographer'. His *Mechanical Exercises* was the first book on the crafts of printing and type-founding. He goes into the whole business in some detail, describing how presses are built, ink made, punches cut, mould and matrices constructed; the proportion of letters; the procedure for furnace work and how type metal should be hardened by the use of stub-nails made of good, soft, tough iron that melts well and how type metal shall be made to run by the addition of antimony. He also gives instructions on composing, correcting, casting-off, presswork, wetting paper, ink balls and how the masters of the chapel should deport themselves! The book, originally published in monthly parts, was intended for the journeyman printer but when it was reissued in one volume it became the standard work for all English printers and publishers. Moxon was on friendly terms with many of the great men of his time including Sir Christopher Wren, to whom he dedicated one of his books. He had a justifiably contemptuous opinion of contemporary English printers, particularly in comparison with those in the Netherlands.

By the end of James II's reign, England had become the most successful manufacturing country in Europe and London had superseded Amsterdam both as a port and as a centre of

At the Court at Whitehall,

The Thirteenth of *October* 1680.

Present,
The Kings most Excellent Majesty,

His Highness Prince *Rupert*
Lord Archbishop of *Canterbury*
Lord Chancellor
Lord President
Lord Privy Seal
Lord Marquess of *Worcester*
Earl of *Sunderland*
Earl of *Clarendon*
Earl of *Essex*

Earl of *Halifax*
Viscount *Fauconberg*
Lord Bishop of *London*
Mr. *Hyde*
Mr. *Finch*
Lord Chief Justice *North*
Mr. Secretary *Jenkins*
Mr. Chancellor of the Exchequer
Mr. *Seymour*

Mr. *Godolphin*.

His Majesty being informed, That notwithstanding His late Proclamation of the Fourth of this instant October, Commanding all Papists, or reputed Papists, to depart from the Cities of London and Westminster, and from within Ten Miles of the same, divers Papists, and Persons reputed Papists, do resort to, and remain in the Cities of London and Westminster, and within Ten Miles Distance of the same ; His Majesty, for the more effectual discovery and apprehension of such Papists, was this day graciously pleased to Declare in Council, That if the Church-Wardens and Overseers of the Poor of any Parish within the City of London, or the Liberties thereof, or within Ten Miles of the said City, shall discover any Papists, Indicted or Convicted, remaining or abiding contrary to Law, within their respective Limits, to Philip Burton Gent. Sollicitor appointed to Prosecute herein, They shall have and receive for the Benefit of the Poor of the Parish where such Papists shall be found, the Moiety of the Hundred pounds Penalty due by Law to His Majesty, and recovered from such Papists upon their being Indicted or Convicted thereof.

JOHN NICHOLAS.

LONDON,
Printed by *John Bill*, *Thomas Newcomb*, and *Henry Hills*, Printers to the Kings most Excellent Majesty. 1680.

commerce. The Dutch, however, as highly successful carriers of seaborne produce were still our most successful maritime rivals. In spite of this, it was very much to England's interests to maintain Dutch sovereignty, for Holland was the only country in Europe either capable enough, or willing to resist Louis XIV's expansionist intentions. Charles II, or his advisers, completely failed to understand this and in 1672 we were at war with the Netherlands and got a 'bloody nose' for our trouble at the battle of Sole Bay. Led by William of Orange, a man of great qualities of leadership, the Dutch also successfully resisted the French attempts at invasion, by opening the dykes and flooding much of their below sea-level country.

Once again we became friends with Holland and their Prince William married Charles's niece Mary. At home the Tory party were persecuting the Protestant Puritans with fearful vigour and indiscriminately clapping into prison hundreds of worthy and devout men, amongst whom were John Bunyan and George Fox, founder of the Quaker movement. It was these Puritans who provided at least part of the manpower for Monmouth's abortive rebellion of 1685. As a result of this insurrection, James II was moved to various acts of tyranny executed 'by Judge Jeffreys in his insane lust for cruelty'.[8]

This time the King had gone too far, the parallel with France was too near for comfort. Louis XIV was, with equal viciousness, persecuting the Huguenots. A real fear of a return to Catholic domination 'gave fresh actuality to John Foxe's *Book of Martyrs*'[9] and caused both Tory and Whig leaders to make common ground. Before they could depose King James, he had fled to France. Prince William of Orange and his wife Mary were offered the throne.

On 5 November 1688, Prince William landed unopposed at Brixham, a fishing port in Devon, and there was not a printer west of Oxford to strike off a Proclamation. Freedom of worship had come to stay, to be joined in 1695 with the freedom of the press and the freedom for any man once again to set up a print shop.

However bad the printing had become by this time and however thin the native talent in the arts of painting and sculpture remained, and however troublesome the times, it was at least a golden age of English architecture. Wren continued in his old age to build fine houses. Amongst his contemporaries Nicholas Hawksmoor, James Gibbs and William Kent were all very talented architects and Sir John Vanbrugh, one of England's few exponents of the Baroque, built three of the greatest houses in Europe.

Vanbrugh, the son of a wealthy sugar broker, was born in the City of London in 1664. When he was nineteen, he went to France for two years, presumably for architectural instruction. He returned to England to take a commission in the Army and then returned to France, only to be arrested at Calais as a spy.

8. *History of England*, G. M. Trevelyan, Longmans, Green and Co. 1926.
9. *English Social History*, G. M. Trevelyan, Longmans, Green and Co. 1942.

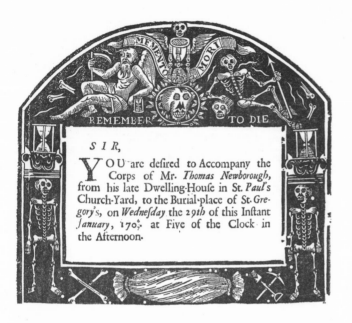

SIR,

YOU are defired to Accompany the Corps of Mr. *Thomas Newborough*, from his late Dwelling-Houfe in St. *Paul's* Church-Yard, to the Burial-place of St. *Gregory's*, on *Wednefday* the 29th of this Inftant *January*, 170⅝, at Five of the Clock in the Afternoon.

He was imprisoned in the Bastille and whilst there, produced the first draft of his play *The Provok'd Wife*, so inspiring a caustic comment from Voltaire who said that he could not imagine what had gained such a comic writer the distinction of detention in such a grim fortress.[10] On his return to England, Vanbrugh wrote *The Relapse* which was first performed on Boxing Day 1696. The success of *The Relapse* resulted in *The Provok'd Wife* being staged. In spite of, or because of its bawdy libertinism, it was hugely successful. However, it called forth a serious attack by Jeremy Collier on Vanbrugh's 'immorality'. In his *Short View of the Immorality and Profaneness of the English Stage* Collier, a non-juring cleric but not a Puritan, berated the immodesty of Vanbrugh's *Relapse* and Dryden's *Amphitryon*. Maybe because of this, Vanbrugh turned once again to architecture, but from that time onwards he combined the two professions of playwright and architect. Apart from Congreve, and perhaps Wycherley, he was the most successful of the Restoration playwrights. By 1699, his plans for the Earl of Carlisle's house, Castle Howard, were complete. It was a grand conception in the French style of a country seat set in the midst of lovely country. Horace Walpole called it 'sublime'.

Vanbrugh was fortunate in his clerk of the works, who was the architect Nicholas Hawksmoor. In 1702, Vanbrugh became Comptroller of the Royal Works (the equivalent of the present-day Office of Works). In the next year he was writing to his Scottish publisher friend Jacob Tonson for a copy of Palladio's book. Castle Howard in due course was followed by the Opera House in the Haymarket and then the huge Blenheim Palace, built in the grand manner as a national monument for the Duke of Marlborough. Half a million pounds was voted by a grateful nation to build it.

If Castle Howard was a grand conception, Blenheim was a grandiose one. The essence of Baroque is extravagance, usually displayed in ornament. Unlike most Baroque architects, Vanbrugh liked bare walls. His extravagance was scale, and he was a master of it. His third great house, Seaton Delaval, built for the 'drunken' Delavals, was largely burnt out in a great fire and stands today a romantic relic near the North Sea coast, amongst the pit-heads and slagheaps of the Northumberland coalfields. It looks like a dramatic stage set and is a fit memorial for this theatrical genius.

Vanbrugh died in 1726, only three years after the 91-year-old Sir Christopher Wren. The first English type-founder of any note had only recently become established in a shop not far from Wren's St Paul's. He was an ex-gunsmith's apprentice called William Caslon.

10. *Lettres Philosophiques sur les Anglais*, F. M. A. de Voltaire, Paris, 1733.

4 Drawing by Sir John Vanbrugh of the Garden Front of
Eastbury Park, Dorset. This drawing was later engraved and
printed in *Vitruvius Britannicus. Victoria and Albert Museum*

5 Seaton Delaval, Northumberland. Designed by Sir John
Vanbrugh, 1720. *National Monuments: Crown Copyright*

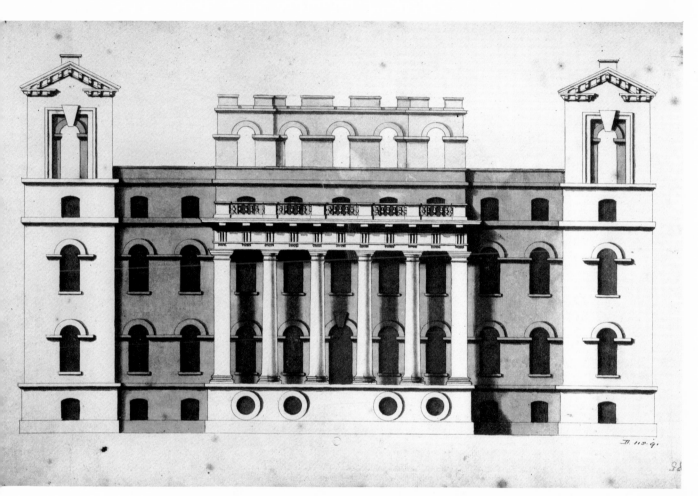

56 The printers' church of St Bride in Fleet Street, designed by
Sir Christopher Wren. Built in 1680. The 'many-tiered' steeple
was added in 1701. *Guildhall Library*

The Ground Platt of the Steeple

A Scale of Feet

The Elevation or Prospect of the West ends of the Steeple of S.t Bridget
als Brides in Fleetstreet London Shewing the Inside and outside Thereof
being 235 feet high S.r Chr: Wren K.t Architect M.r Sam.l Foulks Mason

57 St Paul's Church, Covent Garden. The 'handsomest barn in England', designed by Inigo Jones, 1631 – 38. Engraving by Edward Rooker after the painting by P. Sandby. 1766. *Victoria and Albert Museum*

58 Illustration by Francis Barlow for Aesop's *Fables*

59 Milton's agreement with the publisher of *Paradise Lost* dated
27 April 1667. *British Museum*

60 Title-page from *The Provok'd Husband* by Sir John Vanbrugh
and Mr Cibber. Printed in London, 1728. *British Museum*

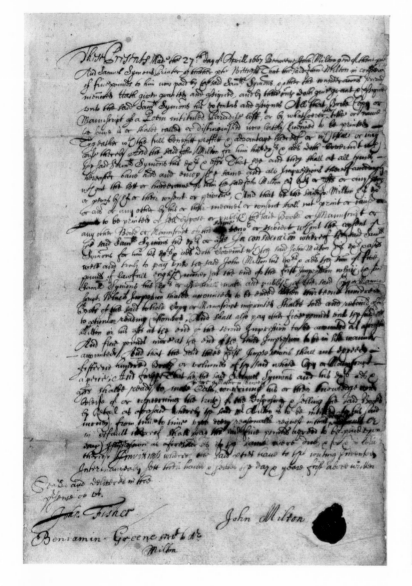

The Provok'd Husband;

OR,

A Journey to LONDON.

A

COMEDY,

As it is Acted at the

THEATRE-ROYAL,

BY

His MAJESTY's Servants.

Written by the
Late Sir JOHN VANBRUGH,
and Mr. CIBBER.

——— *Vivit Tanquam Vicina Mariti.* Juv. Sat VI.

LONDON:
Printed for J. WATTS, at the Printing-Office in
Wild-Court near Lincolns-Inn Fields.
MDCCXXVIII.

61 *Marriage à la Mode*, oil painting by William Hogarth. The scene shows the Countess's dressingroom. *National Gallery*

62 Hogarth's trade card, engraved 23 April 1720, his earliest known work

63 Japanned coffee pot. Pontypool ware. c. 1760. *Newport Museum*

64 Engraving by E. Rooker of Strawberry Hill after a painting by
P. Sanby (sic) showing Walpole's alterations and improvements.
Guildhall Library

65 Engraving by Charles Grignion after a design by Richard
Bentley to illustrate Gray's *Elegy written in a Country Churchyard*.
1753. *British Museum*

66 Specimen slate, letters cut by John Baskerville, c. 1730. *Birmingham Public Library*

68 Engraved portrait of John Bell 'the most resourceful and inventive bookseller of his generation,' at the age of eighty. After the painting by G. Clint

67 Engraved portrait of John Baskerville, the Birmingham type-founder and printer

he life of townsman and countryman in England in 1700 was
tle different from that of the time of Queen Elizabeth I.
here had been no significant change in methods of manufac-
re. The crafts of weaving, furniture-making, pottery-making
d so on, were all on the basis of cottage economy, with a
om in the front room, a lathe in the shed in the garden or a
t-kiln in the back yard. Printing alone, as the first of the mass
roduction industries, on occasions demanded more space,
ough many jobbing printers could run their presses single-
nded, with a composing case and a couple of tables, all in one
om. Their staple trade was the printing of hand-bills, tickets,
sters, ballad sheets etc. The book printer was in a much more
mplicated line of business. He needed space to house his
aff of journeymen and apprentices, he needed space for
oring type and storing paper, for composing and printing
d for drying his sheets, as, until rotary presses came into use,
e sheets were always dampened first before printing (this
ampening made the hand-made paper much more receptive to
npression and lessened the need for make-ready).

ravel and transport were not easy. Roads were still unmetalled.
took a waggon or a coach the best part of a week to get from
lanchester to London. Even though the towns were growing,
was still a mainly rural life; apprentices could go fishing or
aaring rabbits and their masters could shoot wildfowl. Local
ialects, if not as pronounced as in Caxton's time, were indi-
idual and unspoilt by the press, let alone by the radio.

olitically, it was to be a century of consolidating the principles
at had brought about the downfall of the Stuarts. Any kind
f popular political movement was not to be tolerated, yet it
as freedom of speech and a freedom to print what they liked
at separated the British from the more constrictive regimes of
e Continent. Of these privileges, so newly won, and so
nusual a thing abroad, they were justly, and with good
eason, proud.

Vith the freedom of the press, newspapers and journals
roliferated. News reporting became a profession and com-
nentary and literary qualities were to be found in newspapers
s well as in books. In 1709 Richard Steele published the first
umber of *The Tatler*, which soon had Joseph Addison, Steele's
ormer school fellow at Charterhouse, as its main contributor.
n 1711, Addison and Steele dropped *The Tatler* and replaced it
vith *The Spectator*. This was full of good humoured satire on
he manners of the times. *The Spectator* in turn was followed by
The Guardian, again under the direction of these gifted Old
Carthusians. Addison and Steele widened the reading habits of
he English middle classes. 'The Essays of the *Spectator* and the
Tatler were made to order for the man to whom other reading
natter of the age seemed either forbiddingly profane or
ortentously dull.'¹ The circulation figures for the journals were
robably not much more than 3,000 to 4,000 copies a week.

BIRMINGHAM
STAGE-COACH,
In Two *Days* and a half; begins *May* the
24th, 1731.

SET Sout from the *Swan-Inn* in *Birmingham*,
every *Monday* at six a Clock in the Morning,
through *Warwick*, *Banbury* and *Alesbury*,
to the *Red Lion Inn* in *Alderſgate ſtreet*, *London*,
every *Wedneſday* Morning: And returns from
the ſaid *Red Lion Inn* every *Thurſday* Morning
at five a Clock the ſame Way to the *Swan-Inn*
in *Birmingham* every *Saturday*, at 21 Shillings
each Paſſenger, and 18 Shillings from *Warwick*,
who has liberty to carry 14 Pounds in Weight,
and all above to pay *One Penny a Pound*.
Perform'd (if God permit)

By Nicholas Rothwell.

The Weekly Waggon ſets out every *Tueſday* from the *Nagg's-Head* in
Birmingham, to the Red Lion Inn *aforeſaid*, every *Saturday*; and returns
from the ſaid Inn every *Monday*, to the *Nagg's-Head* in *Birmingham* every
Thurſday.

Note. By the ſaid Nicholas Rothwell at *Warwick*, all Perſons may be fur-
niſhed with a By-Coach, Chariot, Chaiſe, or Hearſe, with a Mourning Coach
and able Horſes, to any Part of Great Britain, at reaſonable Rates: And
alſo Saddle Horſes to be had.

Stage-coach notice 1731. *Printed Ephemera*

1. *The English Common Reader*, Richard D. Altick. The University
of Chicago Press, 1957.

Printing house with compositors, pressmen and warehousemen at
work, 1752

A true Representation of a Printing House with the Men at Work.

Engraved for the New Universal Magazine. 1752.

B.Cole sculp.

The eighteenth century in England was an age of letters. In 1712, Pope's *Rape of the Lock* was published. In 1719, Defoe's *Robinson Crusoe* appeared and some seven years later, Swift's *Gulliver's Travels*. Novels were becoming the chief products of the book printers. The first half of the century ended with a string of literary masterpieces: Smollett's *Roderick Random* and Richardson's *Clarissa* in 1748 and Fielding's *Tom Jones* in the following year, each sold in several volumes, at about half a crown a volume. Slowly the standard of printing was improving though the engraved title-pages were in marked contrast to the still rather sloppy letterpress printing. In ephemeral printing, the engraver continued to hold the field for anything of importance. The engraved tradesman's cards and billheads came into popular use in the early years of the century. They were not only engraved by numerous and often anonymous craftsmen, but also by artists of the calibre of William Hogarth. Of the many cards Hogarth engraved, there is one illustrated by Ambrose Heal[2] for a goldsmith called Ellis Gamble, set in a Rococo frame, and another for James Figg the prize fighter. Hogarth's own card, with the words 'W. Hogarth Engraver' set in a frame supported by two standing figures and surmounted by two *putti*, was engraved in 1720. Hogarth, the so-called 'father of English painting', was apprenticed in 1712, not to a painter or engraver, but to this Ellis Gamble, who had workshops at the Golden Angel, Cranbourn Street, Leicester Fields. After serving his time with Gamble, he worked as an engraver of silver and pewter tankards and of copper plates for trade cards and other ephemera, as well as illustrations for books. He also worked at Thornhill's School of Drawing in St James Street, Covent Garden, and there learned to paint in oils. By the time he was thirty, he had taken to painting small conversation pieces, with which he had some success, but the art market for native-born artists, particularly painters, was still not very good, so he returned to his burin and copper plate. He set to work on a series of moral subjects. The first of these engravings was *The Harlot's Progress*, which appeared in 1731. This was followed by *Southwark Fair* in 1733 and *The Rake's Progress* in 1735. *Industry and Idleness*, *Gin Lane* and *Marriage à la Mode* followed in fairly quick succession. Through these brilliantly observed scenes, rakes and pimps, harlots and drunken seamen parade alongside the men-about-town and their pretty ladies.

In 1734, Sir James Thornhill, Hogarth's father-in-law, died. In the following year, Hogarth opened the St Martin's Lane Academy, making good use of the various casts from the antique and other material from Thornhill's School of Drawing. The St Martin's Lane Academy was close to Old Slaughter's Coffee House, a meeting place for artists, authors and actors — a forerunner to such London clubs as the Garrick and the Arts. Hogarth's friends at Slaughter's included David Garrick and

THE

LIFE

AND

STRANGE SURPRIZING

ADVENTURES

OF

ROBINSON CRUSOE,

Of *YORK*, MARINER:

Who lived Eight and Twenty Years, all alone in an un-inhabited Island on the Coast of AMERICA, near the Mouth of the Great River of OROONOQUE;

Having been cast on Shore by Shipwreck, wherein all the Men perished but himself.

WITH

An Account how he was at last as strangely deliver'd by PYRATES.

Written by Himself.

LONDON:

Printed for W. TAYLOR at the *Ship* in *Pater-Noster-Row*. MDCCXIX.

2. *London Tradesmens' Cards of the 18th Century*, Ambrose Heal. Batsford, 1925.

Henry Fielding, as well as many artists and patrons of the arts such as Dr Martin Foulkes, the Vice-Chairman of Captain Coram's Foundling Hospital, who later became President of the Royal Society. Hogarth recruited the staff for his school from artists in this circle. Of these, Francis Hayman taught painting and the history of art, Roubiliac sculpture and Gravelot design. The marked influence of the latter on printed book illustration and the influence of the circle as a whole on the design of printing in eighteenth-century England is referred to in the next chapter.[3]

Hogarth, and in fact the whole of the St Martin's Lane circle, were strongly anti-Lord Burlington and his Palladian followers. They rejected the classical tradition, perhaps linking it with authoritarian and aristocratic patronage. Their interests lay in a return to nature, however fanciful the Rococo attitude to nature might be. Hogarth's link with the Rococo style can be seen both in his paintings and in his engraved work.

The moral implications in all Hogarth's work are obvious. In the design, there runs through most of the engravings a sinuous curving line and a marked lack of symmetry. In 1753 he published the *Analysis of Beauty* where he analysed his approach to design. He was a most sensitive painter; the slight little painting called *The Shrimp Girl* in the National Gallery in London, or his portrait of Captain Coram in the Foundling Hospital would alone assure his fame, yet in *Marriage à la Mode* one comes nearest to his true genius, for he was the most acute of observers and a splendid story teller, in an age of story tellers. The paintings and the engravings can be read like a book. He was a painterly Dickens and always preferred to regard himself as an author rather than as an artist.

Hogarth was somewhat chauvinistic, perhaps like Vanbrugh as a result of being arrested at Calais as a spy. Though he was soon influenced by French Rococo, particularly in his engraved designs, and by Watteau in his painting, he had little feeling for European art. He died in 1764, in the same year that Johann Joachim Winckelmann, the German art historian, published his *Geschichte der Kunst des Alterthums* (History of Ancient Art) and Horace Walpole his Gothick romance *The Castle of Otranto*. Hogarth, with his leanings towards the Rococo, would have heartily disapproved of Winckelmann's Neo-Classicism, and would probably not have been much amused by Walpole's Gothick fantasy; he had little opinion of him as an art critic.

Horace Walpole, youngest son of the politician Sir Robert Walpole, first Earl of Orford, though only a bit-player in the pageant of history, is of importance to this survey for his part in the Romantic movement and for being the owner of the first 'private' printing press in England.

Walpole was one of the originators of the Gothic Revival. Without doubt he was one of the best letter writers of his time. He was educated at Eton and King's College, Cambridge. In

3. See *Hogarth and his friends* by Mark Girouard. A series of three articles in *Country Life*. 13, 22 Jan and 3 Feb. 1966.

company with his fellow Etonian, the poet Thomas Gray, Walpole went on the Grand Tour. When he started to print at Strawberry Hill in 1757, Gray's *Odes* was his first book. His Gothick fantasy, *The Castle of Otranto*, appeared in 1764. This is a strange creaking, horror-comic much praised by both Sir Walter Scott and Lord Byron. Walpole followed *Otranto* by a play, *The Mysterious Mother*, described at the time 'as a tragedy too horrible for representation on any stage'. He printed only fifty copies of it at Strawberry Hill.

133

T H E

Myſterious Mother.

A

T R A G E D Y.

By Mr. HORACE WALPOLE.

Sit mihi fas audita loqui!   VIRGIL.

PRINTED AT STRAWBERRY-HILL:
MDCCLXVIII.

4. *British Architects and Craftsmen.* S. Sitwell. Batsford. 1945.
5. Henricus Stephanus was the Latinized version of Henri Estienne's name.

At the press, Caslon types were in use and the books were tolerably printed, though in their presswork they suffered in comparison with those of his contemporary John Baskerville. Strawberry Hill was at least as remarkable, with its turrets and its fan vaulting, for its architecture as for its printing. When in 1754 Walpole started altering this villa at Twickenham there was hardly a hint of the Gothic in secular architecture, yet with the contemporary taste for the extravagances of Rococo and Chinoiserie and a growing interest in romantic ruins, it was not so surprising that the 'Gothick' should become fashionable. The 'Gothick' as opposed to the 'Gothic', was a term applied to this romantic development of the Rococo. This style of architecture and décor came in with Strawberry Hill, which William Beckford called 'a species of Gothick mousetrap'.[4] (And who was he to talk? with his enormous Gothick Folly at Fonthill Abbey, which had a tower that fell down before they had finished building it, and fell down again after it was rebuilt.)

In the Strawberry Hill books, the Gothick style was evident only in *what* Walpole printed and not in the manner of its printing. Much of the interior decoration at Strawberry Hill was designed by Richard Bentley, a protégé of Walpole's. The workmanship of their interiors may have been somewhat gimcrack, but they were certainly Gothick in style. Before starting on his designs for Strawberry Hill, Bentley, son of the great classical scholar who was a close friend of Walpole's, decorated in a Gothick-Rococo manner an edition of Gray's *Poems*, which through Walpole's influence, Robert Dodsley published in 1753. These illustrations, engraved by Charles Grignion, were framed in crumbling Gothick arches, decorated with Arcadian figures or romanticized garden implements.

Walpole, a fastidious dilettante who ended his days as a gouty old bachelor, spent twenty-five years perfecting his Gothick villa. On the 25th June 1757, four years after the house had come into his possession, he launched his private press, the *Officina Arbuteana*. In a letter to his friend John Chute, Walpole wrote 'On Monday next the *Officina Arbuteana* opens in form. The Stationers' Company, that is Mr Dodsley, Mr Tonson, & Co. are summoned to meet here on Sunday night. And with what do you think we open (Gray's *Odes*) . . . I found him in town last week: he had brought his two *Odes* to be printed. I snatched them out of Dodsley's hands, and they are to be the first fruits of my press . . . Elzevier, Aldus and Stephens are the freshest persons in my memory'. And so with a nod to his illustrious printer-forbears, and Anglicising Stephanus's name,[5] he launched his press. On the title-page of the *Odes* is a charming vignetted view of Strawberry Hill, as it then was, drawn by Richard Bentley and engraved by Charles Grignion for a fee of two guineas. A couple of months later Walpole is writing to another friend, Sir Thomas Mann: 'I am turned printer and

O D E S

B Y

Mr. G R A Y.

ΦΩΝΑΝΤΑ ΣΥΝΕΤΟΙΣΙ--------

PINDAR, Olymp. II.

PRINTED AT STRAWBERRY-HILL,
For R. and J. DODSLEY in Pall-Mall.
MDCCLVII.

THE

WORKS

OF

EDMUND WALLER, Efq;

IN

VERSE AND PROSE.

LONDON:

Printed for J. and R. Tonson, in the Strand.

MDCCLVIII.

have converted a little cottage here into a printing office. keep a painter in the house and a printer – not to mention M Bentley, who is an academy himself.' It seems unlikely tha Walpole ever worked the printing press, though on on occasion he writes that he had been pasting the covers of som books. His first printer was an Irishman whom he dismisse after eighteen months. He had a series of other printers until in 1765 he engaged Thomas Kirgate at a guinea a week. Kirgat printed all but a dozen or so of the forty-two books from Strawberry Hill. Walpole describes him as the only hones printer he had ever had. Kirgate has been accused by subse quent bibliographers of being a forger and a cheat, because, i seems, he reprinted some of the books at the end of Walpole' life, or after his employer's death, before he left Strawberry Hill. As after thirty-two years service Walpole had left him only £100, he may well have felt justified in trying to better hi fortunes before looking for a new job. The whole business o the artificial rarity of limited editions, that stems from Walpole' press, is so contemptible that Kirgate perhaps deserves sym pathy rather than censure. On the other hand, the preceden that Horace Walpole established at Strawberry Hill of the culti vated amateur taking an interest in printing, was ultimately to bring much of value to the trade, not only in England, but in France, Italy and elsewhere.

As for the 'professional' printer-publishers in Britain at this time, the best of these were in Scotland. These were the Foulis brothers, Robert and Andrew, who had been appointed printers to the University of Glasgow in 1743. Using light, open typefaces (from the Wilson foundry in Glasgow) they printed a series of Greek and Latin classics that had a pleasantly fresh appearance. The most successful London booksellers (a term synonymous with publishers) were Jacob Tonson who published Addison, Steele, Dryden and Otway and the later editions of *Paradise Lost*, Bernard Lintot, the publisher of Pope, and Walpole's publisher Robert Dodsley who also pub lished Goldsmith, Gray (including Bentley's decorated edition) and Samuel Johnson. The prices of books remained at about the same level, at least until 1780. Folios and quartos sold at 10s. and octavos at 5s.[6]

Of the London printers, the most interesting from our point of view, apart from Tonson, who was both publisher and printer, was William Bowyer. Bowyer was not a particularly good printer and in 1713 he had the misfortune to have his press in Dogwell Court, Whitefriars, with all his type and machinery, burnt out. It was Bowyer, however, who was responsible for launching William Caslon, the first great English type designer, on his type-founding career.

The only two type-founders of any note in England at the end of the seventeenth century were the Grovers in Angel Alley, Aldersgate Street, and Robert Andrews whose foundry

APOLLONII PERGAEI

LOCORUM PLANORUM

LIBER PRIMUS.

PROPOSITIO I.   *Charmandri.*

SI rectae lineae magnitudine datae terminus unus datus fit, alter terminus tanget concavam circumferentiam pofitione datam.

SIT enim A B magnitudine data, datumque fit punctum A; circulus centro A intervallo A B defcriptus pofitione et magnitudine dabitur [Def. 6. datorum]. Et manifeftum eft hujus circumferentiam Locum effe quem tangit terminus cujufvis rectae quae a puncto A, ipfi A B aequalis ducitur. Et contra, rectam quamcunque a centro A ad circumferentiam ductam, aequalem effe ipfi A B.

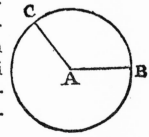

A   PROP.

A SPECIMEN

By WILLIAM CASLON, Letter-Founder, in Chiſwell-Street, LONDON.

ABCD
ABCDE
ABCDEFG
ABCDEFGHI
ABCDEFGHIJK
ABCDEFGHIJKL
ABCDEFGHIKLMN

French Cannon.

Quouſque tan-
dem abutere,
Catilina, pati-
Quouſque tandem

DOUBLE PICA ROMAN.

Quouſque tandem abutere, Catilina, patientia noſtra ? quamdiu
nos etiam furor iſte tuus eludet ?
quem ad finem ſeſe effrenata jac-
ABCDEFGHJIKLMNOP

GREAT PRIMER ROMAN.

Quouſque tandem abutére, Catilina, patientia noſtra ? quamdiu nos etiam furor iſte tuus eludet ? quem ad finem ſeſe effrenata jactabit audacia ? nihilne te
nocturnum præſidium palatii, nihil urbis vigiliæ, nihil timor populi, nihil con-
ABCDEFGHIJKLMNOPQRS

ENGLISH ROMAN.

Quouſque tandem abutére, Catilina, patientia
noſtra ? quamdiu nos etiam furor iſte tuus eludet ?
quem ad finem ſeſe effrenata jactabit audacia ?
nihilne te nocturnum præſidium palatii, nihil
urbis vigiliæ, nihil timor populi, nihil conſenſus bonorum omnium, nihil hic munitiſſimus
ABCDEFGHIJKLMNOPQRSTVUW

PICA ROMAN.

Melium, novis rebus ſtudentem, manu ſua occidit.
Fuit, fuit iſta quondam in hac repub. virtus, ut viri
fortes acrioribus ſuppliciis civem pernicioſum, quam
acerbiſſimum hoſtem coërcerent. Habemus enim ſe-
natuſconſultum in te, Catilina, vehemens, & grave :
non deeſt reip. conſilium, neque autoritas hujus ordinis : nos, nos, dico aperte, conſules deſumus. De-
ABCDEFGHIJKLMNOPQRSTVUWX

Double Pica Italick.

Quouſque tandem abutere, Catili-
na, patientia noſtra ? quamdiu
nos etiam furor iſte tuus eludet ?
quem ad finem ſeſe effrenata jac-
ABCDEFGHJIKLMNO

Great Primer Italick.

Quouſque tandem abutére, Catilina, pa-
tientia noſtra ? quamdiu nos etiam fu-
ror iſte tuus eludet ? quem ad finem ſeſe
effrenata jactabit audacia ? nihilne te
nocturnum præſidium palatii, nihil ur-
bis vigiliæ, nihil timor populi, nihil con-
ABCDEFGHIJKLMNOPQR

Engliſh Italick.

Quouſque tandem abutere, Catilina, patientia noſ-
tra ? quamdiu nos etiam furor iſte tuus eludet ?
quem ad finem ſeſe effrenata jactabit audacia ?
nihilne te nocturnum præſidium palatii, nihil ur-
bis vigiliæ, nihil timor populi, nihil conſenſus bo-
norum omnium, nihil hic munitiſimus habendi ſe-
ABCDEFGHIJKLMNOPQRSTVU

Pica Italick.

Melium, novis rebus ſtudentem, manu ſua occidit.
Fuit, fuit iſta quondam in hac repub. virtus, ut viri
fortes acrioribus ſuppliciis civem pernicioſum, quam
acerbiſſimum hoſtem coërcerent. Habemus enim ſenatuſ-
conſultum in te, Catilina, vehemens, & grave : non deeſt
reip. conſilium, neque autoritas hujus ordinis : nos, nos,
dico aperte, conſules deſumus. Decrevit quondam ſenatus
ABCDEFGHIJKLMNOPQRSTVUWXYZ

Pica Black.

And be it further enacted by the Authority
aforeſaid, That all and every of the ſaid Exchequer Bills to be made forth by virtue o
this Act, or ſo many of them as ſhall from
ABCDEFGHIKLMNOPQRST

Brevier Black.

And be it further enacted by the Authority aforeſaid, That all and every
of the ſaid Exchequer Bills to be made forth by virtue of this Act, or ſo
many of them as ſhall from time to time remain undiſcharged and uncan-
celled, until the diſcharging and cancelling the ſame purſuant to this Act.

Pica Gothick.

ATTA ᚠNSAK ΦN ÏN hIMINAM ᚢᛖIhNAI
NAMᛟ ΦEIN ᚢIMAI ΦINAINASSnS ΦEINS
ᚢAIKΦAI ᚢIAᚷA ΦEINS Sᚢᚷ ÏN hIMINA

Pica Coptick.

ϩεκ οⲩⲁⲣⲭⲏ ⲉϥϯ ⲟⲁⲁⲉⲟ ⲛⲧϥε ⲛεⲗⲗ ⲛⲕ-
ⲁϩⲓ← ⲡⲓⲕⲁϩⲓ ⲁε ⲛε οⲩⲁⲟⲓⲁⲧ ⲉⲣοⲩ ⲡε οⲩⲟϩ
ⲛⲁⲧⲥⲟⲟϯ οⲩⲭⲁⲕⲓ ⲛⲁϭⲭⲏ εϫεⲛ Φⲛοⲩⲛ οⲩⲟϩ
οⲧⲡⲛⲁ ⲛ̄ⲧεϥϯ ⲛⲁϭⲛⲟⲧ ϩⲓϫεⲛ ⲛⲓⲙⲱοⲩ ←-ⲟⲟ

Pica Armenian.

 Սկզբանէ էր Բանն եւ Բանն էր առ Աստ-
ւած եւ Աստուած էր Բանն։ Նա էր ի սկզբանէ
առ Աստուած։ Ամենայն ինչ նովաւ եղեւ եւ
առանց նորա եղեւ եւ ոչ ինչ որ ինչ եղեւն։

English Syrisck.

ܐܝܟܢܐ ܕܟܬܝܒ ܒܐܫܥܝܐ ܢܒܝܐ ܕܗܐ
ܡܫܕܪ ܐܢܐ ܡܠܐܟܝ ܩܕܡ ܦܪܨܘܦܟ
ܕܢܬܩܢ ܐܘܪܚܐ ܩܕܡܝܟ ܩܠܐ ܕܩܪܐ

Pica Samaritan.

ﭏﭏﭏﭏ ﭏ ﭏﭏﭏ ﭏﭏ ﭏﭏﭏﭏﭏﭏ ﭏﭏﭏﭏ
ﭏﭏﭏ ﭏ ﭏ ﭏ ﭏﭏﭏﭏﭏ ﭏﭏﭏﭏ ﭏﭏﭏﭏ

succeeded Joseph Moxon's and who established himself in Charterhouse Street. In 1710 the James Foundry was started by the brothers Thomas and John James. In 1700 Thomas James had been apprenticed to Andrews. He finished his apprenticeship in 1708. Having not much opinion of English type design, he visited Amsterdam and bought a quantity of Dutch matrices and types. He returned to England, finally establishing himself with his brother in Bartholomew Close, near the hospital and a few hundred yards from Charterhouse School and the Andrews foundry where he had learned his trade. None of these foundries had any claims to originality in their type designs. They were only type-casters and rarely if ever cut punches for new types, which were almost always imported from Holland. If there were storms in the North Sea, they had to wait for new matrices, and their customers for new supplies of type.

For a while, the James foundry prospered until a rather unsavoury incident occurred, resulting from the attempts of an

Edinburgh goldsmith called William Ged to produce stereo plates. There were no type-foundries in Scotland and the Scottish printers bought nearly all their type direct from Holland. One of these Scottish printers told William Ged of his difficulties, perhaps thinking he might persuade Ged, a trained metal worker, to set up a type-foundry. Ged, however, put forward a suggestion of duplicating imposed forms of type by taking a mould in gypsum from the completely set pages, then casting a plate from this mould. This is, of course, the basis of modern stereotyping, where *papier mâché* is used for the mould (or flong as it is called). Newspapers are printed from plates cast in this manner. The process had been in use in Holland since 1700. Ged formed a partnership with a London stationer called Fenner, who provided the capital for the project, and introduced him to Thomas James, with whom they formed a company. This was a palpably double-faced act on the part of James, for he did everything in his power to undermine the success of Ged's invention, even to supplying worn and battered types for duplication and bribing the printer's compositors to make silly mistakes in the texts and his pressmen to damage the formes with their ink balls. James's business very rightly suffered as a result of this disreputable affair.

About the year 1720 William Bowyer happened to see some letters on the binding of a book, which had been struck from tools cut by a young Shropshire man called William Caslon. Caslon had established himself some three or four years before this in Vine Street near the Minories, as an engraver of gun-locks and gun-barrels and also occupied himself cutting tools for chasing silver, and cutting punches for bookbinders.

Half a century later, John Nichols described Bowyer's discovery in these words: '(William Bowyer) accidentally saw in the shop of Mr Daniel Browne Bookseller, near Temple Bar, the lettering of a book, uncommonly neat.'[7] On being told that the lettering was from tools cut by Caslon, Bowyer sought him out, and discussed the prospects of his setting up as a punch-cutter and type-founder. As Caslon knew nothing of the trade, Bowyer took him to have a look at the James Foundry. No doubt if they had known what a devastating rival he was to be, they would have found some means of putting him off the scent. However, Bowyer was a valuable client and they could have had no idea who this West Country lad was.

Within twenty-four hours of seeing the James Foundry, Caslon had agreed to start business if Bowyer could procure £500 capital for him. This was quickly forthcoming. Caslon started work in Vine Street, later moving to Helmet Row, Old Street. In 1722, his first commission came from the Society for Promoting Christian Knowledge, to cut an Arabic fount. Commissions for an English size and a pica size roman fount came from Bowyer. The pica first appeared in *Anacreon* in 1725

7. *Biographical and Literary Anecdotes of William Bowyer*, by John Nichols, London, 1782. Nichols was a former apprentice of William Bowyer and from 1766–1777 was a partner of Bowyer's son.

139

DOUBLE PICA ROMAN.
Quousque tandem abutere, Catilina, patientia nostra ? quamdiu
nos etiam furor iste tuus eludet ?
quem ad finem sese effrenata jac-
ABCDEFGHJIKLMNOP

Double Pica Italick.
Quousque tandem abutere, Catili-
na, patientia nostra ? quamdiu
nos etiam furor iste tuus eludet ?
quem ad finem sese effrenata jac-
ABCDEFGHJIKLMNO

and the English size three years later. Caslon then cut a Coptic type for a new edition of the *Pentateuch* under the direction of Bowyer, his patron and instructor. By 1730 he was well established and had received the rights to be the sole supplier of typefaces to the King's printers. He issued his first type specimen sheet in 1734 from Ironmonger Row. This sheet he re-issued in the 1738 edition of Ephraim Chambers' *Cyclopaedia* without alteration except for the address which was now in Chiswell Street.[8]

The great differences between Caslon and the earlier English type-founders were that he was a designer-craftsman who could cut new typefaces whenever a customer requested such a thing, and that his roman and italic founts in all their different sizes were all obviously of the same basic design, which was certainly not the case with types from the other foundries. Also Caslon's roman and italic were fundamentally good designs even if, at least in the case of the roman, they were based on Dutch models, which in their turn were copies of Garamond's designs, which had been based on those cut by Francesco Griffo for Aldus some two hundred years before Caslon set up shop! Caslon was, as John Nichols says 'Universally esteemed as a first-rate artist, a tender master, and an honest, friendly and benevolent man.'[9] He was most hospitable and had many writers amongst his friends. Once a month he gave a music party always on the night of the full moon, so that his guests could travel home safely, no matter how much wine or how many pints of Mr Caslon's home-brewed ale they had drunk. He died in 1766 and was succeeded at the foundry by his son William.[10]

The two great English typographic figures of the eighteenth century were Caslon and Baskerville. Talbot Baines Reed in his monumental *A History of the Old English Letter-Foundries* wrote: 'In 1720, the art of letter-founding had been roused from its lethargy through the genius of a gunsmith's apprentice, so in 1750 the art of printing was to find its delivery in the person of an eccentric Birmingham Japanner.'[11]

This eccentric Birmingham Japanner had been born in Worcestershire in 1706. At the age of twenty, Baskerville had established himself as a writing master in Birmingham. Later he had a school in the Bull Ring and also engraved inscriptions on tombstones. The 'art of the writing master' smacks of Renaissance Florence, but in fact the art had developed in England mainly because of the arrival in this country at the end of the sixteenth century of many Protestant Dutch and Flemish engravers who settled in London. Thanks to these refugees, the crafts of engraving and intaglio printing were soon flourishing in England. Some of these craftsmen were engaged in map-making, and the cursive letters they engraved were the fore-runners of the English copperplate hand.

Cartography and calligraphy were very closely linked and map

8. The bulky two volumed *Cyclopaedia* can still be found in second hand booksellers but it is advisable to look and see that the type specimen has not been removed.
9. *Biographical and Literary Anecdotes of William Bowyer* by John Nichols, London, 1782.
10. The Caslon Type Foundry continued after the death of the last of the Caslons in 1874, finally closing in 1936 when the stock was bought by Stephenson, Blake and Co. of Sheffield, who took on the Caslon name for their Foundry.
11. *A History of the Old English Letter-Foundries*, T. B. Reed, first published 1886; new and revised edition edited by A. F. Johnson, Faber and Faber 1952. How well Talbot Baines Reed wrote, anyone who ever read *The Adventures of a Three Guinea Watch* or *The Fifth Form at St. Dominics*, or any other of his school stories, would remember.

Letters

ON

Several Occasions.

EXTRACTED

From some Original Curious Specimens
of Epistolary Writing, in Prose and Verse,

Compos'd by the best Hands

In order to habituate Youth to an easy and elegant
Expression, as well as a Graceful Manner of
Writing, and Striking by Command of Hand.

Written,

With the friendly Assistance of several of the most Eminent Masters,

And Engrav'd by G. Bickham *Sen.*

Cadmus did first the wondrous Art devise — Of Painting Words, and Speaking to the Eyes.

N.º XLV.

G. Bickham Feci.

Sold by H. Overton at the White Horse without Newgate, London.

141

Detail from an engraved bill-head, showing a jeweller's shop-front
c. 1780

publishers also published writing books. The first of th
English writing books was *A Booke Containing Divers Sortes o
Hands* by John de Beauchesne and John Baildon, published i
1570. This was engraved on wood. From the beginning of th
seventeenth century, copper engraving was used for the print
ing of these books.

By the mid-eighteenth century something like seventy o
eighty English writing manuals had been issued.[12] The finest o
these was George Bickham's *Universal Penman*, published i
parts between 1733 and 1741. The skill of both penman an
engraver shown in this book is breathtaking, with flourishe
developing as naturally as if they had been produced by som
divinely inspired figure skater. Writing masters taught i
schools or gave private tuition. One of these writing master
was George Shelley who published in 1715 a manual calle
Alphabets in All Hands. This book provided Baskerville wit
the impetus that set him on his course of penman, engrave
stone letter-cutter and finally type-designer (but not type
cutter). Whether Baskerville felt he was not earning enough a
a writing master or for some other reason unknown to us, h
suddenly turned from his writing to the japanning trade whic
proved to be most profitable. This japanning which was use
mainly in the manufacture of coffee pots, urns and trays was
relatively short-lived trade. It was carried out in metal workin
centres such as Birmingham, but the finest examples of thi
japanned ware are the delicately shaped, prettily painted piece
from Pontypool in Monmouthshire, where the trade ha
started in 1720.

There was a heavy demand for these japanned goods an
Baskerville, within a few years of entering the trade, ha
amassed a fortune and had become the most important rival o
the Pontypool japanners. His wares, according to contem
porary writers, were beautifully designed and highly finished
They included chestnut urns, tea trays, salvers, bread basket
and candlesticks.[13] None of Baskerville's japanned ware i
known to have survived for it appears that he omitted th
tinning process (probably for reasons of economy). As a resul
of this, the articles would have rusted and eventually disinte
grated.[14]

In about 1750, Baskerville again returned to letters, but thi
time not as a writing master, but as a printer and type-founder
He engaged a very skilful letter-cutter called John Handy an
set himself to designing a completely new typeface. It was six
years before he was satisfied with his new type and during thi
time he had established both a foundry and a press.

In 1754 he announced the publication of his first book, a
quarto *Virgil*, to be obtained from himself or from R. & J.
Dodsley, Bookseller in Pall Mall, London. In April 1757, thre
years later, Dodsley was writing to Baskerville asking him to
hurry up with the book. Within a month or so it was ready for

12. For a fuller account of the English writing masters, see *The English
Writing Masters & their Copy-books* by Ambrose Heal, Cambridge
University Press, 1931; see also *Renaissance Handwriting*, Alfred Fairbank and Berthold Wolpe, Faber and Faber, London: 1960.
13. Japanning is the name given to a method of coating the surfaces of
metal, wood or *papier mâché* with a variety of varnishes, which are
stove-dried to a heat of about 300°F. Black was the most characteristic
background, consisting of pure natural asphaltum, with a proportion
of *gum animé* dissolved in linseed oil and thinned with turpentine. For
fine work, several coats were applied.
14. A. H. Westwood, The Assay Master, Birmingham, in a letter to the
author, 21 Feb. 1969.

ublication and it was worth waiting for. The style of layout as not so different from the books of such publishers as Jacob onson, but much greater care was evident in every part of he production of the book. The title-page was set entirely in apitals, widely and beautifully letter-spaced.

he italic capitals were particularly striking and individual, vith a swash character to some of the letters. The paper was mooth, though not as smooth as the paper in his later books. he text was set in his Great Primer (the modern equivalent vould be 16 point), with about a 2 point lead running through t. The type is open, wider than Caslon's, and very readable. At ast, here is a break with the Aldine tradition. Griffo and all ubsequent type-cutters had based their letter forms on those vritten with an obliquely-cut, broad-edged pen. The eigheenth-century writing masters like Baskerville wrote with a ointed, flexible pen; they could not have drawn all those lourishes otherwise. The marked diagonal stress of weight in n Aldine letter, still maintained by Caslon, is hardly evident ere. In order to show these cleanly cut types to best advantage, Baskerville produced fine, smooth, wove papers and later ntroduced the technique of calendering the sheets by placing hem between hot copper plates as soon as they came off the rinting press.

n the foreword to *Paradise Lost* which he printed in 1758, he xpressed gratitude to his public for receiving his *Virgil* so well; e also said 'The improvement in the manufacture of the *Paper*, the *Colour* and *Firmness* of the *Ink* were not overlooked; or did the accuracy of the workmanship in general, pass unegarded.' He added that his real ambition was to be allowed to rint an octavo Common Prayer Book and a folio Bible. He ollowed up this plea in the same year by applying for the post f printer to the University of Cambridge. He was accepted for he post and given permission to print two editions of the rayer Book and the folio Bible. This appointment, which hould have proved such a pleasurable one for him, was nything but that! As so often has been the case both before nd since, generosity and academic appointments rarely go and in hand. The syndics fairly soaked him with heavy remiums for the privilege of printing Prayer Book and Bible. Meanwhile he continued to produce handsome, finely printed ooks from his press in Birmingham. He was acclaimed abroad. ournier *le Jeune*, the great French type-founder, wrote: 'M. Baskerville, a private individual of means, has established in Birmingham, the town where he lives, and renowned for its netal manufacturers, a paper mill, a printing office and a typeoundry. He has spared neither pains nor expense to bring hese to the highest perfection. His types are cut with much pirit, his italic being the best to be found in any type-foundry n Europe, only the roman characters are a little too broad. He as already printed some editions printed from the new types,

THE

ORDER

FOR

MORNING PRAYER,

Daily throughout the Y E A R.

¶ *At the beginning of Morning Prayer, the Minister shall read with a loud voice some one, or more of these Sentences of the Scriptures that follow; And then he shall say that which is written after the said Sentences.*

WHEN the wicked man turneth away from his wickedness that he hath committed, and doeth that which is lawful and right, he shall save his soul alive. *Ezek.* xviii. 27.

I acknowledge my transgressions, and my sin is ever before me. *Psal.* li. 3.

Hide thy face from my sins, and blot out all mine iniquities. *Psal.* li. 9.

The sacrifices of God are a broken spirit: a broken and a contrite heart, O God, thou wilt not despise. *Psal.* li. 17.

Rend your heart, and not your garments, and turn unto the Lord your God: for he is gracious and merciful, slow to anger, and of great kindness, and repenteth him of the evil. *Joel* ii. 13.

To the Lord our God belong mercies and forgivenesses, though we have rebelled against him:

B

C. CRISPUS

SALLUSTIUS;

E T

L. ANNÆUS

FLORUS.

❋❖❋❉❖❋❋❖❋❉❖❋❋❖❋❉❖❋❋❖❋❉❖❋❋❖❋

BIRMINGHAMIÆ:
Typis J O A N N I S B A S K E R V I L L E.
MDCCLXXIII.

which for brilliancy are real masterpieces. Some are upon hot pressed paper and although they are a little fatiguing to the eye one cannot deny they are the most beautiful things to be seen in this sort of work.'[15]

English printers, probably because they were jealous, had not a good word to say for him. They disliked his typefaces and complained that the smooth, white paper and crisp presswork were enough to blind anyone. Benjamin Franklin, the printer who became the greatest of American diplomats, and who was a firm admirer of the Birmingham printer, wrote a witty letter to Baskerville describing how he had fooled some egregious ass who had been complaining about how Baskerville's work 'blinded' him. Franklin described how he showed this man a Caslon specimen sheet pretending it was Baskerville's, and concealing Caslon's name. Franklin wrote, 'he declared he could not read the type specimen without feeling very strongly the pain!'

Baskerville's folio Bible at length appeared in 1763, set like the *Virgil* in his Great Primer type. It was a fine piece of printing and, with the possible exception of the Bible printed by the Doves Press in 1903, typographically the finest Bible ever to be printed in English.

Baskerville was really printing for the love of it and all the while the returns from his japanning enterprises under-pinned his printing. Even so, in a moment of despondency, he wrote to Horace Walpole in 1762 asking him, as a member of Parliament, if he could persuade the Government to give him some support. Walpole apparently achieved nothing, though he may very well have been sympathetic as a Private Press Printer himself. In 1766, the year Caslon died, lack of support so discouraged Baskerville that he handed over his press to his foreman Robert Martin. However, three years later, he took charge of it once again. He was now sixty-three years old and had only another six years of life ahead of him. He was still a handsome man, he had always been something of a dandy with a tendency to lace cuffs and lace cravats. For many years he drove round Birmingham in an elegant little carriage, which was really a form of advertisement, with brightly japanned scenes on the metal door panels, and drawn by a beautiful pair of cream coloured horses. During his last years, he continued to print as well as ever. In 1775, the year of the Boston Tea Party, Baskerville died, leaving the quite respectable sum of £12,000 to his widow. No one in England showed the least interest in purchasing his types and they finally went to France, bought by Beaumarchais for the Societé Littéraire-Typographique for £3,700. Their first use was for an edition of the complete works of Voltaire. William Hutton writing about Baskerville in 1835 in his *History of Birmingham* said 'in private life, he was a humourist, idle in the extreme; but his invention was the true Birmingham model, active. He could well design,

15. *Manual Typographique*. P. S. Fournier, Barbou, Paris, 1764. Translated by Harry Carter, with the title *Fournier on typefounding*, Soncino Press, London, 1930.

A
SPECIMEN

By *JOHN BASKERVILLE* of *Birmingham*.

I-Am indebted to you for two Letters dated from Corcyra. You congratulate me in one of them on the Account you have Received, that I ftill preferve my former Authority in the Commonwealth: and wifh me Joy in the other of my late Marriage. With refpect to the Firft,

I Am indebted to you for two Letters dated from Corcyra. You congratulate me in one of them on the Account you have Received, that I ftill preferve my former Authority in the Commonwealth: and wifh me Joy in the other of my late Marriage. With refpect to the firft, if to mean well to the Intereft of my Country and to

I Am indebted to you for two Letters dated from Corcyra. You congratulate me in one of them on the Account you have received, that I ftill preferve my former Authority in the Commonwealth: and wifh me joy in the other of my late Marriage. With refpect to the Firft, if to mean well to the Intereft of my Country and to approve that meaning to every Friend of its Liberties, may be confider'd as maintaining

if to mean well to the Intereft of my Country and to approve that meaning to every Friend of its Liberties, may be confider'd as maintaining my Authority; the Account you have heard is certainly true. But if it confifts in rendering thofe Sentiments effectual to the Public Welfare or at leaft in daring freely to Support and inforce them;

approve that meaning to every Friend of its Liberties, may be confider'd as maintaining my Authority; the Account you have heard is certainly true. But if it confifts in rendering thofe Sentiments effectual to the Public Welfare or at leaft in daring freely to Support and inforce them; alas! my Friend I have not the leaft fha-

my Authority; the Account you have heard is certainly true. But if it confifts in rendering thofe Sentiments effectual to the Public Welfare or at leaft in daring freely to Support and inforce them; alas! my Friend I have not the leaft fhadow of Authority remaining. The Truth of it is, it will be fufficient Honor if I can have fo much Authority over myfelf as to bear with patience our prefent and impending Calamities: a frame of Mind not to be acquired without difficulty,

Q. HORATII FLACCI

Hac ego fi compellar imagine, cuncta refigno.
Nec fomnum plebis laudo fatur altilium; nec
Otia divitiis Arabum liberrima muto.
Sæpe verecundum laudafti: rexque, paterque
Audifti coram, nec verbo parcius abfens
Infpice fi poffum donata reponere lætus.
Haud male Telemachus proles patientis Ulyffei;
Non eft aptus equis Ithacæ locus, ut neque planis
Porrectus fpatiis, neque multæ prodigus herbæ:
Atride, magis apta tibi tua dona relinquam.
Parvum parva decent. mihi jam non regia Roma,
Sed vacuum Tibur placet, aut imbelle Tarentum.
   Strenuus et fortis, caufifque Philippus agendis

EPISTOLARUM LIBER I.

Clarus, ab officiis octavam circiter horam
Dum redit, atque foro nimium diftare Carinas
Jam grandis natu queritur; confpexit, ut aiunt,
Adrafum quendam vacua tonforis in umbra
Cultello proprios purgantem leniter ungues.
Demetri, (puer hic non læve juffa Philippi (quis,
Accipiebat) abi, quære, et refer; unde domo,
Cujus fortunæ, quo fit patre, quove patrono.
It, redit, et narrat, Vulteium nomine Menam
Præconem, tenui cenfu fine crimine notum,
Et properare loco, et ceffare, et quærere, et uti
Gaudentem parvifque fodalibus, et lare certo,
Et ludis, et poft decifa negotia, Campo.

but procured others to execute.' If this was the true Birmingham model, we could do with a few more like him.

Baskerville's typefaces, smooth paper and black inks marke
the transitional stage towards the Neo-Classical typography c
Bodoni and Didot. English printing during the eighteent
century moved gracefully from the time of Caslon an
Baskerville to John Bell, 'the most resourceful and inventiv
bookseller of his generation.'16

In 1774 Bell started the long run of 109 volumes of his series c
Poets. In 1776, he launched another cheap series, the *Briti.
Theatre,* which ran through 21 volumes. In 1791 he reprinte
both series and sold them at 6*d* a volume on rather indifferer
paper or 1/6*d* a volume on better paper. These little book
really were cheap, considering that Boswell's *Life of Johnson
published in 1791, cost £2. 2s. od.17

In 1790 Edmund Burke's *Reflections on the Revolution in Fran.
had been published. Burke anticipated the views and the di:
may of the English middle classes at what was happening i
Paris. Published by Dodsley, it ran to 30,000 copies. Within th
year Tom Paine had replied with *The Rights of Man,* 'the cleares
of all expositions of basic democracy.'18 It was printed an
published by J. Johnson in St Paul's Churchyard, and withi
a few weeks had sold over 50,000 copies. Johnson took frigl
at its radical tone and another publisher took over the distr
bution. The power of the printing press was once again makin
itself felt. Parliament tried to suppress it, but only succeeded i
increasing its circulation. The principles of human rights tha
Paine expounded with such lucidity laid the foundations c
nineteenth-century radicalism and twentieth-century democracy
The events in France that led up to the Revolution were in
small way reflected by the style of French printing. The Rococ
frivolities of court life had their counterparts in the illustration
of Boucher and Fragonard and in the typography of Fournie
le Jeune. English printing, apart from the engraved trade cards
showed nothing of this. It was an age of letters. The literar
content called for clear, dignified typography. The types c
Caslon and Alexander Wilson in Glasgow, enabled printer
like the Foulis brothers to print in a manner that did justic
both to authors and type-founders.

16. *John Bell*, Stanley Morison, Cambridge University Press, 1931.
17. *The English Common Reader.*
18. *Printing and the Mind of Man.*

146

The Baroque and the Rococo

The terms Baroque and Rococo were as alien to the English as the architectural movements they designated. The word baroque comes from the Portuguese *Barocco*, which means a rough, ill-shaped pearl. In French it becomes *Baroque* meaning curious or odd. Like Gothic in its original sense, it was used as a term of contempt.

There was little Baroque architecture in England. Vanbrugh was the only real exponent of the style. As for Baroque art, only that under-rated artist Sir James Thornhill could be considered as a native-born Baroque painter. St Paul's Cathedral, the Radcliffe Camera or Seaton Delaval are all superficially Baroque buildings, yet because of an underlying Classicism, lack the fundamental dynamic tensions of Baroque architecture, tensions that produce the feeling of movement in space found in all true Baroque buildings.

One of the reasons why this great architectural movement made so little impact in England was that England never had a Catholic Counter-Reformation. From the time of Elizabeth I, it was a Protestant country.

The Catholic church on the Continent made use of every facet of Baroque art and architecture as a means of inviting Protestants back into the fold. The Baroque was much closer to the Gothic than to classical architecture. It picked up again something of the mysticism and the love of pageantry of the late Middle Ages.

The Baroque contribution to printing was limited to the elaborate engraved title-pages, with which most large quartos and folios were embellished. The formula for these engravings was nearly always an archway to lead the reader into the book. Palladian porticoes gave way to the flat-vaulted Baroque arch which was often supported by Bernini's 'barley-sugar' pillars. At about the end of the first quarter of the eighteenth century, mainly under French influence, the grandeur of Baroque began to merge into the decorative frivolities of Rococo. The word rococo comes from the French *rocaille*, which means shell-work. It was a delicious, absurd, sophisticated style – the antithesis of the classical style with hardly a straight line or a hint of symmetry. Natural forms of leaves, fronds and shells were joined with curling scrolls. The Rococo was the art of the stage designer and the interior decorator. Looking glasses, wall brackets, picture frames all took on absurdly fanciful forms.

The liveliest Rococo interiors are to be found in Bavaria and of these, the two loveliest are in Munich: the little Residenz theatre and the Amalienburg, the hunting lodge in the grounds of the Nymphenburg. Both these exquisite buildings were designed by François Cuvilliés. The Amalienburg was built for the Electress Maria Amalia in 1734–9 and was decorated by J. B. Zimmermann and the Munich wood carver, Joachim Dietrich. This joyous style, however, was not limited to secular buildings.[1]

Engraved border to title-page with Bernini pillars, printed in London, 1596

1. See *From Baroque to Rococo*, Nicholas Powell, Faber and Faber, London, 1959; and *Great Houses of Europe*, edited by Sacheverell Sitwell, Weidenfeld and Nicolson, London, 1961.

Engraved border to title-page with indications of the Rococo,
printed by John Teage at the Sign of the Golden Ball in Paul's
Churchyard, London, 1621

VOX
clamantis.
MARK. I. 3.

A
STIL VOICE,
TO THE THREE
Thrice-honourable Estates
OF
PARLIAMENT:
And in them, to all the Soules
of this our Nation, of what state or
condition soeuer they be.

By *William Loe*, Doctor of Di-
uinitie, and Chaplaine to the Kings
most excellent *Maiestie*.

Printed by *T.S.* for *John Teage*, and are
to be sold at the Signe of the *Golden-
Ball* in *Pauls*. Church-yard, 1621.

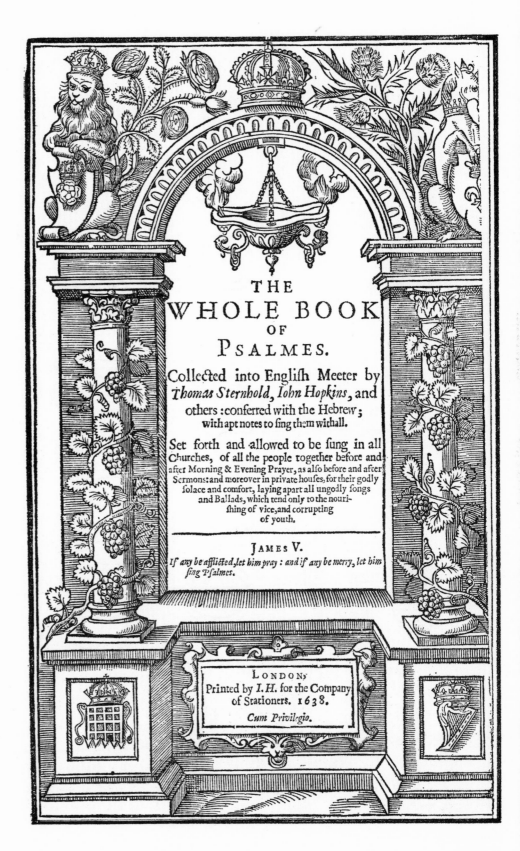

THE
WHOLE BOOK
OF
PSALMES.

Collected into English Meeter by *Thomas Sternhold*, *Iohn Hopkins*, and others : conferred with the Hebrew ; with apt notes to sing them withall.

Set forth and allowed to be sung in all Churches, of all the people together before and after Morning & Evening Prayer, as also before and after Sermons: and moreover in private houses, for their godly solace and comfort, laying apart all ungodly songs and Ballads, which tend only to the nourishing of vice, and corrupting of youth.

JAMES V.

If any be afflicted, let him pray : and if any be merry, let him sing Psalmes.

LONDON,
Printed by *I.H.* for the Company of Stationers. 1638.
Cum Privilegio.

Engraved border to title-page to *The Historie of the Reigne of King*
Henry the Seventh by Viscount St Albans, with baroque cartouche,
London 1641

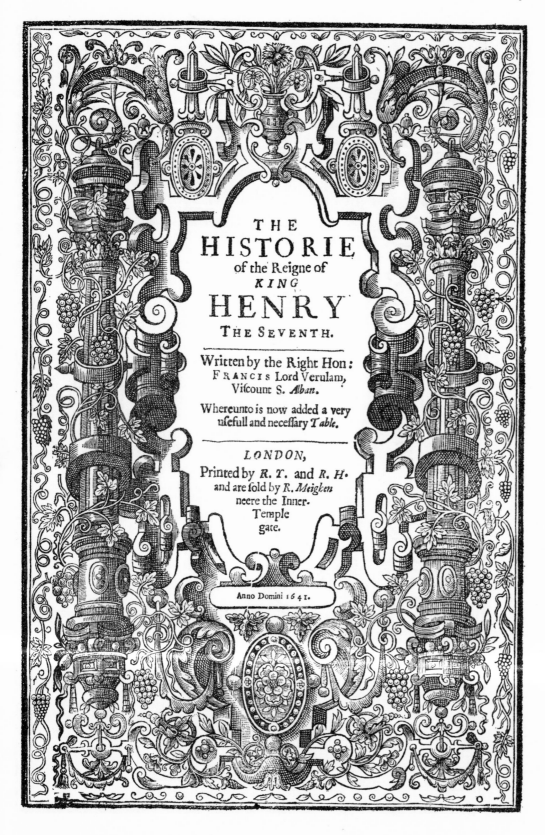

THE
HISTORIE
of the Reigne of
KING
HENRY
THE SEVENTH.

Written by the Right Hon:
FRANCIS Lord Verulam,
Viscount S. *Alban.*

Whereunto is now added a very
usefull and necessary *Table.*

LONDON,
Printed by *R. T.* and *R. H.*
and are sold by *R. Meighen*
neere the Inner-
Temple
gate.

Anno Domini 1641.

The brothers Asam, in churches such as the one at Weltenburg on the Danube, used every kind of Rococo decoration as well as concealed lighting and stucco figures blending imperceptibly into fresco painting. The Rococo was fun, a quality all too rare in architecture. At Weltenburg if you look up at the ceiling, you can see a man in a full-bottomed wig and eighteenth-century costume looking down somewhat quizzically from over the cornice. It is the architect, Cosmas Damien Asam, modelled in stucco and placed there by himself to keep an eye on things.

The Rococo style was in every way artificial, even though it made great play with vegetable and animal forms. Yet though its forms were often wildly extravagant, it was a harmonious style and was in fact a direct ancestor of *l'art nouveau*. The Rococo, Chinoiserie and Gothick were all styles of extreme sophistication, used as playthings by the aristocracy and the courts of western Europe. In eighteenth-century French painting, Watteau, Boucher and Fragonard represented the Rococo style in a Never Never Land of half undressed Arcadian shepherds and shepherdesses. Yet in spite of this escapism, Watteau was as acute an observer of real life as Hogarth, a painter with whom he had much in common.

The asymmetry of the Rococo was the final stage in the movement's rejection of classical ideals. French Rococo developed from the inspiration of J. A. Meissonier, the Paris goldsmith, and Bernard Toro, a woodcarver, whose engraved designs were published in 1716. Both these designers made use of asymmetry, though it has been suggested that this asymmetry was arrived at by chance. The Nuremberg engraver, Paul Decker, issued in the early eighteenth century, some designs for cartouches where the two halves of each design were obviously intended to be halves of *symmetrical* designs. This was merely an economy of space and effort. These combined designs needed very little modification to convert them into asymmetric designs. It is an ingenious theory, at least worthy of consideration.[2]

In the decorative arts in France the tapestry weavers of the Savonnerie carried the Rococo into their designs with flowers, dogs and monkeys, all entwined with tendrils and creepers. The silversmith Paul de Lamerie with other Huguenot craftsmen emigrated to England and worked Rococo forms with much skill into the design of silver tableware – a soup tureen in the form of a turtle or a cake basket like a scallop shell. In Germany the same spirit and same motifs of scroll, shells and foliage could be seen in the Meissen and Nymphenburg figures by J. J. Kändler and F. A. Bustelli respectively. In England the potters of Bow, Chelsea and Derby followed their lead. In British architecture, the most successful exponent of Rococo was the Scottish architect, James Gibbs, who had studied in Italy under a pupil of Bernini. Gibbs was a friend of Wren and was responsible for many Baroque and Rococo London churches

2. *Asymmetry in Rococo Art.* Anon. *The Times* 29th Nov. 1958.

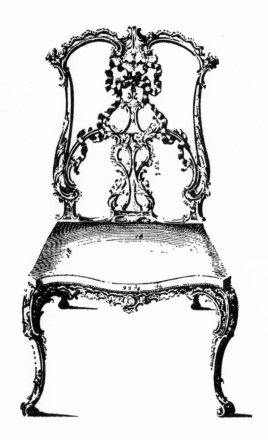

including St Mary-le-Strand. As interior design his Rococo
style hardly compares with the Asams', yet buildings such
as his Senate House at Cambridge have much of the pervading
charm of the movement. The English Rococo was seen at it
most extravagant in little architectural follies and summer
houses such as the shell grotto at Goodwood, and even more
so at Vauxhall Gardens. As David Garrick and George Colman
said in their play *The Clandestine Marriage:* 'There is none of
your straight lines here, but all taste – crinkum crankum – in and
out – right and left – twisting and turning like a worm.'

In 1732 Jonathan Tyers, a friend of Hogarth, opened a
Vauxhall a Rococo entertainment, which he called a *Ridotto a
fresco.* The whole staff of Hogarth's St Martin's Lane Academy
and no doubt some of the students as well, worked on design
for this entertainment.

The Rococo impetus in England must have come mainly from
Hubert François Gravelot, who had come over from Paris in
1732. It was said that he made designs for goldsmiths and
silversmiths (perhaps anticipating Paul de Lamerie), as well as
decorating and illustrating a number of books. He brought a
French charm and sophistication into these engravings and
provided a link between such French Rococo painters as
Watteau and Boucher and the English painters and engravers.
His illustrations for books and song sheets usually had elaborate Rococo frames. Some of Gravelot's work was engraved by
G. Bickham, the author of *The Universal Penman.*

The St Martin's Lane Academy was in the midst of the work-
shops of the leading furniture makers, including Chippendale.
Some of the young craftsmen in these workshops may have
attended Hogarth's school. Amongst the younger pupils at
Hogarth's Academy were Thomas Gainsborough and James
Paine, the architect who had been introduced to the Rococo by
Thomas Jersey, James Gibbs's clerk-of-the-works. Paine had
close links with Chippendale and, though the evidence is
circumstantial, there can be little doubt that the St Martin's
Lane circle must have influenced the furniture trade. Gravelot
never published a pattern book for the furniture makers, but
he was probably the inspiration behind many of the pattern
books and other similar productions which were to pour off
the printing presses in the next quarter of a century.

Thomas Johnson, the furniture designer, and Matthias Lock,
woodcarver, were other designers who followed the style. They
drew out Rococo designs for girandoles, mantelpieces, etc, for
Chippendale. In 1746, Henry Copland, an engraver of trade
cards, published *A New Book of Ornament*, which was chock-a-
block with Rococo designs.

The designers of both the Rococo and Baroque trade cards
make much use of the oval, a form that has inherent dynamic
tensions and which imparts to an engraving a sense of movement and a rhythm lacking in any classical design.[3]

3. See *Baroque Churches of Central Europe*, John Bourke, Faber and Faber,
1958.

69 Rococo Derby porcelain group. c. 1765, copied from a model by Carl Vanloo. *Victoria and Albert Museum*

70 Cosmas Damian Asam peering down from the cornice at Weltenburg

71 Bernini 'barley-sugar' pillars and back-lighting in the Asam church at Weltenburg

72 Baroque stage design; pen and wash drawing by Filippo Juvarra (1685–1736). *Victoria and Albert Museum*

O*

75 *La Pêche Chinoise*, oil painting on paper by François Boucher. Boucher did a series of Tableautins in 1742 with Chinoiserie themes, which served as preparatory cartoons for the Beauvais tapestry works. One of the tapestry sets decorated the apartments of the Marquise de Pompadour. *Boymans-van Beuningen Museum, Rotterdam*

77 The restrained Rococo of St Mary-le-Strand; sepia wash and black line drawing by James Gibbs, the architect of the Church, which was built 1714–27. *Victoria and Albert Museum*

78 Engraving from Sir William Chambers' book *Designs for Chinese Buildings*, 1757. *Victoria and Albert Museum*

80 Rococo design for a panel by Jeremy Wachsmuth (1712–79). *Victoria and Albert Museum*

81 Fragments of cotton textile, printed with designs in the Ch[...] style. English, second half of the eighteenth century. *Victoria [...] Albert Museum*

L'Imprimerie, allegorical engraving by J. V. Schley 1739, showing
Minerva and Mercury granting the art of printing to Germany,
who in turn passes it on to Holland, England, Italy and France

L'IMPRIMERIE, descendant des Cieux, est accordée par **Minerve** *et* **Mercure** *à* **l'Allemagne**,
qui la présente à la **Hollande**, *l'**Angleterre**, l'**Italie**, & la* **France**, *les quatre prémieres
Nations chés les quelles ce bel Art fut adopté*

Robert Legg

Upholder, Appraiser & Undertaker,
at the sign of ye Leg, near Southampton Street in

Holborn

Son of the late Robt. Legg
opposite Bloomsbury Market.

Darly Sculp. Chandos Street.

Taillart M.
de flute Rue Descordeliere
vis avis La Rue haute feuille
a Paris

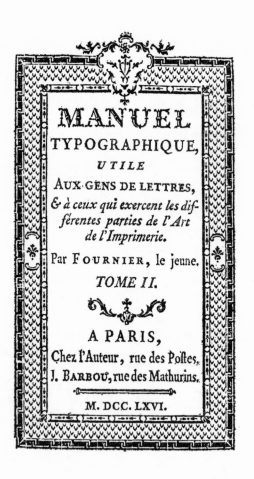

The decorative possibilities of the Rococo, so difficult one would think to render in wood, as Chippendale and others succeeded in doing, was seized upon by the engravers of trade cards, billheads and title-pages. Linen-drapers, peruke-makers and haberdashers were some of the trades represented on cards engraved in the Rococo style. Matts. Darly, painter, engraver and stainer represented his 'Manufactory for Paper Hangings', with a somewhat symmetrical Baroque card. It was Darly who engraved most of the plates for Chippendale's *The Gentleman and Cabinet Maker's Director* (1754–62). The same engraver combined the Rococo with Chinoiserie in a delightful card for Robert Legg, Undertaker.

Chinoiserie, which was a variant on the Rococo, had its origin in the growing interest in distant and exotic places, and in the case of Britain, with a growing trade with China in tea, silk, opium, also porcelain and wallpapers. Some of these papers were quite delightful, with paintings of flowering trees, hung with birdcages and lanterns. Chinese motifs were quickly adopted by European painters and engravers and continued in use for tea merchants' billheads right through the nineteenth century. Boucher's Chinoiserie painting *La Pêche Chinoise* in the Boymans Museum at Rotterdam is the forerunner of these engravings and as idyllic as any Rococo scene of nymphs and shepherds.

In 1757, Sir William Chambers's *Designs for Chinese Buildings* was published, to be succeeded by a later volume, *Dissertations on Oriental Gardening*, which was about Kew and the famous pagoda. Chambers, like Chippendale, adapted Chinese forms to English furniture. A year or so before Chambers published his first book, Jean Pillement, a former designer at the Gobelin factory, arrived in England. Pillement produced a series of black chalk designs showing a variety of Chinoiserie forms. These were copied by various English porcelain manufacturers. These copies included some engraved transfer prints by Robert Hancock for the Worcester factory. Pillement also had a marked influence on the japanning trade. *The Ladies Amusement or the Whole Art of Japanning Made Easy*, which was published by Robert Sayer, had plates of Chinoiserie designs drawn and engraved by Pillement. He also produced another volume, which he called *A New Book of Chinese Ornaments*.

The Rococo influence on printing was more obvious in France than elsewhere. Large folios with ponderous Baroque title pages were replaced by small octavos with vignetted head and tail pieces. Boucher illustrated Molière's *Oeuvres* and Ovid's *Metamorphoses*. Fragonard illustrated the Abbé St Non's *Voyage Pittoresque*, and Oudry illustrated La Fontaine's *Fables*. The charm of these illustrations was matched by the typography with decorative typefaces and arabesques from the Fournier type-foundry.

The Fourniers came of a large family of printers and type

Peu de chofes

de Saint-auguftin.

F G H K

J M L N

founders. The one of most interest to us was Pierre Simon Fournier, called *le Jeune*, to distinguish him from his elder brother Jean Pierre, the manager and ultimately the owner of the Le Bé type-foundry.

Fournier *le Jeune*, born in 1712, came into type-founding via the art school. He had been brought up, away from his brothers, by an aunt. From the time he was fifteen years old, he attended the Academie de St Luc, and was taught drawing by the miniature painter J. B. G. Colson. When he was seventeen, he went to work under his brother at Le Bé's foundry. Here he learned to cut punches and to engrave ornaments. Within a year or so, he had set up as a freelance engraver and punch-cutter. In 1736 he started his own type-foundry in Paris, on the left bank of the Seine. He cut his first fount of type, a *Gros-canon* (44 point), in the same year and in 1737 he published his *Table of Type sizes*, the first attempt at introducing a codified system of type measurement. In 1742, Fournier issued his first type specimen book *Modèles des Caractères de l'Imprimerie*. It was made up of 27 leaves bound up as a landscape quarto. It was a finely printed book and his typefaces had some of the characteristics of the 'modern' face, with flat almost unbracketed serifs. Fournier's italic capitals, in the form of a sloping roman, following Grandjean's precedent, were a complete break with the Arrighi script, which had influenced most of the previous italic designs. Fournier's lower case italics, like Baskerville's, had their origin in the copperplate hand.

Fournier's roman letters, again like Baskerville's, were transitional designs, falling between the old style letters of Caslon, Van Dyck, Garamond and Aldus and the 'modern' typefaces, such as the *Romain du Roi*, and the Neo-Classical typefaces of Bodoni and Didot that came into popular use at the end of the eighteenth century.

Fournier's place in this survey is due to the manner in which he reflected the Rococo movement. This he did by the use of his typographic ornaments, which were supremely decorative. To match these flowery decorations, he designed and cut flowery, decorative capital letters.

Fournier's contribution to book design, was to convert the Rococo engraved decorations of the time into letterpress material, with arabesques and flowers cast on type bodies, so that the printer could handle them as if they were cast letters. His 'flowers' combined most happily into patterns, rules and borders. Printing in this pretty manner became an aristocratic and fashionable hobby at court. In 1718 a little printing office was opened in the Tuileries. Here Louis XV, at the age of eight, learned to set type and pull proofs. There was another press at Versailles where Marie Joseph of Saxony, Louis XVI's mother, printed. Madame de Pompadour, in addition to her other talents, was a clever artist and etcher. She had yet another press set up for herself in the north wing at Versailles.

he opening pages of the first volume of J. Papillon's *Traite*
istorique et Pratique de la Gravure en Bois, engraved in 1743 and
ublished in Paris in 1766. *St Bride Printing Library*

A MONSIEUR
LE MARQUIS DE BOYER DE BANDOL,
Chevalier d'Honneur de l'Ordre de Saint Jean de Jérusalem,
Commandeur & Grand'Croix de l'Ordre de Saint Michel de Ba-
viere, Chambelan de feu Son Alteſſe Séréniſſime & Eminentiſſime
Monſeigneur le Cardinal de Baviere, Evêque & Prince de Liege,
&c. &c. &c.

ONSIEUR,

OTRE Goût pour les beaux
Arts, la protection que vous ac—

In 1756, Pompadour still a close friend, if no longer mistress, of the King, commissioned Fournier to print 'a tasteful little edition of the psalms for the King's chapel'. For this book he cut a 5-point fount of type.

Fournier lived in a house in the Rue des Postes, which had been occupied by Philippe Grandjean, a former type-cutter to the Royal Printing House. Fournier was as interested in printing as he was in type-cutting, but under the 'Bookselling and Printing Code' of 1723 he was debarred from setting up as a printer. However when he pleaded that he wished to further the craft of printing, and was not intending to take the bread out of the mouths of the other printers, he was granted admission as a supernumerary printer for Paris. And so he entered the printing shop of Barbou in the Rue St Jacques. Here he printed the two volumes of the *Manuel Typographique*. In the first volume, issued in 1764, Fournier describes in detail the technicalities of punch-cutting, matrix-making and type-founding. The second volume came out two years later and is mainly taken up with type specimens including many pages of ornaments. They are pretty little books, each page framed in decorative rules. Fournier had intended two further volumes, but he did not live to finish them. In 1768 he died from overwork; for twenty-nine years he had been doing most of the work of the foundry himself.

The Rococo had a short-lived effect on printing, but the little books that appeared in this style are very appealing.

Many-tiered wedding cakes and ornamental pastry may be more enduring and popular manifestations of the Rococo than printing, yet in spite of its eccentric extravagances, the Rococo was a harmonious printing style.

The end of the Rococo style came about through two causes. One was the fact that it had become the plaything of the aristocracy and the French Revolution put an end to all that. The other was a revived interest in classicism, brought about by the excavations at Pompeii and the writings of Winckelmann and Mengs.

The Neo-Classical was to be the next great design movement; it spanned the years 1780–1830. This was also the finest period of printing since the time of Gutenberg and Fust and Schöffer.

83 Neo-Classical mural painting by Zucchi for the Eating room at
Osterley Park, designed by Robert Adam. *Photograph: Victoria
and Albert Museum, Osterley Park*

After the grandeur of the Baroque and the sheer joy of the Rococo, the Neo-Classical movement comes like a cold douche. France in the last quarter of the eighteenth century was heading for political anarchy. Once again, as in the Carolingian epoch and at the time of the Renaissance, Europe turned back to the world of classical antiquity, confusing on this occasion the *art* of the Romans and the ancient Greeks with Roman and Greek *law and order*.

A spur had been given to this movement by the excavations at Herculaneum, and the writings that resulted from these archaeological finds. Johann Joachim Winckelmann (1717–68), the first great German art historian, published his *Geschichte der Kunst des Alterthums* in 1764. This history of ancient art was soon translated into French and English. Even though Winckelmann's knowledge of Greek art was mainly from Roman copies, he provided the basis of a new aesthetic, by directing his contemporaries to renounce instinct, to look away from real life and to look back towards the concepts of antiquity. Neo-Classicism was an intellectual movement. It was all brain and no belly. Viewed in this light, it is possible to understand the outrage felt by the great English potter, Josiah Wedgwood, when, as legend has it, he found John Voyez, the most skilful of his modellers, actually modelling from the life a naked village maiden. It may have been Wedgwood's aesthetic prejudice, rather than his prudery, which was so upset. He sacked him on the spot. (He continued to pay him his salary, so that he should not work for anyone else.) At this moment, Voyez was arraigned at the Stafford Assizes and sentenced to three months' imprisonment and a flogging, whether for this offence is not clear.

In 1761 Anton Raphael Mengs (1728–79), the son of a Dresden court painter and a friend of Winckelmann, was working in Rome where he painted his *Parnassus*. This mural design for Cardinal Albani was based on drawings from the antique. *Parnassus* was a complete break with the Baroque and was the first full scale demonstration of Neo-Classical painting. In the following year, Mengs published his Neo-Classical treatise, *Beauty in Painting*, which before it was even printed had been pirated and published in England. Yet as a painter, Mengs was of little importance compared with his contemporary Tiepolo, who was still decorating walls and ceilings in the Rococo manner. It needed painters of the stature of David and Ingres to confirm Neo-Classicism's importance as a movement. The essentials of their philosophy were an insistence on symmetry and the strict observance of the use of line and volume rather than colour. Yet already the Neo-Classicist painters were in some confusion because of a strong undercurrent of Romanticism. Painting was too intuitive an art to be shackled by all this backward-looking cerebration.

Architecture on the other hand provided the perfect means of

Neo-Classical dress and furnishings. Engravings by Henry Moses from *Designs of Modern Costume etc.* by Henry Moses, published by Henry Setchel and Son, Covent Garden, London. c. 1805

expression for this movement. The finest and earliest examples of the style are in France; the finest exponent of the style was Ange Jacques Gabriel (1698–1782). His buildings for the Place de la Concorde and the École Militaire, both in Paris, and the exquisite Petit Trianon at Versailles, completed in 1770 for Madame Dubarry and later to be Marie Antoinette's favourite house, are all immaculate in proportion and severely restrained. The Petit Trianon though, because of its diminutive scale, is a jewel of a house, possessed of a charm one does not usually associate with the movement.

In 1812, *Recueil de décorations intérieures* was published. This collection of designs for rooms and furniture was by Charles Percier and Pierre-Leonard Fontaine. The plates in this book had been issued serially since 1801. These began with designs based on Pompeian wall decorations, which the authors called Etruscan. This book did much to establish the Neo-Classical 'Empire' style as the proper method of interior decoration for the courts of Europe. The aristocracy and the *haute bourgeoisie* followed suit. The dogmatic insistence on symmetry and a rigid grammar of design produced a style that was somewhat arid. It developed in Germany into the Biedermeier style, which 'combined the picturesque with the comfortable, the two guiding spirits of Biedermeier decoration.'[1]

In England an interest in Palladio had been revived by William Kent (1684–1748), perhaps at the instigation of his patron Lord Burlington. Kent was nothing if he was not eclectic, working as happily in the Gothic or the Baroque as in the Neo-Classic style. It would seem likely that Lord Burlington, even if he was only a gifted amateur, was the real innovator (or renovator) of the classic style.

Lord Burlington's 'Palladian Circle' included William Kent and the Scots architect Colin Campbell, who both built copies of Palladio's Villa Capra, one at Chiswick, the other at Mereworth in Kent, and very chilly they must have been, with their high, dark halls lit only by clerestory windows. Other architects in the Circle were the ex-chimney sweep Isaac Ware who built numerous Palladian houses in various London squares; Flitcroft (if he had a Christian name the authorities have forgotten it) who was responsible for the spire of St Giles-in-the-Fields, and who drew Lord Burlington's attention to himself by falling off some scaffolding and breaking his leg! We have no small Palladian house to compare with the Petit Trianon, but we have two lovely miniature Palladian bridges, one at Wilton Park in Wiltshire, designed by yet another nobleman, the Earl of Pembroke, assisted by the architect Robert Morris, and another almost as good at Stowe. We also still have Kent's last important group of buildings, the Horse Guards in Whitehall. Whatever weaknesses the Neo-Classical style can show in the fine and graphic arts, it can at least stand proudly by these superb Palladian buildings.

1. *La filosofia dell'arredamento*. Mario Praz. Trs. W. Weaver (English title *An Illustrated History of Interior Decoration*). Thames and Hudson, London, 1964.

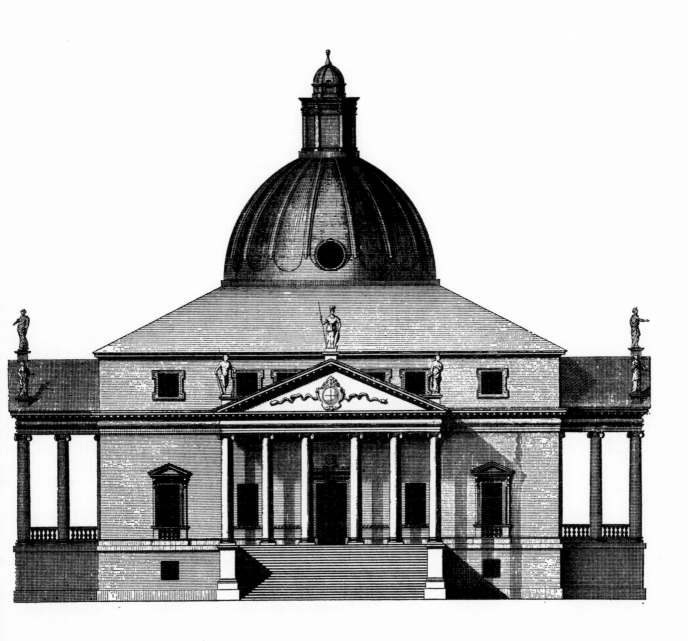

In England (where through insularity or plain ignorance many ephemeral movements of Continental taste and fashion have been either neglected or belatedly acknowledged) the Neo-Classic movement really caught on. It inspired not only the work of the architects we have discussed, but that of their successors, Wyatt, Nash and particularly Robert Adam. In the 'fine' arts, the sculptor John Flaxman became the English equivalent of Antonio Canova. The movement spread to the furniture designs of Hepplewhite and Sheraton, and to the jasper and cream ware of Josiah Wegwood. It finally left its enduring and deadly imprint on all the academies of art, with their besotted studies from the antique.

163

The key figure in the later phase of English Neo-Classicism was Robert Adam. William Kent had died in 1748 when this Scots architect was just twenty. A couple of years or so later, Robert Adam was in Italy where he spent three years studying ancient Roman architecture. He also became close friends with Piranesi. The climax of his studies came when in July 1757, he visited the ruins of Diocletian's palace at Spalato, in company with the French architect-antiquary C. L. Clérisseau and a couple of draughtsmen. In little over a month, Adam had assembled a mass of drawings, plans and measurements resulting in his book *The Ruins of Diocletian at Spalatro* (sic) which appeared in 1764.

The Adam style in architecture, and particularly in interior decoration, owed much to these studies. He was a brilliant designer, of everything from great interiors such as those at Syon House and Harewood House to the smallest pieces of furniture, even to the dog kennels, that graced those mansions. He will however probably be best remembered for his town houses with their pretty fanlights and Palladian porticoes. The Adam style, originally so elegant but so often repeated and so often debased, has come to be associated with the salons of *haute couture*. The real Adam had much more vigour than this. The spindly swags and cornices and those marble bas-reliefs of ice-cold, sexless semi-draped female figures by Flaxman frozen onto so many overmantels, though typical of Neo-Classicism, were only a part of this man of parts. Some indication of his industry can be seen at the Soane Museum in London, where nearly nine thousand of Adam's designs are bound up in fifty-three large folio volumes. These designs had wide influences on all the domestic arts including pottery making. Following the Neo-Classical fashion, Wedgwood called his pottery Etruria. As well as employing the wayward Voyez, he had the sculptor John Flaxman under contract. Generations of tea tables were to groan under the weight of Wedgwood's jasper ware cake stands, teapots and biscuit jars, around which Flaxman's pallid classical ladies so decorously tripped. The same Neo-Classical motifs soon found their way into printing.

As in the fifteenth-century Venice of Jenson, Ratdolt and Aldus the cry had gone out for the roman letter, based on the handwriting of a previous rebirth of Roman culture, so in the case of Neo-Classicism, a new style of letter was once again demanded from the printers. By what stretch of imagination the actual typefaces of Bodoni and Didot can be said to answer this need, it is hard to see. The most likely association is that the Neo-Classical engravers who were to illustrate the folios of these printers used letters with sharply defined thick and thin hairline strokes. These letters, so simple to engrave on copper, but, one would think, so difficult to cut in relief on the hard steel of the punches, and even more difficult to cast in soft type metal, were taken up with avidity by the punch-cutters. Yet the first

AaBbCcDdEefgG
Holding ESTATE

Neo-Classical and Old Style typefaces

ypeface in this style antedated the Neo-Classic movement by ver half a century. This was Grandjean's *romain du roi*, cut for he Royal Printing House between 1693 and 1745. (It is identiiable by an idiosyncratic horizontal projection set mid-way lown the left side of the small letter 'l'.) Baskerville's typefaces olayed a part in the development of the Neo-Classical letters, by ntroducing a more vertical stress, greater contrast between hick and thin strokes, and much cleaner cutting of the letters. Fournier's typefaces however provided the final point of departure for the first real Neo-Classical typefaces, which were cut by the great Italian printer G. B. Bodoni.

During his lifetime Bodoni achieved success and wide fame. Kings and emperors honoured him. Napoleon gave him a medal. The nobility of many countries patronized him. His Ducal Press at Parma was one of the sights of the Grand Tour. Pensions were showered on him. He was justly proud, perhaps even a little vain of his position – a vanity that any self-made man might have had. Yet underlying this vanity was the humility of the great craftsman – and Bodoni was a great craftsman, judged as a typographer, a printer or a type-cutter. He achieved this eminence and productivity mainly by the fact that his press – the Stamperia Reale at Parma – was a private press and though it was the private property of the Duke of Parma, after 1790 Bodoni had an agreement permitting him to print for anyone he liked. Now the private press is the only kind of printing establishment where a policy of perfection can be successfully followed. The history of printing is studded with the failures and bankruptcies of the *commercial* printing houses who allowed themselves to be seduced by such an ambition. Bodoni in the enviable position of not having to run a commercially viable enterprise produced works which are magnificently impressive – and far finer than the Jensonites and Aldinites and the other devotees of Old Face have allowed. Giovanni Battista Bodoni was born on the 16th February 1740 at Saluzzo, a small town in the province of Piedmont, some forty miles south of Turin. His father was a printer, and apparently at a very tender age Bodoni started to learn the trade and also showed an aptitude for engraving on wood and sold prints of his woodcuts in Turin.

When he was twelve years old, he further revealed his artistic bent by designing and producing for a local festival, illuminations on the façade of his father's house. This effort filled the people with admiration and wonder for his youthful precocity. By the time Bodoni was eighteen, he was a competent compositor and well versed in the other sides of printing. Something or other must have fired his curiosity to see the Missionary Press in Rome – the Propaganda Fide, which printed ecclesiastical works in every language and distributed them to all parts of the world.

In company with a friend, another Saluzzo lad, he set out for

Roman Print

Aabcdefghijklmnopqrſstuvwxyz.
ABCDEFGHIJKLMNOPQ
RSTUVWXYZ.

C'eſt le ſujet de cette Médaille. On y voit Pallas, tenant un Javelot preſt à lancer; le fleuve de l'Eſcauld effrayé s'appuye ſur ſon Urne. La Légende, HISPANIS TRANS SCALDIM PULSIS ET FUGATIS, ſignifie, *les Eſpagnols défaits & pouſſez au-delà de l'Eſcauld.* L'Exergue, CONDATUM ET MALBODIUM CAPTA. M. DC. XLIX. *priſe de Condé & de Maubeuge. 1649.*

Rome. When they arrived there it took Bodoni some time to get permission to see the Propaganda Press, but at last he was admitted, and his boyish enthusiasm so impressed Ruggieri the printer, that he took him on as a compositor.

The Propaganda Fide owned a fine series of exotic characters cut in the time of Pope Pius Sixtus V by the Frenchman Granjon. These, however, had been hopelessly pied for many years. Ruggieri gave Bodoni the job of clearing this typographic Augean stable. He took up the study of oriental languages and set about the mammoth task of putting the jumble of sorts, matrices and rusty punches to rights. His interest in both punch-cutting and exotics was intensified by this work. He was soon cutting punches himself – his first were unsuccessful, but after further efforts he finally produced a set of capital letters that received some acclamation in Rome.

Bodoni, from all accounts, was an attractive and likeable young man. He made many friends, some of whom were influential men. Fr. Mario Paciaudi, the librarian to the head of the Propaganda Fide, was to be directly responsible for Bodoni's appointment to the Stamperia Reale at Parma.

With the death of Ruggieri (who had shot himself) Bodoni felt that he could work no longer in Rome. So in 1767 he left the Propaganda Fide and set out for England, where with perhaps Baskerville's example as the impetus, he may have felt there would be better opportunities for fine printing than anywhere else. But he was never to reach England, for en route he fell in with tertian fever and broke his journey at his parents' house at Saluzzo. Whilst he was convalescing from this illness, an offer came to him from Du Tillot, the minister of Ferdinand, Duke of Parma, to establish a private printing press at the Ducal Court. Bodoni had been recommended for the post by Father Paciaudi; the former librarian of the Propaganda Fide had by this time become librarian to the Parmesan court.

Ferdinand of Parma, even though he was a young man, was a great supporter of the arts, and had already established an Academy of Fine Arts and founded a very fine library. Not content with these efforts, and influenced by Du Tillot, he decided to have his own royal printing press. This was no doubt in emulation of the royal printing establishments in Paris, Madrid, Rome, Turin and many other places.

On 24th February 1768, Giambattista Bodoni arrived in Parma and started to build the handpresses, lay out the composing room, buy type, engage compositors and pressmen, make arrangements with paper merchants and binders, and to establish a type-foundry, with his brother Joseph as manager. His career as a printer and type-founder had begun. In 1771 he issued his first specimen of type – *Fregi e Majuscole* – a pretty little specimen book based unashamedly on Fournier's *Manuel Typographique*, with a collection of borders and decorated letters which are either copies, or supplied by the French type-founder

The early Bodoni work was quite unlike the conception that most people have of Bodoni's printing. Books in small format, full of charm, and highly decorated – greatly influenced by Fournier in layout and in the style of types and use of ornament. Yet already in this early work, Bodoni's handling of capital letters and brilliant use of white space was becoming apparent. In some subtle way, he was converting the sugary quality of the Fournier typography into something – still decorative – but rather more astringent.

In 1775, Bodoni issued his first book in the grand manner – an *Epithalamium*, which was set in various exotic languages. Five years later he showed further evidence of his Neo-Classic tastes by producing the works of Raphael Mengs, who had died the previous year. The average length of run of the Stamperia Reale productions was between 400 and 500 copies. In 1785, Bodoni published a letter in French and Italian to the Marquis de Cubières, in stout defence of his typefaces, which had been criticized in France. He sent a copy of this letter to Benjamin Franklin. This evoked a charming reply, delighting Bodoni, even though Franklin had criticized his script capital letters.

Printing orders came pouring in from all over Europe – even from London. From Mr J. Edwards the London bookseller, he had orders for editions of 250 copies of a dozen classical poets and in 1791 for the same publisher he printed Horace Walpole's *The Castle of Otranto*. Walpole in writing to a friend said: 'I am glad you did not get a Parmesan *Otranto*. A copy is come so full of faults that it is not fit to be sold here.' This inaccuracy was Bodoni's Achilles' Heel. Though a man of fastidious tastes, he saw his printed work through the eyes of a creative artist and not of a scholar. This lack of critical scholarship and slipshod proof-reading is evident in much of his work, but Walpole was a bit hard on him. The Bodoni *Otranto* is a brilliant piece of design, superbly printed and set in a narrow measure of 17½ Ciceros, deeply leaded and widely margined. The only concession to decoration in these immaculate pages is in the folios, which are in swash italic characters, centred at the head of the text.

Bodoni was now fifty-one years old. He was established, highly esteemed and happy in his work. At this age, he took himself a wife, a Parmesan lady of quality, who proved a wonderful companion, devoting herself not only to her husband's creature comforts, but also to understanding his work.

In 1793 the King of Spain granted Bodoni a pension of 6,000 reals a year – though as far as we know he had never printed anything for him. In this year he printed an Italian translation of Gray's *Elegy* and, in English, Gray's *Complete Poems*. Also a two volume edition of Virgil, which the French type-founder Firmin Didot criticized on the grounds of its textual inaccuracies. By the turn of the century, Bodoni was getting very deaf and rather infirm. He was, however, greatly helped both by his

IN CELEBERRIMAM VICTORIAM

AUSTERLITII

RELATAM A GALLIS

DUCE

NAPOLEONE MAXIMO

ODE ALCAICA

PLACIDI TADINI

SCHOLARUM ALEXANDRIAE MODERATORIS,

GYMNASII PATAVINI

PROFESSORIS EMERITI.

PARMAE

~~~~~~

TYPIS BODONIANIS

MDCCCVI.

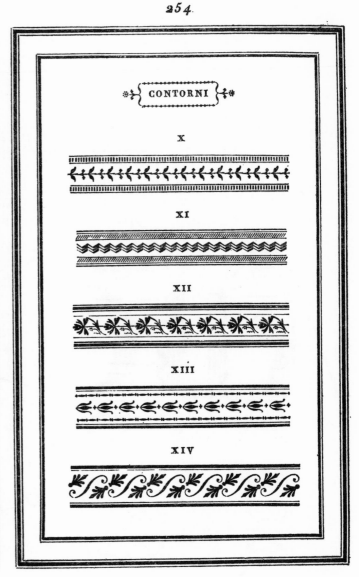

wife and his foreman Luigi Orsi, who was indeed responsible for the design of many of his books.

In 1802, the city of Parma honoured their printer citizen and struck a medal in his honour. Bodoni's last important publications were, in 1806 *The Lord's Prayer* in 155 languages, in 1808 a *Homer* and in 1813 the works of Racine. In the winter of 1813 he died, leaving unfinished the second edition of the *Manuale Tipografico*.

From all that one reads about him, Bodoni appears to have had a lively good humour and an equally lively temper and an Italianate, carefree attitude that gave him such grand if sometimes inaccurate results.

ABC

Bodoni large display capital letters from the *Manuale Tipografico*

Bodoni is said to have cut by his own hand over 10,000 punches. If this figure is true, which seems rather unlikely, it meant something like twenty years work for a punch-cutter, cutting two punches a day. However many punches he actually may have cut is immaterial. Certainly, this side of his work was Bodoni's greatest contribution to the art of printing. It was the side of the work he was most interested in – leaving the typography and presswork of many of his books to the admirable Luigi Orsi.

Only for rather special works, such as the *Homer* and the *Manuale*, did he devote much care to the layout and production of the printed page.

When Arthur Young, the social and political observer and the greatest of all English writers on agriculture, visited Bodoni in 1789, he says the Stamperia Reale had over 30,000 matrices. The punches that Bodoni did not cut himself were produced by various workmen, including Andrea Amoretti, who later, with his brother, established his own foundry.

The range of sizes shown in the *Manuale* was from Parmigianina (or $3\frac{1}{2}$ point) to Papale (or 80 point) and even some 96 point capital letters, each size blending with the greatest subtlety with the next, so that he was not faced with that problem so common to typographers today, of, for example, knowing that in the case of most typefaces 14 point is too small for a large folio and yet 18 point is too large.

In addition to this gradual variant of sizes, he cut two faces for each size, one a full face with strong contrasts and one less condensed and less bold. A single Bodoni fount had 380 punches to it. A contemporary witness stated that Bodoni 'conceived his designs with a very broad and very sharp-edged pen, though in fact his types were more like copper engravings than penmanship'.

In his preface to the 1818 *Manuale Tipografico*, Bodoni gives instructions for the proportions of letters: 2/7ths for ascenders, 2/7ths for descenders and 3/7ths for x-height. This is a definite break away from the proportions of the Old Face. He states what he considers to be the four principles of good type design in this preface:

'Regularity due to the standardization of everything that is not distinctive, including the individual units from which each letter is made up.

Smartness and neatness; perfect matrices; clean type with a surface as smooth as a mirror, terminating boldly at the corners with a knife edge. Good impression and the use of *new* type.

Good taste: choosing best forms most congenial to national and temporal situation.

Charm: letters giving the impression of being written not un-willingly or with hostility, but painstakingly, as a labour of love. Free of affection.'

As the habit of condensing or narrowing typefaces tends to be aid at Bodoni's door, his remarks on width in the same preface are of interest. Of width, he says, 'the greater the width, the clearer the script, but the fewer letters you can get to the line'. He continues 'This may be intolerable for verse, where each line must be unbroken. Condense your letters, but do not shorten them.'

Caught up in the movement of the time with its strong reaction against the Baroque and the Rococo, Bodoni finally dispensed with the use of printers' flowers, arabesques and borders. He designed a page depending for its qualities entirely on proportion and the placing of black type on white paper. To this classical severity he added the more and more refined versions of Fournier's typeface.

What leads one more firmly to the conviction that Bodoni's classical types developed from the Fournier model is that for the 1818 edition of the *Manuale Tipografico*, Bodoni worked on, altered, and modernized every punch used for characters printed in that book. Many of those punches must have been over thirty years old.[2]

Bodoni's printing methods were those of his time: the normal wood press, leather-covered ink balls, dampened paper and the use of calendering plates or cylinders;[3] and his runs were no greater than those of the fifteenth-century Venetians.

Bodoni's typographic layouts were not at all common to his age, when in the 1790's he started to use his second style. In the preface to the *Manuale*, he gives some important pointers to typographic usage:

'Spacing: Do not set too closely nor too widely; space evenly. Take great care with evenness of impression: look out for broken sorts (a necessary instruction in view of the fine hair lines in his types, though these were more robust than those of Firmin Didot).

Footnotes to be equally distributed on verso and recto, to produce symmetrical spreads.

Good paper is the most important thing of all (he favoured wove or *papier velin*).

Care with calendering, not too shiny but merely a smooth surface; take care not to distort the print or dirty the paper.'

After Bodoni it might seem that there was not much more to say about Neo-Classical printing. In fact the final stages of this typographic movement were worked out in France and England.

In France the two great type-founding and printing families of the eighteenth century were the Fourniers and the Didots. The most important members of the Didot family, with regard to the Neo-Classic movement, were Firmin and his brother Pierre, the sons of François Ambroise Didot, the type-founder who perfected Fournier's point system of measurement. Firmin was born in 1764; in due course he took over his father's type-foundry and produced the final version of the Neo-

2. Dr. Giovanni Mardersteig of the Officina Bodoni in Verona has handled all these punches and says it is quite easy to see which have been altered. If any character in a fount was not appearing in the new *Manuale*, Bodoni left the punch unaltered.
3. Dr. Mardersteig has a letter that Bodoni wrote to his supplier, giving details of a press he wanted which was in no way out of the ordinary. There is no record that he ever used any of the early iron presses, though they had come into use some years before his death.

Classical typeface, which today we call 'Modern'. The Didot typefaces became almost violent in their contrast between the thick and thin strokes, with hair-line serifs and thin strokes of extreme fragility.

These Neo-Classical types were very perfect and very dazzling and they demanded excellent presswork, which, in truth, they were usually given. They were the perfect counterpart for the engraved classical illustration.

Pierre Didot succeeded to the Didot printing office. In his great folio volumes such as the works of Horace, published in 1799, the Flaxman-like illustrations and headpieces of Charles Percier (the co-author of *Recueil de décorations intérieures*), match most perfectly the Neo-Classic typefaces of Didot. This is typography for the book to be looked at on the table. Exhibitionist typography, demanding slow reading, admiration and even respect.

Benjamin Franklin's grandson wrote in his diary in 1785, 'My grandpapa has prevailed upon M. Didot, the best printer of his age, and even the best there has ever been seen, to consent to take me into his house to learn printing.' And Firmin taught the youth how to cut a punch. Updike sums up this Neo-Classical French printing with: 'Men of that day saw in Didot's great folios antiquity. To us the only interesting thing about them is that they exhibited Didot's idea of it.'[4]

The heights of Neo-Classical typography were scaled by Pierre Didot with his three folios of Racine's works illustrated by 'The great artists of the Davidian school (who) were anxious of the honour of seeing their drawings reproduced as illustrations.'[5] One of these artists was Pierre Paul Prud'hon who carried his Neo-Classical tastes into interior decoration, designing the furniture and décor for the bridal chamber of the Empress Marie Louise.

In Didot's superbly cut typefaces, the finest hair-lines contrasted abruptly with the solid black downstrokes. Such a style could not be taken any further. The only other French typefounder of this time who has a bearing on the movement is J. G. Gillé *fils* whose type specimen issued in 1808 has not only Didot-like types but also a fine series of Neo-Classical borders. In England the movement towards good printing that Baskerville had started in the late 1750's did not really come to anything until towards the end of the century. The first important English type designer after Baskerville was William Martin, who had learned his trade at Baskerville's foundry, and was a brother of Robert Martin, Baskerville's foreman. The printer who reintroduced 'fine printing' to this country was the Northumbrian William Bulmer, the English Neo-Classical counterpart to Bodoni or Didot.

Bulmer was born in Newcastle upon Tyne in 1757 and was apprenticed to a Newcastle printer. Here he met Thomas Bewick who was some four years older than himself. Bulmer

4. *Printing Types*, D. B. Updike, Harvard University Press, Cambridge, Mass. 1922.
5. *Ibid.*

actually pulled the proofs from some of Bewick's first blocks. Bulmer is also credited with having suggested to Bewick that the background of his designs should be lowered to produce a more delicate effect. Bulmer and Bewick were to remain life-long friends. After serving his apprenticeship, Bulmer left Newcastle for London, and then travelled to Paris 'to improve his taste and technique'.[6] How long Bulmer spent in Paris and whether he worked for the Didots or any other printer is not known, but in the 1780's he was back in London working for John Bell the publisher of *British Poets* and *Bell's Edition of Shakespeare.*

6. Robert Pollard, *Newcastle Magazine.* October, 1830.

Page from the Boydell *Shakespeare*, printed by William Bulmer
between 1791 and 1810 showing William Martin's typefaces

SCENE II

CAPULET'S GARDEN.

Enter Romeo.

Rom. He jests at scars, that never felt a wound.——
                      [Juliet appears above, at a window.
But, soft! what light through yonder window breaks!
It is the east, and Juliet is the sun!——
Arise, fair sun, and kill the envious moon,
Who is already sick and pale with grief,
That thou her maid art far more fair than she:
Be not her maid, since she is envious;
Her vestal livery is but sick and green,
And none but fools do wear it; cast it off.——
It is my lady; O, it is my love:
O, that she knew she were!——
She speaks, yet she says nothing; What of that?
Her eye discourses, I will answer it.——
I am too bold, 'tis not to me she speaks:
Two of the fairest stars in all the heaven,
Having some busineſs, do entreat her eyes
To twinkle in their spheres till they return.
What if her eyes were there, they in her head?
The brightneſs of her cheek would shame those stars,
As daylight doth a lamp; her eye in heaven
Would through the airy region stream so bright,

1787, Bulmer was introduced to George Nicol, the book-
ller to George III. Nicol was already negotiating with Messrs
oydell for the production of a rather grandiose edition of
hakespeare's *Works*. Bulmer must have had evidence to show
s printing and organizing abilities, for within a few months
oydell and Nicol had established him in Cleveland Row, St
ames's Street, as W. Bulmer and Co., the Shakspeare (*sic*)
rinting Office. William Martin had been working for Nicol
nce 1786 cutting types in the manner of Bodoni and Didot.
he idea for the famous Boydell Shakespeare originally came
om Nicol, who was a prominent member of literary circles
nd a personal friend of the Duke of Roxburghe.
hen William Bulmer set up his Shakspeare Printing Office off
t James's Street, Martin moved to nearby premises in Duke
treet running his foundry as a private connection to the press.
nd here, to some extent under the guiding hand of Bulmer,
Iartin worked for the next twenty years, producing his
iodernized versions of Baskerville's typefaces. The Martin
ypes are an interesting hybrid, having something of the stress
nd weight of the Didot faces yet retaining the good calli-
raphic qualities of the Baskerville letters.
he production of the Boydell Shakespeare between the years
791 and 1810 in nine magnificent volumes was a striking
dvance in English typography and English printing. T. F.
Jibdin, the contemporary Vice-President of the Roxburghe
lub, writing about the work of this press says with some
nthusiasm 'there is scarcely one perceptable shade of variation
rom the first page of the first volume to the last page of the
vork, either in the colour of the ink, or the hue of the paper, or
he clearness and sharpness of the type.' Some of this quality at
east in the later volumes, may have been due to Bulmer
istalling in 1800, a Stanhope press, the first printing press to be
iade of cast iron, with a lever-principle.
hough much of the success of the Bulmer books is due to
heir excellent typography and layout and good presswork, yet
Iartin must claim some share in his work as the punch-cutter
vho cut the punches for all the types that were used. Although
Iartin's foundry was owned by the Shakspeare Press, he
iccasionally supplied typefaces to outsiders, including John
AcCreery, the author of *The Press*, a poem published in 1803 as
specimen of printing. McCreery was a very able printer him-
elf and does ample justice to Martin's types in this specimen.
n the preface to the book the author pays tribute to William
Iartin's ability: 'Mr Martin, whose abilities are so conspicu-
usly displayed in the production of the Shakspeare Press, is a
upil of that celebrated school (of John Baskerville). By the
iberality of George Nicol Esq., I am enabled to boast of being
he first who has participated with Mr Bulmer in the use of
hese types, a mark of kindness for which my warmest acknow-
edgements are the least recompense he has the right to expect.'

THE

PRESS,

A

POEM.

PUBLISHED AS A SPECIMEN OF TYPOGRAPHY.

BY JOHN MᶜCREERY.

Liverpool:

PRINTED BY J. MᶜCREERY, HOUGHTON-STREET.

AND SOLD BY

CADELL AND DAVIES, STRAND, LONDON.

1803.

Martin, unfortunately, did not live to see the completion of a
Bulmer's typographical masterpieces. He died in 1815 and wa
buried in St James's Church, Westminster.

Nicol, writing in the advertisement to the Boydell Shakespear
says: 'With regard to the typographical side of the work, th
state of printing in England when it was first undertaken i
1786, was such that it was found necessary to establish
printing house in order to print the work, a foundry to cast th
types, and even a manufactory to make the ink'. The sam
conditions obviously were still prevailing as when Baskervill
was at work.

Bulmer produced a number of books using Martin's typefaces
the two most pleasing being the *Poems by Goldsmith and Parne*,
and Somerville's *The Chase*. These books were issued in 179
and 1797 with illustrations by the Bewicks, with the secon
editions in 1802 and 1804 respectively. The second edition o
The Chase as a piece of printing is more interesting than th
first. It is printed in a very rich black on a not particularl
smooth paper and shows to better effect than any other book
the Bewick engravings. These were designed by John Bewick
the younger and less famous of the two brothers, but because o
his untimely and early death, were cut by his brother Thomas
If you compare Bulmer-printed Bewicks with any of th
Bewicks' work printed by other printers it makes one grieve t
think that all their work had not been handled by Thoma
Bewick's Northumbrian friend. Bulmer paid Thomas Bewick
£60 for engraving the illustrations to *The Chase*. Whether or no
he paid John Bewick anything for the designs is not known
Bulmer was said to have been a hard business man. Maybe h
and the Bewicks came from a hard school. There can be n
question that he was a fine printer, whose work stood out eve
from that of his very able rivals, T. Bensley at Bolt Court and C
Whittingham at the Chiswick Press. Bulmer died in 1830 and
was buried in St Clement Dane's church in the Strand.

By the time of Bulmer's death, the Neo-Classic movement i
England, typographic and otherwise, had become submerge
by the rising tide of Romanticism. Romanticism has been de
scribed as the pursuit of some ideal that is always unattainable
If it ever could be attained, its value would evaporate. In th
fine arts, the Romantic movement helped to free the artist from
the academic limitations which had so devitalized Neo-Clas
sicism.

In architecture and in the applied arts, including printing, th
Romantic movement showed itself in an idealization of th
Middle Ages and a revival of Gothic styles. Neo-Classicism
was soon quite dead. The second Gothic Revival had muc
wider ramifications and perhaps much deeper roots than
sophisticated Neo-Classicism.

84 Palladian Bridge at Stowe. *Photograph: James Mosley*

85 *Le Petit Trianon* designed by Ange Jacques Gabriel and built in 1763 for Madame Dubarry. *Photograph: Edwin Smith*

86 Sepia drawing by William Kent of the Horse Guards Parade, 1751. *Victoria and Albert Museum*

87 Engraving by P. Santini from Robert Adam's *The Ruins of Diocletian*

86 Sepia drawing by William Kent of the Horse Guards Parade, 1751. *Victoria and Albert Museum*

87 Engraving by P. Santini from Robert Adam's *The Ruins of Diocletian*

88 Giovanni Battista Bodoni. An engraving by F. Rosaspina from a painting by A. Appiani

89 Neo-Classical trade card, engraved by Varley

90 Josiah Wedgwood's first pattern book, begun in 1769 and completed in 1814 with contemporary plates showing some of the Neo-Classical borders. *Wedgwood*

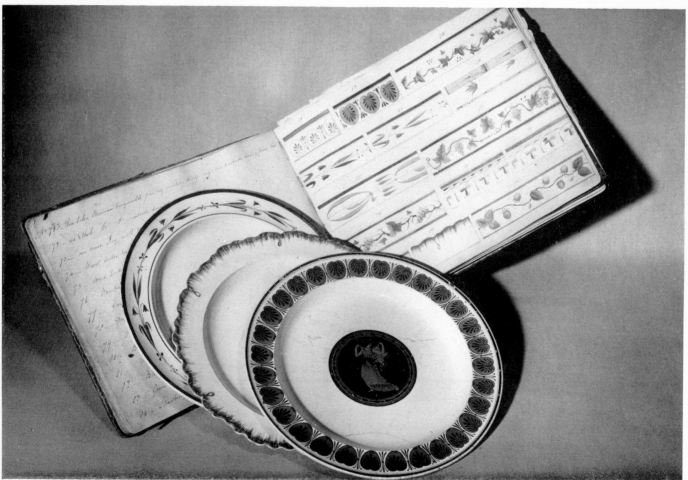

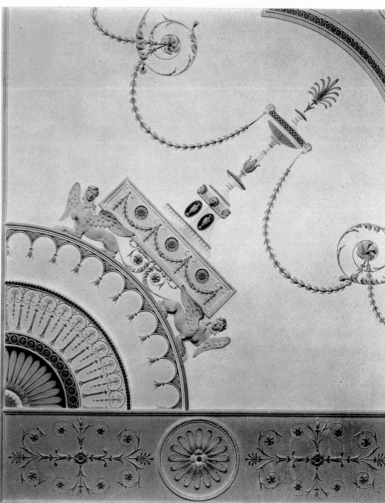

93 Didot typography and Neo-Classic illustration in a page from
Horatius Flaccus Quintus: Opera, printed and published in Paris in
1799 by Pierre Didot. The typefaces were cut by Firmin Didot and
the engraving, involving a separate printing operation, is by Charles
Percier. *Victoria and Albert Museum*

QUINTI

HORATII FLACCI

CARMINUM

LIBER PRIMUS.

ODE I.

AD MAECENATEM.

MAECENAS, atavis edite regibus,

O et præsidium et dulce decus meum!

Sunt quos curriculo pulverem Olympicum

Conlegisse iuvat; metaque fervidis

Evitata rotis, palmaque nobilis,

Terrarum dominos evehit ad Deos:

Hunc, si mobilium turba Quiritium

Certat tergeminis tollere honoribus;

94 Engraving by Marais after the design by Pierre Paul Prud'hon illustrating Racine's *Oeuvres*, for the Edition de Louvre, printed between 1801 and 1805 by Pierre Didot. *British Museum*

THE BOY'S OWN PAPER

No. 1.—Vol. I.   SATURDAY, JANUARY 18, 1879.   Price One Penny.

MY FIRST FOOTBALL MATCH.

BY AN OLD BOY.

IT was a proud moment in my existence when Wright, captain of our football club, came up to me in school one Friday and said, "Adams, your name is down to play in the match against Craven to-morrow."

I could have knighted him on the spot. To be one of the picked "fifteen," whose glory it was to fight the battles of their school in the Great Close, had been the leading ambition of my life—I suppose I ought to be ashamed to confess it—ever since, as a little chap of ten, I entered Parkhurst six years ago. Not a winter Saturday but had seen me either looking on at some big match, or oftener still scrimmaging about with a score or so of other juniors in a scratch game. But for a long time, do what I would, I always seemed as far as ever from the coveted goal, and was half despairing of ever rising to win my "first fifteen cap." Latterly, however, I had noticed Wright and a few others of our best players more than once lounging about in the Little Close where we juniors used to play, evidently taking observations with an eye to business. Under the awful gaze of these heroes, need I say I exerted myself as I had never done before? What cared I for hacks or bruises, so only that I could distinguish myself in their eyes? And never was music sweeter

"Down!"

The Gothic Revival and the Industrial Revolution in England

At the time of Waterloo, England was still a predominantly rural country, of small towns and pretty villages. Though towns were growing in size the country was always at the town-dwellers' back door, or at least at the end of the street. In the few large cities it was somewhat different, for mean streets of back-to-back houses were beginning to spring up, particularly in the new industrial cities of the North. In 1767, Thomas Bewick moaned dreadfully at leaving his beloved home, Cherryburn House, on the banks of the Tyne, to be apprenticed in Newcastle, a mere ten or twelve miles away. In the country, folk still enjoyed life. In his *Memoir*, Bewick says: 'I had the opportunity of witnessing the kindness and hospitality of people. The countenances of all, both high and low, beamed with cheerfulness.'[1] Ralph Beilby's little workshop in St Nicholas Churchyard in Newcastle to which Bewick was apprenticed, must have been typical not only of contemporary engravers' shops but also of those of printers and other trades. There were just Beilby and his apprentice Thomas Bewick. The principle of master and man was customary for nearly all trades. That it was not always a happy situation for the apprentice was shown by the poet Crabbe in *The Borough*. He describes how the brutal fisherman Peter Grimes bought his apprentices from the workhouse-clearing men for some trifling sum, then proceeded to work or starve the wretched boys to death. Another Grimes, the sweep in Kingsley's *The Water Babies*,[2] was not exactly a kind task-master either.

As for the kind of work done by engravers in Newcastle in the 1770's, Beilby and Bewick undertook everything from the coarsest kinds of steel stamps and pipe moulds to clocks and plates for doors and coffins. They cut bookbinders' letters, chased silver and engraved bills of exchange, bank notes and letterheads. For printing, they engraved on steel, copper and wood.

As Beilby disliked engraving on wood, and in fact had little talent for it, such humble work was pushed across to Bewick. The result we all know. As far as book illustration went, Bewick practically put copper engravers out of business by not only his own woodcuts, but later by those of his apprentices. Following the pattern of his master's workshop, his woodcuts were also widely used for commercial printing, for trade cards, billheads, etc.

The distillation of the Northumbrian countryside into the compass of Bewick's little wood engravings, is one of the great achievements of English graphic art. These cuts helped to foster at least one side of the Romantic movement – a return to nature – though Bewick himself the greatest of nature lovers would have scorned any such association.

On 10th September 1828, after a visit to London, Bewick wrote: 'The real cockneys, seem to me to be no way altered in character, since I left them about 51 years ago – they are still fond of

Head and tail pieces from *British Birds* 1797. Wood engravings by Thomas Bewick

1. *A Memoir of Thomas Bewick*, 1862. Newcastle upon Tyne.
2. Charles Kingsley's *The Water Babies*, published in 1863, brought about the passing of the 'Chimney Sweepers Act' of 1864, which ended the practice of sending little boys up chimneys.

Intaglio engraving on copper by Thomas Bewick for a trade card
for The King's Arms Inn, Ross-on-Wye. (Enlarged.)

WALL,
The KINGS-ARMS INN,
ROSS.
WINES, STIRE-CYDER, PERRY,
Brandy Rum & Compounds
neat & Genuine.
Accommodations for Excursions on the
WYE.
Neat POST CHAISES & able Horses.

T.B. dire

high living and talk in the same way about "Good Wittals".'
He had been up to London to sell the remaining part of th
last editions of his *Quadrupeds* and his *British Birds*. Two month
later he died, whilst still working on his large woodcut of th
dying horse. Prophetically it was titled 'Waiting for Death'
He had made the sketch for this in 1785.[3]

When Bewick died in 1828, the Romantic Movement was i
full swing. The popular vogue for Gothick romances tha
began with *The Castle of Otranto* was carried to a much wide
audience by the novels of Sir Walter Scott, and the revival o
Gothic features in buildings such as Walpole's villa at Straw
berry Hill and Beckford's great house, were the starting point
of the Gothic Revival, combining as they did romantic and
antiquarian interests. But these interests, as McLuhan ha
pointed out, 'Later unfolded into a serious aesthetic with
Ruskin and the French symbolists. This Gothic taste, trite and
ridiculous . . . was a Pre-Raphael or Pre-Gutenberg quest for
unified mode of perception.'[4]
It is perhaps not so odd that in the time of the greatest change

3. *Bewick to Dovaston: Letters* 1824–28. Pub. Nattalie & Maurice, 1968.
4. *The Gutenberg Galaxy*, Marshall McLuhan, University of Toronto,
Canada; Routledge and Kegan Paul, London, 1962.

nd inventions in the history of man, that the most powerful
design influence should have been the Gothic.

The real pioneer of the Victorian Gothic Revival was the
architect Augustus Welby Pugin, who was born in 1812, the
son of another architect of Gothic tastes. Pugin was a fine
draughtsman and a designer who worked for the stage and
designed furniture for Windsor Castle and also designed silver-
ware. In addition to this he was a pamphleteer who made clear
that his ideas on design were inseparably linked with his
Christian beliefs. He thought that a society that could produce
beautiful buildings like the cathedral at Chartres must be a
better place to live in than the one that built the Coke Towns of
England. Pugin, having begun his career, like Inigo Jones
before him, as a scene designer (he was responsible for the sets
for a successful stage production of Walter Scott's *Kenilworth* at
Covent Garden), went on to work under Sir Charles Barry on
the rebuilding of our Neo-Gothic Houses of Parliament. He
followed this up by designing and building over sixty churches
in the Gothic style. In 1841 he published *The True Principles of*

179

London. Published by John Weale, 59 High Holborn, 1841.

THE TRUE PRINCIPLES

OF

Pointed or Christian Architecture:

SET FORTH IN

TWO LECTURES DELIVERED AT ST. MARIE'S, OSCOTT,

BY

A. WELBY PUGIN,

ARCHITECT,

AND PROFESSOR OF ECCLESIASTICAL ANTIQUITIES IN THAT COLLEGE.

EN AVANT

LONDON: JOHN WEALE.

M.CC XLI.

Pointed or Christian Architecture, in which he established the fitness-for-purpose axioms, that 'all ornament should consist of enrichment of the essential construction,' and that 'there should be no features . . . which are not necessarily for convenience, construction or propriety.' Like many other writers on design, his preaching was more eloquent than his practice was effective.

Great movements in design – and the Gothic Revival was a great movement – are always allied to great beliefs, however mistaken those beliefs may appear to a later generation. The fantastic burst of invention that caused the Industrial Revolution coincided with an age of revived Christian beliefs. In England, the Victorian age was an age of heavy piety and also of intolerable factory conditions. It was an age of expanding commerce and an age of much hypocrisy.

The nineteenth century introduced the craving for speed. Speed on the road, speed on the rail, speed on water and above all speed of production. Until the time of the first steam engines and steamboats, the speed of travel had not varied much from the time of the Romans. It was the speed on land of about four to six miles an hour of a trotting horse pulling a carriage and on sea of a tubby sailing ship sailing off the wind at perhaps even or eight knots. It had taken Thomas Bewick three weeks in 1776 to get from Newcastle to London in a collier brig. The macadam-surfaced roads and the stagecoach for a brief and, if we are to believe Charles Dickens, a glorious period, stepped up these speeds to about twelve miles an hour. Stage-coaches like Mr Tony Weller's London-to-Ipswich coach, which decanted Mr Pickwick at the doors of the Great White Horse Inn under the statue of 'that insane carthorse', used to take seven hours, to make the journey of 72 miles from Aldgate Pump.

Then came the steam engine, and in no time trains were hustling along at forty, fifty and even sixty miles an hour. The water power and the great water wheels were replaced by steam engines. An inexhaustible supply of coal provided steam, gas and ultimately electricity to drive the machines of the Lancashire cotton mills and the looms of Bradford and the other Yorkshire wool towns. In 1814, the first steam driven cylinder printing press was installed by *The Times* newspaper, raising the rate of impression from a paltry 250 to 1,100 copies per hour. Fifty years later and the rate was twenty times as fast. All this while, architects were building houses and factories covered in pinnacles and pointed arches, and at the same time building the cotton mills of Lancashire in a fine classical idiom, and printers were doing their best with gothic typefaces and spiky gothic borders and manufacturers were covering every kind of machine with Gothic decoration. That steam engines, sewing machines and wood-turning lathes should be decorated with such Gothic ornaments struck some contemporary obser-vers as a bit odd. Amongst these was William Morris, at that time a seventeen-year-old schoolboy.

The majority of the middle classes did not bother their heads about such things. They were complacent and well-to-do. England after all was the 'workshop of the world'. In 1870, barely a hundred years ago, her export trade was greater than that of France, Germany and Italy together. It was four times that of the United States.[5] When the Great Exhibition of 1851 opened in its Crystal Palace in Hyde Park, thousands thronged to it to acclaim and to praise.

A youngish and not particularly successful architect called Owen Jones (1809–74) was appointed Superintendent of the Works for the Great Exhibition. He was also in charge of the section of exhibits which included sculpture and plastic art, mosaics and enamels. With this exhibition he made his name. He was a fine decorator and designer. His work covered all aspects of interior design, including wallpaper, textiles and furniture. In 1856, Jones published his *Grammar of Ornament*, an encyclopaedic work on decoration of all periods and countries. The *Grammar of Ornament* became the standby for all designers for the next fifty years. The folio edition of 1856 was followed by a large quarto in 1868 and it continued to

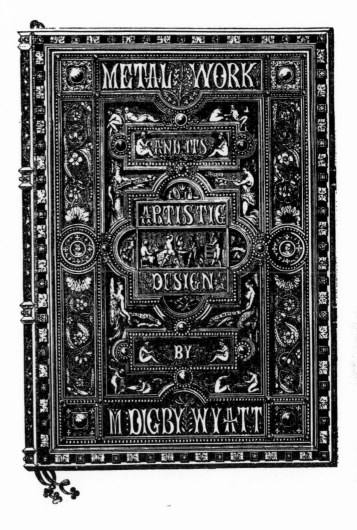

5. *English Social History*, G. M. Trevelyan, Longmans, Green and Co., 1942.

The Crystal Palace in Hyde Park, 1851. Contemporary wood engraving

6. Ruari McLean writing on Owen Jones in his *Victorian Book Design* (Faber and Faber 1963) says: 'He had in fact founded a new industry, and was for several years the chief supplier of that characteristic early Victorian product the chromo-lithographic illuminated Gift Book.'

reprint until 1910. It was printed and published by Day and Son. Jones was an experienced lithographer who had run his own small lithographic print shop, first in John Street, Adelphi, and later in Argyll Place, off Regent Street.[6] No doubt he kept a sharp eye on the production of the *Grammar of Ornament*. The hundred-odd plates were superbly drawn in separate colours on the stone by the chromo-lithographer Francis Bedford and his assistants. This massive tome was bound up from single leaves by Leighton Son and Hodge (and soon came apart, for this was before the age of flexible synthetic glues). It is a landmark both for its colour printing and for its being the first comprehensive reference book on decorative design.

John Ruskin was the literary champion of the Gothic Revival. Prolific writer though Ruskin was, more ink has been spilt by critics in explaining Ruskin or describing his curious domestic

Gothic bookcase in carved oak, designed by B. Bernardis and
J. Kraner and built by Carl Leistler and Son, all of Vienna. From
the catalogue to the 1851 Exhibition

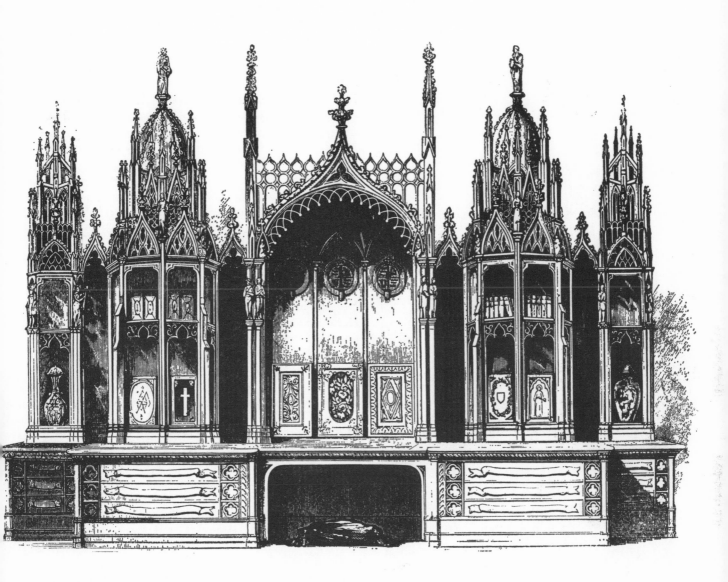

life than he could ever have used himself. Yet today, this towering figure of the nineteenth century, who was an inspired critic
of both art and architecture, the first to recognize the greatness
of Turner, one of the greatest social reformers of his time, and
a superbly eloquent writer of English prose, is today hardly
read at all. He was certainly a strange and difficult man, with the
seeds of madness scattered through his genius. In spite of his
championship of Turner, his influence on the general stream of
European painting was minimal, but as an influence on the
Pre-Raphaelites and William Morris, he was of the utmost
importance. His most significant utterance, the key to his philosophy (foreshadowing the Dadaists and John Heartfield), was,
'If you wanted a different kind of art, you would have to begin
by producing a different kind of society.' He was convinced
that the people of the Middle Ages had the secret of happiness,

183

in dedicating their lives and their work to God, and that this
happiness was achieved by actually making things with their
own hands.

Ruskin made clear in *The Nature of Gothic* (first published as a
chapter in *The Stones of Venice* in 1847) the real appeal the Gothic
had for the Victorians – and this had nothing to do with
Horace Walpole's antiquarianism. 'The vital principle is not
the love of Knowledge, but the love of Change. It is that
strange disquietude of the Gothic spirit that is its greatness;
that restlessness of the dreaming mind, that wanders hither and
thither among the niches, and flickers feverishly around the
pinnacles and frets and fades in labyrinthine knots and shadows
along wall and roof, and yet is not satisfied . . .'

It was 'this restlessness of the dreaming mind' that inspired the
Pre-Raphaelites to their synthesis of the Gothic Revival and
the Romantic Movement. The Pre-Raphaelite Brotherhood was
founded in 1848 with John Everett Millais, William Holman
Hunt and Dante Gabriel Rossetti as the first members.
Amongst their associates, if not actually members of the
Brotherhood, were Ford Madox Brown and Arthur Hughes.
Apart from Millais, if the Pre-Raphaelite idea had never been
formulated, it is quite possible that none of these painters
would ever have been heard of again. They set out in search of
a fantasy, a dream world of the Middle Ages that never existed.
Their knowledge of painting before the time of Raphael was of
the slightest. Swept up in the Romantic Movement and the
Gothic Revival of Pugin and Ruskin, like all liberals, they were
against the Industrial Revolution and what they thought to be
its devastating effects on the lives of the working classes.

They were also affected by the religious revival and the back-to-
nature poetry of Wordsworth and Keats. They established
their credo as 'Truth to Nature'. This extraordinary hotch-
potch of dreams, ideas and misconceptions led to an achievement more massive than the sum of their not particularly
remarkable talents. These starry-eyed young men set to
painting their super-real, every-blade-of-grass-made-visible
and every-minute-detail-seen pictures, using their friends and
families as models. Millais had the whole Millais family in his
'Christ in the House of His Parents', Rossetti used old Mrs
Rossetti for St Anne and his sister Christina as the Virgin
Mary, for one of his paintings. Others joined in and in due
course Arthur Hughes, who was never a member of the
Brotherhood, out-painted the lot with his girl in the blue
skirt standing by an ivy-covered wall. He called the painting
'April Love'. Morris was later to buy it. Holman Hunt provided
the strongest religious element in the Pre-Raphaelites in combining his religious beliefs with truth to nature. He spent moonlight night after moonlight night in an orchard at Ewell
painting 'The Light of the World', which was to appear as a
frontispiece to so many prayer books. As if this was not

enough, he then went off to Syria and Palestine to paint on the shores of the Dead Sea that unfortunate 'Scape Goat', which dropped down dead before Holman Hunt had finished the painting.

Meanwhile in 1857, Millais had been elected an associate of the Royal Academy and had deserted the Pre-Raphaelite Brotherhood. Encouraged by John Leech, the *Punch* illustrator, he had taken up fox hunting. He liked the life of an English country gentleman, left his Bohemian life behind, became a friend of Anthony Trollope and in time illustrated a number of the Barchester novels. With this defection of their most talented member, it would seem as if the Pre-Raphaelite movement would come to an end, but it was not quite dead. In the same year as Millais was elected to the Royal Academy, two young undergraduates of Exeter College, Oxford, were reading Ruskin and particularly Ruskin on the Pre-Raphaelites. They were Edward Burne-Jones and William Morris. Together they studied what Pre-Raphaelite paintings they could see, they read poetry and they wrote poetry and significantly they read Malory's *Morte d'Arthur*. With their minds filled with dreams of the odd goings-on of Launcelot and Gwenever, they went to northern France and fell in love, at least Morris did, with the medieval architecture of Chartres, Amiens and Rouen.

Morris graduated (with a pass degree) and putting aside possible ideas of going into the Church apprenticed himself to G. E. Street the Gothic architect who later was to build the Law Courts in the Strand, one of the last great Neo-Gothic buildings. Burne-Jones, set on becoming a painter, contrived to meet Rossetti and in turn to introduce Morris to him. The Bohemian Rossetti captivated them, with his brilliant talk and his belief that art was the thing that mattered above all else and that all men should become artists. He was a very mature twenty-eight, Burne-Jones was twenty-three, Morris twenty-two, but their difference in experience of life was much more than the five or six years that separated them. Rossetti, with his Mediterranean blood, must have been born old, he was a man by the time he was sixteen, and a very mature man of the world at twenty-eight.

In 1857, Rossetti embarked on a scheme for decorating the new Oxford Union Debating Rooms. The themes for the painting were to be drawn from *Morte d'Arthur*. He swept Morris and Burne-Jones into the scheme and Arthur Hughes and others as well. The scheme proved abortive. They were painting in distemper on damp walls. None of them knew anything of fresco and Morris with all his genius was no painter. He was practically everything else. In 1858 his first book appeared, a volume of poems called, not improbably, *The Defense of Guinevere*. By this time he had forsaken architecture as a profession and was on the point of marriage. His close friend Philip Webb, a young architect he had met in Street's office, built him a house in

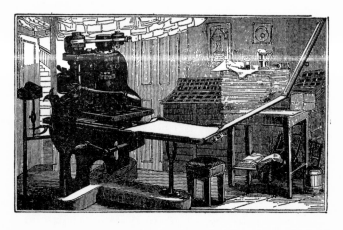

Kent. Morris disliking the kind of furniture that could be
bought at that time, designed all his own furniture, curtains and
wall-hangings. He had found his *métier*. It was to be another
thirty-two years before he turned his attention to printing.

It was Ruskin, by showing that art and life were indivisible
and not separate activities, who had inspired Morris, himself
the great pioneer both of the modern movement in design and,
which is very much to our purpose, the key figure in the revival
of good printing. It was Morris who put the craft of printing
back on the rails and inspired two utterly divergent developments. His preoccupation with quality and workmanship and
his refusal to accept shoddy materials provided the basis for
the English Private Press Movement and led to a renaissance of
good book printing in England and Germany. This, combined
with his obsessive interest in medievalism, in the Gothic and in
gothic typefaces, and his rejection of the Italian Renaissance
provided the springboard for modern design and modern
typography.

The modern typeface of today is the grotesque – one of its
original names was the gothic. Its proportions are much closer
to black letter than to the roman. Here is a connecting link.

The Renaissance and the Neo-Classic movement were based on
intellectual preoccupations, perhaps misconceptions, of the
Classical past. To repeat Ruskin 'the vital principle (of the
Gothic) is not the love of Knowledge but the love of Change.'
The modern movements in architecture and design followed
the same desire for change, the same rejection of classic rules
and the academic rule book. The printers somewhat tardily
followed suit.

Until the end of the eighteenth century, the larger printing
houses devoted most of their production capacity to printing
books. With the expansion of commerce caused by the Industrial Revolution, the situation changed in a radical manner. The
print shops were called in by industry to help sell commodities,
services, property and entertainment. They were soon to be
asked to print labels and packages. The printing and typographic equipment available was no match for the challenge.
New and faster machines were needed and typefaces that would
catch the eye and compel attention.

Earl Stanhope's first iron hand press was made just after the
turn of the century. Though very strongly built, it still depended to some extent on the principles that Gutenberg had copied
from the Rheingau wine presses. The first real step forward
came with the Columbian and the Albion presses. These two
hand presses superseded all other jobbing presses during the
first half of the nineteenth century. The Columbian press was
designed and built by George Clymer of Philadelphia and was
first introduced into Europe in 1817. The Albion press was
invented by R. W. Cope in about 1820. Cope was a manufac-
turer of hydraulic presses, with premises off Finsbury Square.

186

CONCERT

OF

Sacred Music.

Miss HILL (of the London and New York Concerts and Sacred Music Society) begs leave to announce to her friends and the public that a performance of

CLASSICAL SACRED MUSIC

will take place at the **UNITARIAN CHURCH**, on *Monday Evening, the 16th inst.*---To commence at 8 o'clock, precisely.

Organist & Conductor,---Mr. W. H. COPE, (*late Organist of the Moravian Church in New York.*)

Miss HILL deems it proper to state, that she has from infancy endured the *privation of sight.*

PROGRAMME.

PART 1.		PART 2.	
OVERTURE—MESSIAH,	*Handel.*	ORGAN VOLUNTARY—Mr. COPE—Extemporaneous.	
DUET. Miss HILL and Mr. COPE—Forsake me not.	*Spohr.*	ARIA. Miss HILL—But thou did not leave his soul in Hell.	*Handel,*
ARIA. Miss HILL—A Holy Spirit loving goodness.	*Romberg.*	RECIT. } Miss HILL—Ye sacred Priests.	
ORGAN VOLUNTARY. Mr. COPE—Adeste Fideles, with Var's.	*Adams.*	ARIA. } Farewell ye limpid springs. *Handel.*	
RECIT. } Miss HILL—Comfort ye my people.		ORGAN DUET. Miss HILL and Mr. COPE—The marvel'ous work.	*Haydn.*
ARIA. } Ev'ry valley shall be exalted. *Handel*		ARIA. Miss HILL—Let the bright Seraphim.	*Handel.*
DUET. Miss HILL and Mr. COPE—"Shew us thy Mercy."	*Boyce.*	ORGAN VOLUNTARY—Mr. COPE.	

TICKETS, 50 cents each, to be had at the Hotels and Bookstores. *Springfield, July 14th, 1838.*

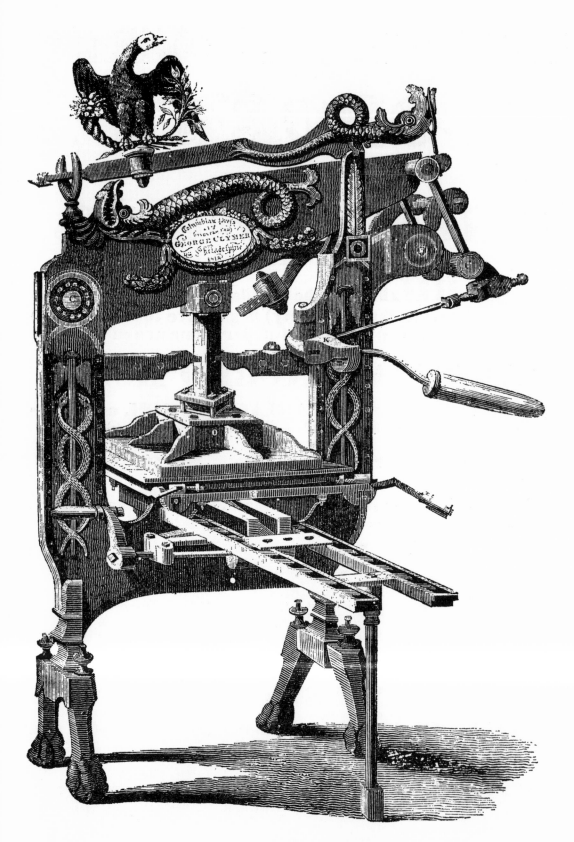

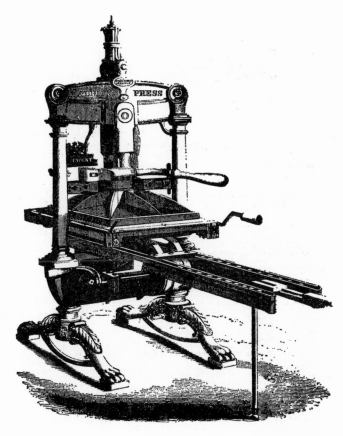

The Columbian and Albion presses, relatively simple, mechanically sound, lever-operated printing machines, were the basic equipment for all the nineteenth-century jobbing printers, who printed the posters, handbills, notices, letterheads and every other kind of ephemera. It was not until 1819 that ink rollers, made up of a composition of molasses, glue and a portion of tar, began to replace the old pelt balls that had been used for inking type from the earliest days of the craft. The ink roller improved the performance of the hand press but only to a small degree. It was not until the platen machines came into the hands of the job printer that he could exceed by much the production of the old wooden hand press. What he gained by the use of the Albion and Columbian presses was much better presswork. Some of the finest letterpress printing ever done has come off these machines (William Morris used three Albions at his Kelmscott Press). A hundred million handbills and posters owed their clarity and clear impression to these simple printing machines, which could print larger areas, with firmer impressions than the old wooden presses.

In 1827, two of *The Times* employees improved on Koenig's Steam Press, the first practical power-operated cylinder printing press, with one that could run off between four and five thousand copies in an hour. In 1868, *The Times* installed the first rotary web-fed printing press which raised the rate of production to over 20,000 sheets an hour. They really were forging ahead, though type still had to be set by hand.

The Times had been started in an attempt to popularize a new type setting method. In 1785, to speed up type setting, John Walter had evolved a system of making logotypes, which consisted of a number of letters cemented together, providing useful syllables or terminations to words. To this end he had reduced the 90,000 words of the English language to less than 5,000. He failed to find support for his ingenious idea, so launched a newspaper, *The Daily Universal Register*, to exploit his logotypes. On the front page of the first number, John Walter addressed a lengthy leader 'To the Public', where he declared his paper as non-party and that 'Nothing shall ever find a place in *The Universal Register*, that can tend to wound the ear of delicacy, or corrupt the heart: vice shall never be suffered there to wear the garb of virtue.' He devoted much space to the prompt advertising service he was offering. He also proudly announced that his paper was 'printed logographically'! Three years later he changed the title to *The Times or Daily Universal Register*, a month or so later he dropped the latter part of the title and it became *The Times*. Because of the compositors' objections (oddly enough they were paid on piece-work), his system of logotypes was soon dropped. Type setting was to remain a bottleneck in newspaper production until the end of the nineteenth century.

The job printer's work had already begun to increase by the

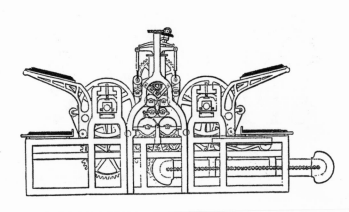

THE *Universal* DAILY *Register,*

Printed Logographically · DIEU · ET · MON DROIT · *By His Majestys* Patent.

NUMB. 1.]   SATURDAY, JANUARY 1, 1785.   [Price Two-pence Halfpenny.

The SIXTH NIGHT.
By His MAJESTY's Company
AT the THEATRE ROYAL in DRURY LANE, this present SATURDAY, will be performed

A *New* COMEDY, called
The NATURAL SON.
The characters by Mr. King, Mr. Parsons, Mr. Bensley, Mr. Moody, Mr. Baddeley, Mr. Wrighten, and Mr. Palmer. Miss Pope, Miss Tidswell, and [Miss Farren.
With new Scenes and Dresses.
The Prologue to be spoken by Mr. Bannister, jun.
And the Epilogue by Miss Farren.
After which will be performed the last New Pantomime Entertainment, in two Parts, called
HARLEQUIN JUNIOR;
Or, The MAGIC CESTUS.
The Characters of the Pantomime, by Mr. Wright, Mr. Williamson, Mr. Burton, Mr. Staunton, Mr. Williames, Mr. Palmer, Mr. Waldron, Mr. Fawcett, Mr. Chaplin, Mr. Phillimore, Mr. Wilson, Mr. Alfred, Mr. Spencer, Mr. Chapman; and Mr. Grimaldi. Mrs. Burnet, Miss Burnett, Miss Tidswell, Miss Barnes, Miss Cranford, and Miss Stageldoir.
To conclude with the Repulse of the Spaniards before The ROCK of GIBRALTAR.

To-morrow, by particular desire, (for the 4th time) the revived Comedy of the DOUBLE DEALER, with the favorite Masque of ARTHUR and EMMELINE.
On Tuesday the Tragedy of VENICE PRESERVED: Jaffier by Mr. Brereton, Pierre by Mr. Bensley, and Belvidera, by Mrs. Siddons: And on Friday the Carmelite. Massinger's Play of the MAID of HONOUR, (with alterations and Additions) is in Rehearsal and will soon be produced.

SHIP- -PING
ADVER- -TISEMENTS

For NICE, GENOA, and LEGHORN,
(With Liberty to touch at One Port in the Channel,)
The N A N C Y.
THOMAS WHITE, Commander,
BURTHEN 160 Tons; Guns and Men answerable. Lying off the Tower, and will absolutely depart on Saturday the 8th instant.
The said Commander to be spoken with every morning at Sam's Coffee-house, near the Custom-house; at Will's Coffee-house, in Cornhill; and at Exchange hours on the French and Italian Walk, or
WILLIAM ELYARD, for the said Commander, No. 16, Savage-Gardens.

Direct for LISBON,
The N A N C Y.
JOHN RACKHAM, Commander,
BURTHEN 300 Tons, Men answerable. Lying off Horslydown Chain; Seven-eighths of her Cargo absolutely engaged, and is obliged by Charter-party to depart on Saturday the 8th instant.
The said Commander to be spoken with every morning at Sam's Coffee-house, near the Custom-house; at Will's Coffee-house, in Cornhill; and in Exchange hours in the French and Italian Walk; or
WILLIAM ELYARD, for the said Commander, No. 16, Savage-Gardens.

To the Public.

TO bring out a New Paper at the present day; when so many others are already established and confirmed in the public opinion, is certainly an arduous undertaking; and no one can be more fully aware of its difficulties than I am: I, nevertheless, entertain very sanguine hopes, that the nature of the plan on which this paper will be conducted, will ensure it a moderate share at least of public favour; but my pretensions to encouragement, however strong they may appear in my own eyes, must be tried before a tribunal not liable to be blinded by *self-opinion:* to that tribunal I shall now, as I am bound to do, submit these pretensions with deference, and the public will judge whether they are well or ill founded.

It is very far from my intention to detract from the acknowledged merit of the Daily Papers now in existence; it is sufficient that they please the class of readers whose approbation their conductors are ambitious to deserve; nevertheless it is certain some of the best, some of the most respectable, and some of the most useful members of the community, have frequently complained (and the causes of their complaints still exist) that by radical defects in the plans of the present established papers, they were deprived of many advantages, which ought naturally to result from daily publications. Of these some build their fame on the length and

Parliament has been engaged in the discussion of an important question till after midnight, the papers in which the speeches of the Members are reported at large, cannot be published before noon; nay, they sometimes are not even sent to press so soon; consequently parties interested in *sales* are essentially injured, as the advertisements, inviting the public to attend them at *ten* or *twelve* o'clock, do not appear, on account of a late publication, till some hours after.—From the same source flows another inconvenience; it is sometimes found necessary to *defer* sales, after they have been advertised for a particular day; but the notice of putting them off not appearing early enough, on account of the late hour at which the papers containing it are published, numbers of people, acting under the impression of former advertisements, are unnecessarily put to the trouble of attending.—It will be the object of the *Universal Register* to guard against these great inconveniences, without depriving its readers of the pleasure of learning what passes in Parliament. —It is intended, then, that the debates shall be regularly reported in it; but on the other hand, that the publication may not be delayed to the prejudice of people in trade, the speeches will not be given on a large scale; the *substance* shall be faithfully preserved; but all the uninteresting parts will be omitted. I shall thus be enabled to publish this paper at an early hour; and I propose

---

aRt. *Soulby's* SPECIMEN

Detail of type specimen from J. Soulby, printer, Ulverston, 1811, showing fat face letters, *Museum of English Rural Life*

latter part of the eighteenth century, but his typefaces as well as his typographical equipment were woefully inadequate. From the early 1500's until the beginning of the nineteenth century, printers had to be content with roman, italic or black letters, rarely cast in a size above 60 point, though in the 1760's William Caslon the younger produced some roman types that were of 7, 9 and 11 lines pica. Bodoni showed some 96 point capitals in his *Manuale Tipgrafico* and in 1794, Robert Thorne, at the Cottrell Foundry in London, showed some even larger roman letters which had been cast in sand. The same Robert Thorne, in 1803, issued the first real display letter – a Fat Face. This was based on the Bodoni style of capital letter but with greatly increased contrasts between thick and thin strokes. In 1808 Thorne removed his foundry to Fann Street off Aldersgate. Display types poured forth from this foundry, first under Thorne's management and then after his death in 1820, under that of William Thorowgood.

Vincent Figgins was an equally prolific producer of display letters. The Figgins works were in Smithfield. In the United States, Horace Wells at the Cincinnati Type Foundry in time outstripped his British rivals in the variety of his display types, but it was Robert Thorne who was the real innovator.

The Fat Face, with its vulnerable hair lines and fine serifs, was succeeded by the Egyptian, first produced by Vincent Figgins in 1817. This was the ideal display typeface, much more suitable for rough presswork and massive display than the Fat Face. The next fundamental change in type form was the sans serif, which at the beginning was called either Gothic or Grotesque (it was also called Doric and Sans Surryphs). Caslon issued a light version in 1816, Figgins a heavy one in 1830. By the 1850's they were in wide use. All these basic forms appeared in three-dimensional and decorated versions.

Innumerable typographic variations followed, with decorated letters, and letters showing Gothic, Rococo, Chinoiserie and rustic influences. In 1845 Robert Besley, again from the Fann Street Foundry, produced a bold typeface to be set in conjunction with normal roman text faces, for dictionaries, catalogues, etc. This little dark letter was named Clarendon; it was in the nature of a bracket-seriffed Egyptian and may well have been based on the kind of letters that were cast for street name plates. The next variation on the basic forms of Grotesque, Egyptian and Fat Face was the Tuscan, a capital letter design, with bifurcated serifs, a witty, light-hearted face that appeared in many forms, yet one which has never been revived.

Demands for colour printing, particularly for labels and packages, caused the printers to turn from their letterpress machines to some other method of printing. Various experiments had been made in printing from separate engraved wood blocks, a method ultimately perfected by Edmund Evans, the printer of Kate Greenaway's work and the Routledge Yellow Back novel covers. However, it was Senefelder's lithographic process (invented in 1797) that met the colour printer's needs. Lithography had been re-introduced into England by Rudolph Ackermann in 1818. It was soon in wide use for both book illustration and commercial printing. Printing rates must have been very low, for many lithographed labels and posters had a dozen or so printings, each colour meticulously drawn by the chromo-lithographer.

Letterpress began to diverge from lithographic printing, though many printers used both processes. Letterpress and lithography were the two sides of the trade. The book printer never combined the two, the job printer sometimes had both activities under one roof. It is only recently that these two processes have begun to merge with the introduction of photo-typesetting and the wide use of lithographic offset presses for printing both pictures and texts.

The job printer in the nineteenth century usually confined his printing to single sheet work. Once the collating of sheets came into the business, it ceased to be real jobbing work. Every small town had at least one print shop of this order,

Egyptian typefaces, both expanded and condensed, 1878

Sans serif typefaces from the Cincinnati Typefoundry. c. 1880

To be Sold

BY AUCTION,

At the Ulverston Canal Head,

On Saturday, the 6th of August,

1825;

At 10 o'Clock in the Morning:

A QUANTITY OF OLD

CORDAGE,

Sails &c.,

Being the remaining part of the
Wreck of the Schooner Sally.

[J. Soulby, Printer, Market-place, Ulverston.]

sometimes allied to the business of stationer. Even grocers or wine merchants have been known to have had a printing department.[7]

After Foudrinier had set up the first paper-making machine in England in 1803, paper became much cheaper and supplies much more plentiful.

A cross section of the work of a job printer in the first quarter of the nineteenth century can be seen at the Museum of Rural Life at the University of Reading in Berkshire, England. This material printed by John Soulby of Ulverston ranges from tickets for balls and assemblies, auctioneers' posters for sale of farm produce or of property, booksellers' catalogues or hotel menus, to shipping notices and posters for post coaches. It is a microcosm of the English social life of a provincial town in the years of the Regency, and during the reign of George IV. John Soulby's little printing business including bookbinding, bookselling and stationery. It was typical of many such small concerns, and was the pattern jobbing print shops followed for the next hundred years.[8] The introduction of the typewriter-typesetter and inexpensive 'office' lithographic offset machine was ultimately to put most of them out of business.

7. Two East Anglian printers, Jarrolds of Norwich and Cowells of Ipswich carried on both letterpress and lithographic printing alongside these other activities.
8. Another example of the work of a small-town printer is shown in *Victorian Delights* by Robert Wood, Evans, London, 1967. This is a selection of entertainment posters, etc, from the spike-files of J. Procter, Printed by Steam Power, Hartlepool.

Top: Lithographed billhead for coal and coke merchant with drawn
design. Birmingham 1878

Below: Letterpress receipt form with stock block for the Railroad
Corporation, Boston, Mass. 1870

TRUCK LOADS TO ANY STATION.

Fol. 673   Head Office 123, New Street,

BIRMINGHAM   1 Nov 1878

Mr C. A. Baxter

Stourbridge

Bought of G. J. Eveson

Coal, Coke, Lime, Limestone, Iron, Iron Ore & Paint Ore Merchant,

DEPÔTS FOR SALE OF COAL & LIME, AT STOURBRIDGE, WORCESTER, HAGLEY, BRIDGNORTH, HENWICK. & DROITWICH,

RAILWAY WAGGONS FOR SALE OR HIRE.

TERMS.   NONE BUT PRINTED CHEQUE RECEIPTS ARE VALID.

Pt Ashbury

RAILROAD CORPORATION.

Boston, _____ Nov 30 1870

HOLLIS & GUNN, Prs.

MARKS AND NUMBERS.

Received from SILAS PEIRCE & CO.

In good order,

JHS
Assabet.

5 Bbls Sugar

John Catnach was a contemporary of Soulby's. He had a printing shop in Alnwick in Northumberland and printed much of Bewick's work. His son James, who was always known as Jemmy, as a boy worked as a shepherd, wandering the Northumberland hills accompanied by his dog Venus and carrying a notebook in which he wrote verses about the countryside.

In 1813, John Catnach moved to London and the boy Jemmy accompanied him, leaving his northern sheep fells with some reluctance. The father set up a printing business and took Jemmy in as an apprentice. In 1816, John Catnach died and Jemmy, caring little about jobbing work, set up on his own as a printer of street literature in the Seven Dials near St Giles' church. This street literature consisted of sheets of doggerel or songs, or descriptions of murders and the 'Last Dying Confessions' of convicted felons. Jemmy had as a rival Johnnie Pitts of the 'Toy and Marbel Warehouse' in Great St Andrews Street. Jemmy felt that with his facility for writing verse and his training as a printer, that he could more than hold his own against Mr Pitts. He had not reckoned with Johnnie Pitts's mother, who was a retired bum-boat woman from Portsmouth and described in the neighbourhood as 'a coarse and vulgar personage'. She lampooned little Jemmy Catnach unmercifully calling him 'Catsnatch, Catblock, Cut-throat' and other less printable names. In time he learned to give as good as he got. In 1819, Jemmy Catnach was had up at Bow Street for libelling a certain Mr Pizzey, a sausage maker of Drury Lane. Perhaps with the ideas of the Abominable Pieman in mind, Catnach had implied that Mr Pizzey's sausages were largely made up from human remains. He got six months in Clerkenwell House of Correction for his scandal-mongering. His mother and sister continued to run the press whilst he served his time. Once out of prison he steadily prospered, though the various 'runners' who sold his sheets said he was pretty tight-fisted.

At the time of Queen Caroline's trial, Catnach had three or four presses running day and night to keep pace with the popular demand for accounts of the previous day's hearing. Catnach was an unashamed literary pirate, lifting his copy wholesale from the daily papers or any other likely source. Twelve hours after the publication of Pierce Egan's *Life in London*, which was illustrated by George Cruikshank, Catnach had an edition on the streets with copies (back to front) of Cruikshank's cuts.

In 1824, Catnach cleared over £500 from the sale of his printed sheets describing the murder of Mr Weare by John Thurtell. Each of his four presses was working for twenty-four hours a day, printing two formes at a time. Catnach was issuing over 250,000 copies in a week. 'There is nothing beats a stunning good murder after all', said a running patterer.[9]

In the same year, there was a gruesome murder of an unfortunate young lady called Maria Marten, whose remains were

THEATRE-ROYAL, NORWICH.

FOR THE BENEFIT OF

R. Battley,
FRUITERER.

On THURSDAY, 12th May, 1836,
Will be performed the POPULAR PLAY, of The

CASTLE
SPECTRE.

Earl Osmond....Mr. MADDOCKS

Reginald ....Mr. HAMERTON	Kenric....Mr. G. SMITH
Earl Percy....Mr. NICHOLS	Saib......Mr. HARRISON
Father Philip..Mr. GRAY	Muley ....Mr. BRYAN
Motley ......Mr. GILL	Hassan....Mr. NANTZ.

Angela ....Mrs. G. SMITH
Alice......Mrs. WATKINSON | Evelina ....Miss HONEY.

END OF THE PLAY.

A COMIC SONG
BY MR. MARTIN.

To conclude with the NAUTICAL DRAMA, of The

PILOT,
OR, A
STORM AT SEA!

The Pilot, Mr. MADDOCKS
Barnstable, Mr. G. SMITH—Captain Boroughcliffe, (a regular ankee), Mr. GILL
Long Tom Coffin, Mr. NANTZ
Captain of the Alacrity, Mr. HAMERTON—Colonel Howard, Mr. GRAY
Lieutenant Griffith, Mr. TAYLOR—Serjeant Drill, Mr. NICHOLS.
Sailors, Soldiers, &c.
Kate Plowden, Mrs. PLUMER—Cecilia, Miss HONEY
Irish Woman, Mrs. WATKINSON.

DAVY & BERRY, PRINTERS, ALBION OFFICE.

9. The 'runners' or 'running-patterers' were the men who sold the sheets on the street, usually singing the songs, or reciting the doggerel.

Woodcut from a song sheet entitled *The Life and Sufferings of Jane Wade a young lady of pleasure and fashion*. Printed by J. Catnach, Monmouth Court, London. c. 1825

U U stands for Umbrella, that
upset Sammy Snub. U

Illustration to one of Catnach's Juvenile Books. c. 1832

concealed in the Red Barn at Polstead, Suffolk. Catnach disposed of 1,166,000 copies of the last dying speech of William Corder the murderer.

The industry and ingenuity of the printers of street literature like Jemmy Catnach and his successor W. S. Fortey, and Johnnie Pitts, were worthy of a better cause. Catnach used woodcuts by Bewick and other engravers both for his sheets of songs and also for his farthing, halfpenny and penny children's books. These were not without charm. Catnach himself also engraved many of the portraits of his murderers, often using the same block over and over again, with maybe slight modifications, such as taking out a moustache or putting in a beard. Catnach retired from the street literature business with a modest fortune in 1838, and bought a pub. He lived for only another three years.

The reading public increased very quickly in the early years of the nineteenth century. In 1810 Sir Walter Scott's *Lady of the Lake*, published at 42s., sold over twenty-thousand copies in the first twelve months – an extraordinary figure for a book of poems, particularly at such a price. In 1821, Scott's publishers

196

Foxcoat, near Stourbridge.

OAK, ASH, ELM, & BEECH

TIMBER

TO BE

Sold by Auction,

BY

MR. DAVIES:

AT THE VINE INN, STOURBRIDGE,

In the County of Worcester,

On FRIDAY, the 8th of January, 1841,

At 5 o'Clock in the Afternoon,

THE UNDERMENTIONED

VALUABLE TIMBER

NOW GROWING AND PART LYING ON THE FOXCOAT ESTATE,

In the Parish of Oldswinford, in the County of Worcester,

In the following or such other Lots as may be agreed upon at the time of Sale, viz.—

LOT 1. 13 Oak, 43 Elm, 4 Ash, 3 Beech, *1 sycamore* numbered with white paint from 1 to 63, inclusive.

LOT 2. 18 Oak, 12 Elm, 13 Ash, 5 Beech, *3 sycamore* numbered from 64 to 111, inclusive.

LOT 3. 25 Oak, 50 Elm, 8 Ash, 8 Beech, *3 sycamore* numbered from 112 to 202, inclusive.

LOT 4. 12 Elm, 5 Beech, lying on said Estate, also 2 Oak, and 1 Elm, now growing near the house, *marked ✗*

The above Timber is generally of large dimensions, sound, and clear.

Mr. Brookes, the Tenant, will cause the respective Lots to be pointed out, and for further particulars apply to Mr. DAVIES, Land Agent, Stourbridge.

J.HEMING, PRINTER, HIGH STREET, STOURBRIDGE.

UNCLE
TOM'S CABIN.

BY

HARRIET BEECHER STOWE.

WITH

Twenty-seven Illustrations on Wood

BY

GEORGE CRUIKSHANK, ESQ.

EVA AND TOPSY.

LONDON:
JOHN CASSELL, LUDGATE HILL.
1852.

issued his novel *Kenilworth* at a guinea-and-half, a high price that was maintained for new novels for some years.

Circulating libraries helped to establish these high prices. However in 1836, Charles Dickens reached a great new reading public with his *Pickwick Papers*, which was issued in 1s. monthly parts. By No. 15 and the appearance of Sam Weller, the circulation had reached 100,000. This same pattern of issuing books in monthly parts was soon followed by many publishers, including those of Thackeray and Trollope.

By the 1840's, steam was replacing hand-power in both book and periodical printing. William Clowes at his press in Stamford Street, London, had nineteen presses at work, each printing 1,000 sheets an hour. American publishing was beginning to infiltrate the English market. In 1852 *Uncle Tom's Cabin*, Harriet Beecher Stowe's book about the slave trade, 'touched off the biggest sensation the publishing trade had ever known.'[10] Ten editions were published in the first two weeks and 150,000 copies were sold within six months.

These huge runs were being printed from stereotyped plates. Plaster-of-Paris stereos had been invented in 1802 and were in general use by 1820.

The spread of railway travel helped the spread of the habit of reading. The success of George Stephenson's locomotives opened up the possibilities for rail travel. By the early 1840's, there were two thousand miles of railway in Great Britain and by the time of the Great Exhibition this had increased to over 5,000 miles. This railway system with its fast trains combined with the electric telegraph made a national press possible. This had not been achieved in Continental America at this period. In 1839 *Bradshaw's Railway Time Table* was issued and remained in print until 1961.

The early Victorian railway bookstall produced an outlet for a flood of salacious and shocking literature, comparable to the paperbacks to be found on any railway bookstall today. By the 1850's, when W. H. Smith achieved a virtual monopoly of the bookstalls, Routledge's Railway Library and the Yellow Backs designed by the colour printer Edmund Evans in 1853, filled the place of the more outrageous 'shockers'. These Yellow Backs, striking examples of economical colour printing, were usually printed from three or four wood blocks, on a yellow glazed paper, with illustrations by such artists as Birket Foster, George Cruikshank and Walter Crane. In contrast to these gaudy productions, attractively illustrated books were being produced by such publishers as William Pickering and printers like Charles Whittingham at the Chiswick Press. The introduction of the Arming Blocking Press in 1832 had led to a spate of richly decorated, heavily Gothic, board covers to gift books and keepsakes.

The railways also provided a great incentive to periodical publishing. A public unused to reading found (and still does)

10. *The English Common Reader*, Richard D. Altick, University of Chicago Press, 1957.

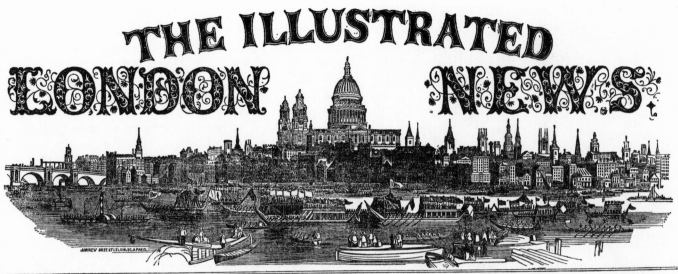

THE ILLUSTRATED LONDON NEWS

No. 149.—VOL. VI.   FOR THE WEEK ENDING SATURDAY, MARCH 8, 1845.   [SIXPENCE.

THE GAME LAWS.

A COMMITTEE of the House of Commons is about to begin an inquiry into the operation and effect of the Game-laws. So many committees have inquired into so many things, with no other result of their labours than a Report, never used as the foundation of any legislative measure, that we begin to look on the appointment of a Committee rather as a form of acknowledging the existence of an evil, than as a step to-"beginning of the end" of the Game Laws has not arrived; they have a long lease of existence yet; the growth of many centuries and the legacy transmitted to us from the Norman conquerors, they will not disappear in a single session, nor vanish at the bidding even of the League. If the landed interest only acts with a little fairness and liberality in the matter, we may go the length of saying that the Game Laws are in no danger at all. The feeling against them has arisen as much from errors and abuses connected with them that do not spring from the law, as from the law itself.

No one will dispute the right of a landowner to resist a trespass on his property of any kind, whether in pursuit of game or not; it is the mere protection the law extends to all property of every kind, and to take it away from land would be a gross injustice. The owner of that land so protected may also preserve the game—birds or animals—upon it. To say that doing so is a temptation offered—that great mischief may be done even by a few score of hares.

To show how prompt and full payment of such damage alleviates the grievance of a Game-law, we will describe the system that prevails throughout a large portion of Germany; we have not yet seen it alluded to in connection with this question, but it might be worth some consideration, even by the recently appointed committee.

In Howitt's "Rural Life in Germany," he says—"The popular division of the land is a dead hindrance to hunting; it has been here and there attempted, and English packs of hounds have been imported by the princes, but the peasants put it down wherever it appeared in a very little time. The German bauers and farmers have no faith, and it is quite impossible to persuade them, as it has been attempted to persuade the farmers in England, that it does their corn good to have it in the winter trodden over and torn to

---

the newspaper or magazine less intimidating than books. In 1836, the Newspaper Tax had been reduced to 1*d*. and in 1855, it was repealed. Six years later the duty on paper was abolished, and at last the press was free of taxes. Newspapers dropped in price. The cheapest was *The Daily Telegraph* which had been 1*d*. since 1853. This resulted in huge increases in circulation. In 1838 *The Illustrated London News* was started. It was the first periodical to devote more space to the illustrations than to the text. This journal employed a number of artists who travelled to far places as special correspondents. Their sketches were translated into printing surfaces, often with as much invention as skill, by the trade wood engravers in London. *Punch or the London Charivari* appeared in July 1841 in emulation of the Parisian *Charivari* with the introduction 'This guffaw-graph is intended to form a refuge for destitute wit – an asylum for the thousands of orphan jokes.' Yet the familiar *Punch* joke with its lengthy caption is absent from the early numbers. The humour, such as it was, was in the writing, the cartoons by John Leech and Alfred Croquill were political and much concerned with the mushroom growth of the railway companies.

Punch: illustration from the title-page of the first volume, 1841

Hard Times by Charles Dickens. Woodcut by Dalziel from a drawing
by Frederick Walker. 1881

11. *Talbot Baines Reed.* Stanley Morison. Privately printed Cambridge
University Press, 1960.

In 1850, Dickens's Magazine *Household Words* started off with
an assured circulation of 100,000. His novel *Hard Times* was
serialized in it, and anyone (and there were plenty of them) who
wanted to read the latest Dickens novel had to buy the
magazine.

John Cassell, the founder of the publishing house of Cassell
and Co, was one of the pioneers in popular periodicals. A re-
formed drunkard, he became a temperance orator and, on the
side, a dealer in teas and coffees. Instead of selling his tea or
coffee by the case, as was the custom, he packed it up in shilling
packets. In order to label these he bought a small hand-printing
press. On this same little press, he printed his first periodical
The Teetotal Times. This understandably not very successful
venture was followed in 1850 by *The Working Man's Friend* at
1*d.* a copy. This found a ready market and within a year the
circulation had reached 50,000. On the success of this, Cassell
set off into a wide field of popular journalism. His productions
eventually included, amongst many others, *Cassell's Family
Magazine*, *The Quiver* and *Little Folks*.

In 1879, the market for improving literature for the young was
tapped with remarkable shrewdness by the Religious Tract
Society, who issued the weekly *Boy's Own Paper*. On the title-
page of the first number are the words 'For pure and enter-
taining reading'! It sold at 1*d.* a copy and was most ably edited
by G. A. Hutchinson, assisted by Dr James Macaulay. Amongst
the contributors to the first number were W. H. G. Kingston,
with a stirring tale of the Royal Navy called *From Powder
Monkey to Admiral*, the redoubtable Captain Webb who described *How I Swam the Channel* and Talbot Baines Reed with the
first of his many school stories, which he modestly signed 'By
an Old Boy'. Reed's first serial, *The Adventures of a Three Guinea
Watch*, came out in 1880, to be followed by numerous of his
other stories of school life, including the most famous of all,
The Fifth Form at St Dominics in 1887, the same year that the
first English edition of Karl Marx's *Das Kapital* appeared. (*Das
Kapital* had been first published in Hamburg twenty years
earlier). It was also in 1887 that Talbot Baines Reed completed
A History of the Old English Letter Foundries, on which he had
been working intermittently for the previous ten years. This
masterpiece was, and still is, the only documented account of
typefounding in England and has no equivalent in France or
Germany.[11] Talbot Baines Reed was by profession a type-
founder, being the managing director of the famous Fann
Street Foundry.

The great age of the type-foundries was drawing to a close, for
in the same year that Reed's book on the old English letter
foundries came out, the first mechanically-set book arrived
from America, set on the Mergenthaler (Linotype) machine. At
last, the bottleneck had been cleared.

The effects of new movements in painting and sculpture are sometimes reflected obviously and quickly in printing. This was not the case with the movement in painting that began in Paris at about the time when the Pre-Raphaelites were moving through their fantasy worlds of the Middle Ages. This new movement was first noticed at the Salon des Refusés in 1863, when Manet's *Déjeuner sur L'Herbe* caused something of a stir. This must have been more for its subject matter than for the way in which it was painted. The sight of a party of young men having lunch with their nude model aroused some anger and perhaps a little envy. With Manet as leader, a group of experimentally minded young painters banded together. In 1874 they held their first show and because there was a painting by Claude Monet called *Impression, Soleil Levant* some critic dubbed them Impressionists and the name stuck. None of this had the slightest effect on the look of printing, or on the design of printed graphic work. However, when the Impressionist painter Seurat systematically broke down his painting into dots of pure pigment, with colours based on the contemporary scientific findings about the spectrum and the nature of light, and so arrived at his Pointillist theory, he was prophetically foreshadowing practically all foreseeable photo-colour methods of graphic reproduction.

The Impressionists had evolved a new visual method of interpreting realism, but already the symbolist poets Mallarmé and Verlaine were rejecting realism in their poetry. In 1886, Jean Moréas published the Symbolist Manifesto in *Figaro Littéraire*, not only summarizing the ideas of these poets but also stating that realism should be rejected in art as well as in poetry.

The artist closest to the symbolist poets was Odilon Redon, painter and pioneer lithographer, and friend of Mallarmé. Redon expressed his ideas indirectly, by allusive and decorative shapes. Redon worked on an unpublished work of Mallarmé's for which he drew four lithographed illustrations, whilst Mallarmé set the type, so as to match the rhythms of the poetry, foreshadowing Apollinaire's *Calligrammes* by some forty years. Redon's and Mallarmé's ideas were developed by Gauguin and by the *Nabis* (Bonnard, Vuillard, Roussel and Denis). Maurice Denis was the theorist of this little group. In 1890 he wrote: '. . . a picture is essentially a flat surface covered with coloured pigments arranged in a certain order.' The connection with printing and particularly the lithographed poster immediately becomes obvious. In 1869 Manet had drawn a poster – *Les Chats* for a bookseller advertising *Champfleury*, which had a brilliantly simple design of black and white cats amongst silhouetted chimney pots.

In 1889, Gauguin made some zincographs, and later some woodcuts which were startlingly new in their flowing shapes, but again with the same contrasts of black and white. Three

Poster *Les Chats* by Edouard Manet for Champfleury, 1869. *Les Affiches Illustrées*

The second device for the cover design for *The Studio* by
R. Anning Bell 1894, which replaced Beardsley's design of the
previous year. Anning Bell was the Professor of Design at the
Glasgow School of Art

years later Felix Valloton carried Redon's ideas and Gauguin's
simple 'flowing shapes' into commercial printing with some
posters for concert halls.

The 1890's was the great age of the French poster. Jules
Chéret, H. de Toulouse-Lautrec, Steinlen and a few others working for theatre, concert hall and ice rink, as well as other commercial concerns, brought art to the man in the street. And running
through all their work was the sinuous, curving line of *art
nouveau*.

So much has been written about *art nouveau* over recent years
that one hesitates to add to such a mountain of words. This
decorative movement, which might so easily have been limited
to the work of a few sophisticated interior decorators, became
one of the starting points of twentieth-century architecture. It
also provided one of the key elements in modern graphic
design (and so in modern printing). This, particularly in
British *art nouveau*, was the conscious use of white space. As
for the origins of *art nouveau*, quite apart from obvious Japanese
influences, the archetype *art nouveau* line appears in Gothic glass
and medieval illumination. Its origins do *not* lie in classical Rome
nor in the art of Renaissance Italy. Just as towering Gothic
arches may owe their origins to forest walks, so the slack
curving line of *art nouveau* can be seen in the curling tendrils of a
vine. The closest likeness to this line is in the writhing column
of smoke from a smouldering joss stick. In an attempt to get
away from formalism, *art nouveau* ended up with a perfect
evocation of a natural form.

Apart from the slack curving line the most telling factor in *art
nouveau*, at least in Great Britain, is the use of white: white walls
in interior decoration and areas of white space in printing. The
interior of Whistler's house, which the architect William
Godwin built for the artist in Tite Street, Chelsea, in 1877, had
plain white or yellow walls to the rooms, a startling innovation
in an age of pattern and clutter. This quality of whiteness became one of the dominant themes in English and Scottish *art
nouveau*, whether for interior decoration and painted furniture,
or for book illustration and even book covers. This whiteness
and a certain angularity of design separated it from continental
art nouveau. The contrast is at its most obvious in a Beardsley
illustration, often with great empty white spaces, and an
Alphonse Mucha design, where every corner is filled, if not
with his hefty women, then with trailing vines and exotic
plants.

In 1893 the first number of *The Studio* was published, the first
magazine of the new movement which was soon to spread like
rabies across Europe. Its effect on designers everywhere, from
Turin to Budapest and from Venice to Moscow was electric, and
particularly on Charles Rennie Mackintosh and the Group of
Four in Glasgow. The impact of *The Studio*, with photographs
of C. F. S. Voysey's architecture and decorations, the painting

The Three Brides by the Dutch-Indonesian artist Jan Toorop, and Beardsley's drawings for *Le Morte d'Arthur*, was to provide the first great formative impulse to Mackintosh, himself one of the key figures in the final stages of this movement.[1]

In 1895, Samuel Bing opened his Paris *art nouveau* shop in the Rue de Provence with the exterior covered in Brangwyn's paintings, and exhibiting glass by Tiffany, paintings by Bonnard, Maurice Denis and Seurat (who also decorated cigar box tops at 100 fr. a time), and books illustrated by Beardsley and Gordon Craig. The settings in Bing's shop were designed by Henri van de Velde, the Belgian painter and architect. In 1900 Charles Rennie Mackintosh, by this time the architect of the famous Glasgow Art School, and other members of the Group of Four, exhibited in Vienna and made a lasting impression on German and Austrian architects.

The review *Jugend* was first published in Munich in 1896 and gave its name to the German *art nouveau* movement. In the following year in Berlin, Julius Meier-Graefe the German art critic brought out his *art nouveau* journal, *Pan*. In 1897 Meier-Graefe opened an *art nouveau* shop in Paris. Bing's shop had yet another rival in London in Liberty's, the Regent Street store. Italy repaid the compliment to England by referring to *art nouveau* as *Stile Liberty*.

The decorative possibilities of *art nouveau* lent themselves to wrought and cast iron, which were used not only for fire screens and bedheads, but also for doors and balconies, such as in the tea shops Mackintosh designed in Glasgow and the houses Victor Horta designed in Brussels. The cast-iron surrounds to the entrances of the Paris Metro, designed by Hector Guimard in 1900, are an enduring monument to the vitality of the style.

The English, who had started the movement, soon lost interest. The faithful followers of William Morris and the Arts and Crafts Movement protested violently when some continental *art nouveau* objects were exhibited at the Victoria and Albert Museum in 1900. Walter Crane spoke of 'that decorative disease known as *art nouveau*',[2] yet in Crane's own work could be seen the germs of that 'disease'. Viewed at this distance of time, there seems to be much that is stylistically similar in the work of many of Morris's followers and the artists of *art nouveau*. Their differences at the time were marked by the craft-based attitudes of Morris and the Arts and Crafts Movement, and the aesthetics of *art nouveau*, where art could be accepted for art's sake. Yet, oddly enough, Morris was one of the influences behind continental *art nouveau*, but so was Charles Rennie Mackintosh. The Munich architect Peter Behrens was influenced by Mackintosh. Behrens in turn was to pass on this influence to the founding fathers of modern architecture – Gropius, Le Corbusier and Mies van der Rohe.

The influences that have shaped twentieth-century printing,

1. These influences on Mackintosh were suggested by Jessie Newbery, the wife of Francis H. Newbery, the head of the Glasgow School of Art and prime inspirer of the young Mackintosh.
2. *William Morris to Whistler*, Walter Crane, London, 1911.

KELMSCOTT PRESS, UPPER MALL, HAMMERSMITH.

February 16th, 1897.

Note. This is the Golden type.
This is the Troy type.
This is the Chaucer type.

Secretary:
S. C. Cockerell, Kelmscott Press, Upper Mall, Hammersmith, London, W., to whom all letters should be addressed.

apart from *art nouveau*, were the work of William Morris and the members of the Arts and Crafts Movement and the Private Presses. Morris can be isolated from the Private Press Movement both because his influence on design was far more widespread than any of the other press printers and also because his tastes for medievalism were quite contrary to those of Emery Walker, Cobden-Sanderson and most of the other private press printers. Yet there were people in the Private Press Movement who in their work were closer to Morris than to the Jensonist ideals of the Doves Press – figures such as C. R. Ashbee at Essex House and St John Hornby at Ashendene with respectively their Arts and Crafts and Neo-Gothic typeface interests, and there was Ricketts the practitioner of *art nouveau* at the Vale Press. None of these fit too neatly into the Renaissance conception of such presses as the Doves.

In their different ways the most influential of the presses were Morris's Kelmscott, with his determined return to incunabula and gothic types, and the Doves Press, with Emery Walker and Cobden-Sanderson and their immaculately dull post-Jensonist typography.[3] In simple terms, Morris represents a rejection of the culture of the Italian Renaissance and a return to the values of the late Middle Ages; Cobden-Sanderson and Emery Walker present the opposite viewpoint, with a complete acceptance of the roman typeface and the printing styles of Jenson, Aldus and the other early Venetians.

Morris and Emery Walker and Cobden-Sanderson were on common ground in their insistence on high standards of workmanship and the use of good materials. They brought back into printing a feeling for craftsmanship that had been widely neglected since the time of Bulmer and Bensley. As designers, they produced nothing new. That was left to Charles Ricketts, who in turn had been influenced by the typography of James McNeill Whistler. Ricketts was both private pressman and one of the first professional book designers. Ricketts was in turn to be succeeded by Talwin Morris, a friend of the Group of Four and art director to Blackie's, the Glasgow publishers. Talwin Morris was the *art nouveau* book designer *par excellence*.[4] His first job had been on the London weekly, *Black and White*, which showed the work of such artists as Walter Crane, Charles Ricketts and G. F. Watts. In 1893 Morris moved to Glasgow to become Art Director of Blackie's. He soon made friends with Mackintosh, MacNair and the Misses Macdonald. Unlike the Group of Four, Talwin Morris had a ready outlet, in Blackie's, for his designs. His output of cover designs and title-pages was prodigious. The designs are immaculate in their linear simplicity. He made constant use of sans serif letter forms, but never attempted to design a typeface.

It was left to the Germans to produce the first real *art nouveau* typeface which appeared when the typefounder Klingspor commissioned Otto Eckmann to design a typeface 'appropriate

3. I have written too much about this dichotomy elsewhere to do more than touch on it here. See *The Twentieth Century Book*, Studio Vista, 1967.
4. *The Art Nouveau Book in Britain*, John Russell Taylor, Methuen, 1966.

In Nov. 1909 will be published at The Doves Press
No. 15 UPPER MALL HAMMERSMITH

WILLIAM CAXTON

A paper read by George Parker Winship, Librarian
of The John Carter Brown Library, Providence,
Rhode Island, at a Meeting of the Club of Odd
Volumes in Boston, Massachusetts, U.S.A., in February, 1908. ⹂Sm. 4to. Printed in black and red. 300
copies on paper, bound in boards, paper sides & vellum backs, at 10s.; or in morocco or sealskin at
£2. 10s.: 15 copies on vellum, bound in boards, at
£2. 10s.; or in morocco or sealskin at £4. 12s.

ORDER FORM

Of the above please supply (hereunder state the
number of copies desired on paper and on vellum, or
one or other, and how bound, quoting description
and price from the above):

Name:

Address:

Standing orders and orders already received:

THE ASHENDENE PRESS
will shortly have ready for publication
I FIORETTI DI SAN FRANCESCO
the Italian text, with 54 woodcut illustrations
from drawings by Charles M. Gere. The book
consists of viij. & 240 pages measuring about
eight & three-quarter by six inches. It will be
bound in limp vellum with silk ties.

⹂The edition is limited to 240 copies on
paper and 12 on vellum.

⹂There are for sale
200 copies on paper at 4 guineas.
9 copies on vellum at 16 guineas.

Orders may be sent through a Bookseller or
direct to
C. H. St J. Hornby, Shelley House,
Chelsea Embankment, London, S. W. 3

⹂An Order Form is enclosed herewith.

February, 1922.

for the printing of books in the new style'. This typeface was
called Eckmann-Schrift. It was an *art nouveau* development of
the German gothic typefaces.

In general commercial printing, the invention of photographic
methods of reproduction, for line in 1876 and half-tone in 1888,
brought about a revolution in the appearance of popular
journalism. Photographs began to take the place of drawings
and the trade wood engravers were almost put out of business.

Die zehnte Muse

Dichtungen vom Brettl
⹂ und fürs Brettl ⹂

Eckmann-Schrift, designed by Otto Eckmann, 1900

Blew Cap
FOR
MEE.

ANNO.M.DCCC.
•L•XXX•III•

5. *Artistic Printing*. Vivian Ridler, *Alphabet and Image* 6.

Popular illustrators in England in the 1890's were still very numerous. There was perhaps only one genius amongst them and that was the *Punch* artist Phil May, who more quickly than anyone saw the possibilities of the line block. Charles Keene, the greatest of all *Punch* artists, died in 1891. George du Maurier continued to work for the same journal in the same old way, though his work had by this time become somewhat mannered. There were almost as many magazines as there were illustrators and new ones kept springing up. *The Strand Magazine*, for instance, which had been founded by George Newnes in 1891, rushed to success when Conan Doyle's first stories about Sherlock Holmes appeared. These were illustrated with vignetted half-tones by Sidney Paget.

In ephemeral printing, there was a shortlived battle between two styles, the Artistic and the Antique.[5] Both these movements were largely confined to compositors and pressman and were supported by Andrew Tuer at the Leadenhall Press. In 1880, Tuer had issued the first of a series of albums of work submitted by printing tradesmen, which was called *The Printers' International Exchange*. The Artistic movement made much use of decorative rules and decorated typefaces. The Antique movement, using battered old typefaces and crude woodcuts by Joseph Crawhall, harked back to the eighteenth-century chapbook and was to provide the formative influence for Lovat Fraser, a stage designer and book decorator who had a brief but dazzling career.

In the United States of America, type-founding and commercial printing boomed, the circulation of journals and magazines such as *Harper's*, *The Century* and *Scribner's* reached new heights. In 1895, Bruce Rogers joined the Riverside Press, at Cambridge in Massachusetts. Rogers, one of the greatest of American typographers, was to have a strong influence on the revival of good printing that followed the English Private Presses. He was an eclectic *pasticheur*, moving happily from one early style to another, yet he had enough of the creative artist in him to enable him to breathe life into this derivative typography. In 1900, the American printer Theodore de Vinne published *Plain Printing Types*, foreshadowing by nearly a quarter of a century Daniel Berkeley Updike's incomparable *Printing Types*. Two years before Bruce Rogers had joined the Riverside Press, Updike had left that press to start his own Merrymount Press in Boston, which became renowned for the quality of its work. Updike designed his books and his printed matter in what was later to be called 'the English Style'. It was a traditional and well-mannered style, that, for books to be read in the hand, has not yet been surpassed.

In 1901, Grant Richards, a young and somewhat shaky London publisher, started his series of cheap reprints, which he named *The World's Classics*. Five years later Dent's *Everyman* series was started. By this time Grant Richards was in trouble (not the

OF THADUENT OF OUR LORDE.

HE tyme of thaduent or comyng of our lord in to this world is halowed in holy chirche the tyme of iiii wekes in betokenyng of iiii dyuerse comynges. ¶ The i was whan he came and apierid in humayn nature and flessh. The ii is in the herte and conscyence. The iii is at the deth. The iiii is at last Jugement. The last weke may vnnethe be accomplissed. For the glorye of the sayntes whiche shal be yeuen at the last comyng shal neuer ende ne fynysshe. And to this signyfyaunce the first responce of the first weke of aduent hath iiii verse to rekene ¶ Gloria patri & filio for one to the reporte of the iiii wekis, and how be it that there be iiii comynges of our lord, yet the chirche maketh mencion in especial but of tweyne, that is to wete, of that he came in humayne nature to the world, and of that he cometh to the Jugement & dome, as it apperith in thoffyce of the chirche of this tyme. And therfor the fastynges that ben in this tyme, ben of gladnes and of joye in one partie, & that other partie is in bitternesse of herte. By cause of the comynge of our lorde in our nature humayne, they ben of joye and gladnes. And by cause of the comyng at the day of Jugement they be of bitternes and heuynes.

Stowchyng the comyng of our lord in our bodyly flessh, we may considre thre thynges of this comyng. That is to wete thoportunyte, the necessyte & the vtylyte ¶ The oportunyte of comyng is taken by the reson of the man that first was vanquysshyd in the lawe of nature of the default of the knowledge of god, by whiche he fyll in to euyll errours, & therfore he was constrayned to crye to god ¶ Illumina oculos meos, that is to saye, lord gyue lyght to myn eyen. After cam the lawe of god whiche hath gyuen commandement in which he hath ben overcome of Impuissance, as first he hath cryed ther is non that fulfilleth, but that comandeth. For ther he is only taught but not delyuerd fro synne, ne holpen by grace, and therfore he was constrayned to crye, ther laketh non to comande

DER KÜNSTLER-
KOLONIE IN
DARMSTADT
GEWIDMET

first or the last of his troubles) and the Oxford University Press took over *The World's Classics* series, no doubt to their lasting benefit. These handy little books soon achieved vast sales and remained unchallenged until the advent of the paperbacks in the 1930's.

The influence of the English private presses was widespread. In 1905 Emery Walker was invited to design a series of German classics for the Leipzig firm of Insel Verlag. These books were planned on classical lines, to the proportions of the Golden Section. Their influence spread to the work of a number of other continental publishers.

Printing by the 1900's had taken on certain well-defined characteristics. Most well-printed books in England, Germany or America were in the English style. *Art nouveau* influences were mostly reflected in cover designs. It is surprising how many books had white covers, either of cloth or artificial vellum, blocked with simple *art nouveau* shapes. In the popular press, in magazines and in ephemeral printing there was little evidence of any conscious attempt at design. Whilst the first tentative modern movements were taking place in architecture and three-dimensional design, printing remained static, or under the private press influence, or under that of Mr Tuer at the Leadenhall Press, took a turn backwards into the past. In Germany, *Jugendstil* became the universal style. Whilst England had slowly rejected *art nouveau* and, as far as printing went, had replaced it with a variety of derivative styles, Germany had at least one important designer who could take *art nouveau* a step further. This was Peter Behrens (1868–1940) who had studied as a painter and then, though virtually untrained, practised as an architect and became the leader of the modern movement in Germany. In 1901 he designed his first building, a house at Darmstadt, and also in 1901 designed a typeface for Rudhard'sche Giesserei (later to become the Klingspor typefoundry) at Offenbach. Both house and typeface have something of Charles Rennie Mackintosh's angularity and indeed Behrens's debt to Mackintosh is obvious.

The time of transition was over. The purity of English (or Scottish) *art nouveau* was to provide a basis for modern design. The Private Presses were to give not only to English, but also to German and Swiss printing, both a style and a standard of quality worth emulating. Post-Impressionist and later developments in French painting were to alter beyond recognition the graphic work of the western world. Constructivist attitudes in Russia were to change twentieth-century architecture and typography entirely. But there was to be a war and a revolution before all these different influences could be resolved in modern design and modern printing.

99 *Woman in Snake Doorway*, design by Odilon Redon, 1890.
Rijksmuseum Kröller-Müller, Otterlo

T*

101 Poster for *Job* cigarettes by Alphonse Mucha, 1897
The French Poster, Studio Vista, 1969

104 and **105** Charles Rennie Mackintosh: design for wall
decoration, furniture and the principal bedroom at the Hill House,
Helensburgh, 1903

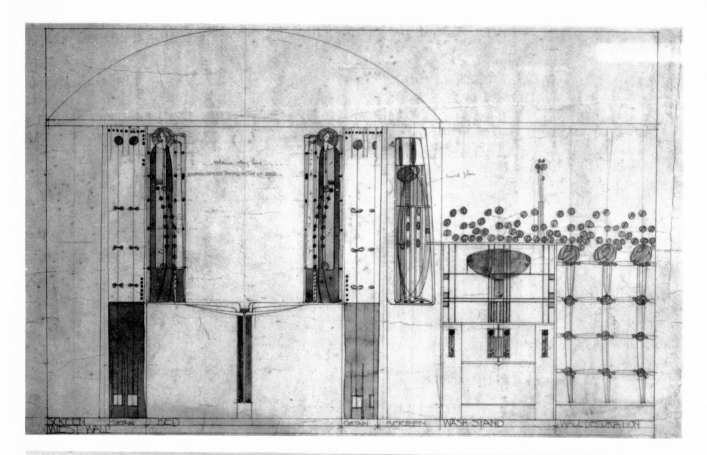

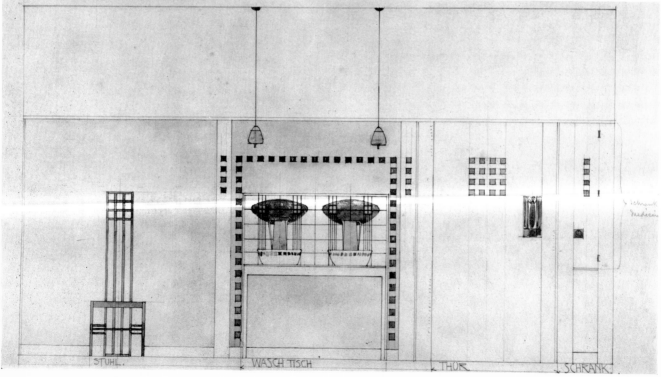

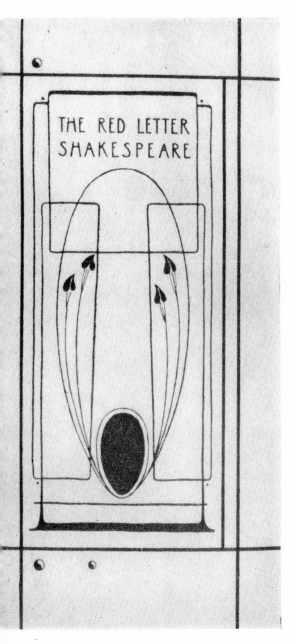

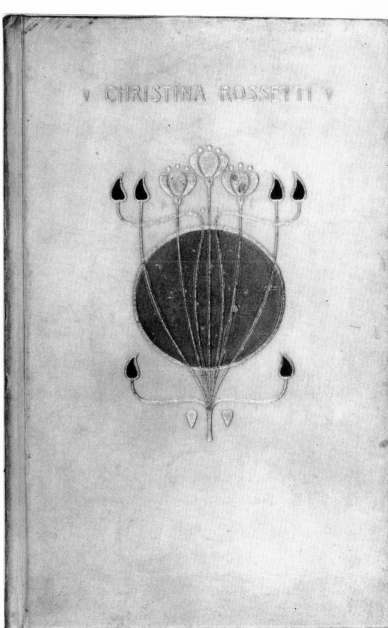

Behrens=Initialen

Original
Erzeugnis

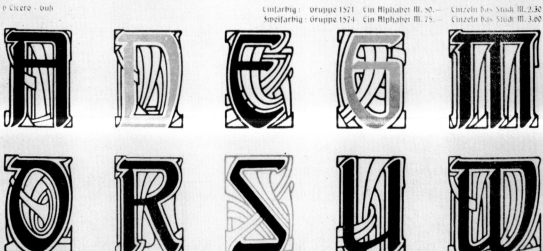

STIMME AUS DEM SUMPF

Fotomontage: John Heartfield

„Dreitausend Jahre konsequenter Inzucht beweisen die Überlegenheit meiner Rasse!"

115 '. . . in their long-bonneted Hispano-Suizas and Isotta-Fraschinis.' Drawing for the cover of *The Autocar* by F. Gordon Crosby, 1926

116 Tut-ankh-amen ornament: a gold cloissonné pectoral with the winged scarab protected by Isis and Nephthys. *Photograph: F. L. Kennett*

PRINTING TYPES

THEIR HISTORY, FORMS, AND USE

A STUDY IN SURVIVALS

BY

DANIEL BERKELEY UPDIKE

WITH ILLUSTRATIONS

"Nunca han tenido, ni tienen las artes otros enemigos que los ignorantes"

VOLUME I

CAMBRIDGE

HARVARD UNIVERSITY PRESS

LONDON: HUMPHREY MILFORD

OXFORD UNIVERSITY PRESS

1922

The Rime of
the Ancient
Mariner

BY

SAMUEL TAYLOR
COLERIDGE

OXFORD

At the University Preß

1930

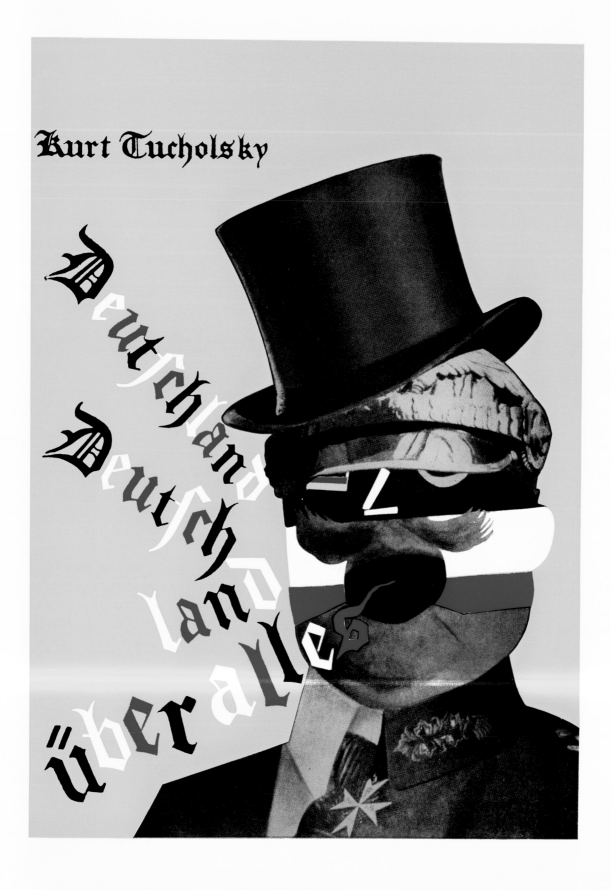

f the invention of photography did not put the painter out of business, it at least drove him to re-examine the purposes of his craft. The camera's job clearly was not picture-making, however laboriously Oscar Gustav Rejlander and others assembled models for complicated compositions. The camera's purpose, it was soon apparent, was to record faces, places and events. This recording, particularly of events, brought a new dimension to printing. Newspapers and magazines copiously illustrated with photographs, became the daily fare of millions of readers. The post-Gutenberg literate reader was once again becoming a viewer of pictures. Text reached minimal proportions and picture dailies developed their own iconography of pop stars, pin-ups and strip-cartoons.

The Great War of 1914–18 gave the printing press its last un-rivalled chance as a medium of propaganda. Atrocity stories and pictures in the daily newspapers diverted momentarily the attention of the readers from the fearful casualty lists. The entire resources of every combatant country were soon mobilized. From the poster hoardings of England, Kitchener's pointing finger backed up by glaring eyes and grotesque moustaches informed anyone who had not joined up that his country needed him. France with conscription in force did not need such moral persuasions, but directed her propaganda to National Loans. In 1916 the writer's father came home on leave from the Western Front with Jules Abel Faivre's poster in his kit-bag. Faivre, a close friend of Renoir, had produced in his drawing of the *poilu* shouting '*On les aura!*' the finest of the war posters. From the eastern front Biro's brutal design for the Hungarian War Loan of a symbolic figure of a worker swinging a sledge hammer, was an omen of things to come.

Switzerland was the one European point of refuge from the war. Zurich was full of those who could not or would not support their governments. Amongst these was Lenin. There were also many young artists from France, Germany and Russia. The meeting place of these artists was the Cabaret Voltaire and here Dada was born. Marcel Janco expressed their feelings when he said 'who on earth in those days of collapse, was still ready to believe in eternal values, in the canned goods of the past, in the academies, the schools of art?... to hell with beauty.'

The Dadaists used Picasso's and Braque's Cubist collages as a starting point for their work. The use by these French painters of actual pages torn from *Le Figaro* and other journals led to the Dadaists making use of typography for picture making. Sententiously, they regarded it as an uncontaminated medium. Dada with its rejection of art was rejecting the society that accepted such art. Dada had a cathartic effect, it was also an expression of horror at a world capable of the genocide of Ypres and Passchendaele. The movement spread from Zurich to Cologne and Berlin and on to New York. By its furious

First World War poster by Alfred Leete, 1914

Pelikan, trademark by Kurt Schwitters, Hanover, 1928

denial of anything positive in art it might soon have destroyed itself. It did not, but left behind an indelible and disrupting mark on the art and the literature of the West. Dada also has had a lasting and sometimes enlivening effect on typography.

In 1916, Helmut Herzfeld, released from the German armed forces, anglicized his name to John Heartfield, as a protest against the hate propaganda of war. From 1913 to 1919, in collaboration with the satiric draughtsman George Grosz, he made a number of collages using advertisements, illustrations, headlines, labels and photographs. In 1918, Heartfield joined the Communist party and a year later became co-founder of the Berlin Dada group. But unlike the Dadaists he worked for the definite objectives of publicity and propaganda. Heartfield's work is loaded with Marxist overtones. The essence of Heartfield's photo-montage was literary and depended on a juxtaposition of photography and typography. This juxtaposition of picture and often irrelevant caption is the key to his work. It reveals some very telling truths. His designs, unlike those of most of his contemporaries, cut through woolly abstraction to bring home a doctrinaire message. They hurt, intentionally.

The immediate derivative from Dada was Surrealism, a movement with a name taken from Apollinaire's play *Les Mamelles de Terésias: drame surréaliste*. The movement was founded by the French poets André Breton and Louis Aragon, its themes dredged up from the subconscious mind. Such Dadaists as Duchamps, Klee and Ernst became Surrealists and were in time joined by the painters Miro, Dali, Chirico, Tanguy, Man Ray and Magritte. The most notorious exponent of Surrealism was Salvador Dali, incidentally perhaps their least significant painter. Max Ernst's use of old printed engravings from catalogues of hardware fittings brought both an element of Dada and unexpected poetry into his Surrealist pictures. He helped to add another dimension to graphic communication.

In 1918, Guillaume Apollinaire's *Calligrammes (Poèmes de la Paix et de la Guerre)* was published. These poems were typographically arranged in a manner that symbolized their content and were by many years forerunners of Concrete Poetry, where poets use words in a purely visual way. Lewis Carroll had done the same kind of thing in *Alice in Wonderland* and so had Sterne in *Tristram Shandy*.

Symbolism, Cubism, Dada, Constructivism, Suprematism and Mimetic Typography (such as that shown in *Calligrammes*) were all to affect the appearance of printing in the years after the Great War. Russia had contributed both Constructivism and Suprematism, when in the first years after the Revolution political fervour was matched with revolutionary ideas about art and design. Constructivism was based on the importance of movement and tensions in space. The Baroque architects of the Voralberg school had demonstrated the same thing nearly two centuries before.

Collage illustration by Max Ernst from *La Femme 100 Têtes*.
Edition du Carrefours, Paris 1929

In 1920, a Constructivist exhibition was held in Moscow.
Amongst the exhibitors were Naum Gabo, Antoine Pevsner
and Moholy-Nagy. The latter was to become one of the key
figures in the new movement in typography. Suprematism, a
purified geometrical form of Cubism whose chief exponent was
Kasimir Malevich, was to influence Joseph Albers who taught
with Moholy-Nagy at the Bauhaus, and also the Russian typographer Lazar Lissitzky, who was a professor at the Moscow
Academy. Lissitzky's typography showed its Suprematist
origins in his use of a limited range of primary colours and such
geometrical elements as the circle, the square and particularly
the diagonal axis that became such a lasting cliché in press
advertising. Once the Revolution had established itself in
Russia, there was a sharp reaction against revolutionary art. A
stodgy Social Realism took the place of the new movements and
there was a quick exodus of artists including Kandinsky,
Chagall, Gabo, Pevsner and Lissitzky.

El Lissitzky was one of the great pioneers of modern printed
design. Before his time display typography had rarely gone
beyond the bounds of the simply displayed handbill, given
variety on its central axis only by variation of weight and variety
of typefaces. Lissitzky was one of the first to synthesize the

Top: Advertisement design from the Bauhaus by Herbert Bayer

Below: Herbert Bayer's Universal alphabet designed at the Bauhaus in 1927

ANBAU MÖBEL

Entwurf: Walter Gropius, Prof. Dr. E. H.

Ges. geschützt

Die moderne Hausfrau, an die in dem erschöpfenden Trubel des modernen Lebens heute soviel mehr Anforderungen gestellt werden, als früher, und die sich in den seltensten Fällen ausreichende Haushaltshilfe beschaffen kann, wird es dankbar begrüßen, wenn sie sich in ihrem Heim nicht mehr einer überwältigenden Fülle von nutzlosen Gegenständen und verschnörkelten Möbeln gegenübersieht, deren Pflege ihr die Zeit stiehlt und die doch nur einen altmodischen, überholten Begriff von „Gemütlichkeit" geben. Ihr werden die Vorteile der neuen „Anbaumöbel" am schnellsten klar werden. Ebenso wie es uns nicht einfällt, im Rokokokostüm über die Straße zu gehen, statt in unserer modernen Kleidung, ebenso wünschen wir uns auch unser erweitertes Kleid; die Wohnung, befreit von sinnlosem, raumsperrendem Kram und überflüssigen Verzierungen. Der Willkür der Stile sind wir satt geworden, von der Laune zur Regel geschritten und suchen nun in klaren, knappen und einfachen Formen, die der Art unseres heutigen Lebens entsprechen, den

wesentlichen und sinnfälligen Ausdruck unserer häuslichen Umgebung.
Der leitende Gedanke für die Gestalt unserer neuen „Anbaumöbel" ist die Erfüllung der praktischen Bedürfnisse in knappster und zeitsparendster Weise, so daß sich die Lebensvorgänge im Hause entsprechend der Schnelligkeit unseres heutigen Lebens zweckmäßig und dennoch komfortabel abspielen.
Für die Bestimmung der Größenverhältnisse und Höhen der verschiedenen Möbel sind die natürlichen Maße des menschlichen Körpers, seine natürlichen Bewegungen und Funktionen maßgebend. Unser Leben ist heute ein anderes als das unserer Vorfahren, unsere Gesellschaftsverhältnisse haben sich gewandelt. Die Stellung der heutigen Frau im Erwerbsleben, die verminderte Seßhaftigkeit und die knapperen Wohnverhältnisse stellen bestimmte Forderungen, die Erfüllung heischen. Wir haben keine Zeit dafür, aus falscher Sentimentalität vergangene Gesellschaftsformen und Lebensweisen nachzuahmen, die für ganz andere Voraussetzungen geschaffen wurden. Unsere Großeltern brauchten andere Möbel als wir im Zeitalter der Autos und Eisenbahnen. Nicht wir sind um der Möbel willen da, wie es vielfach heute den Anschein hat, sondern umgekehrt. Das „Anbaumöbel" befreit uns von dieser Tyrannei.

modern art movements and convert them usefully to typographic ends, so that the relationship of forms, the dynami tensions of diagonals against verticals, the purity of primar colours, the studied organization of the pages and the repetitiv rhythm of carefully placed units would all help to clarify an increase the force of the copy.

Lissitzky was closely associated with a number of the fathe figures of modern design. He worked with Kurt Schwitters o the Dada magazine *Merz*, contributed to *De Stijl* and als worked with Mies van der Rohe, Theo van Doesburg and Har Arp, with whom in 1925 he produced *Die Kunstismen*. In thi publication various artists attempted to define the contem porary movements in art. In 1922, Lissitzky visited the Bauhau His typographical ideas had the sharpest effect on Gropius school, where his East European Suprematism came face t face with the immaculately serene doctrine of *De Stijl*, reflectin Constructivism in the West with Piet Mondrian's paintings. was Lissitzky who influenced Lazlo Moholy-Nagy, the fir great teacher of *Die Neue Typographie*, who in his turn added t the art of printing all the creative possibilities of photograph and photo-collage.

The Bauhaus preoccupations with functionalism, which w something that Pugin and Ruskin had talked about nearly

abcdefghi jklmnopqr stuvwxyz a dd

century earlier, only took fire when it was allied to Constructivism. This functionalism, governed by Constructivist principles, provided the essentials of the Bauhaus typography.

From 1925 to 1928 the typography workshop at the Bauhaus was run by Herbert Bayer, a former student. The impetus and the credo had come from Lissitzky, via Moholy-Nagy. The essential features of this Bauhaus typography were order, asymmetry and a basic rectangular grid structure. Decoration was limited to the use of heavy rules, circles and rectangles of typemetal. The sans serif typeface was regarded as an essential feature. Both Herbert Bayer and Josef Albers designed sans serif founts. In 1925, the use of capital letters was dropped. Bayer was the instigator of this idea and apparently still supports it, if the superb catalogue he designed for the 1968 Bauhaus exhibition is any guide to his feelings.[1]

Bayer's idea of a single alphabet has certain factors, including economy, to recommend it, but the sans serif lower case alphabet is certainly not the answer. A modern half uncial might be nearer the mark. Cassandre's type *Peignot* is an interesting if not altogether successful attempt at solving the problem in this way.

In 1928, Jan Tschichold's *Die Neue Typographie* was published. The title-page to this book was set in a heavy sans, with an off-centre arrangement and facing the solid black verso to the half-title. Tschichold was never connected with the Bauhaus but was one of the first to formulate the basic principles of the New Typography. He greatly refined the rather ponderous Bauhaus work but in time felt that he had exhausted its possibilities and returned to an immaculate and classic style of typography.

The New Typography that started with such panache at Weimar and Dessau, after 1928 went into cold storage for about twenty years. It was no coincidence that the second volume of Adolf Hitler's *Mein Kampf* had been published the year before. The gross sentiments of the Nazis soon obliterated the Bauhaus doctrines and discredited anything that was to come out of Germany. There were protests and of these, John Heartfield's fearsome photo-collage portraits for bookjackets were not the least effective. They still have a powerful impact today.

To the west of the Rhine, there was a kind of Gaderene-swine-downhill-only race to the Riviera and the Jazz Age was carrying all before it. Paris was still the centre of the art world. Diaghilev's *Ballets Russes*, a survival of pre-1914 Paris, was continuing to excite and shock the audiences at the Théâtre des Champs-Elysées, with Léon Bakst's barbaric sets, glowing with rich jades and crimsons; also there were new ballets such as the Ballets Suédois presentation of *La Création du Monde* by Blaise Cendrars with music by Darius Milhaud and sets by Léger, or Jean Cocteau's *Le Train Bleu*, with sets by Henri Laurens, a drop curtain by Picasso and a score by Milhaud. *Le Train Bleu* was a ballet of life on the *plage*. It was symptomatic of this frantic,

IN illo tempore : Dixit Jesus discipulis suis : Hoc est præceptum meum, ut diligatis invicem, sicut dilexi vos. Majorem hac dilectionem nemo habet, ut animam suam ponat quis pro amicis suis. Vos amici mei estis, si feceritis quæ ego præcipio vobis. Jam non dicam vos servos : quia servus nescit quid faciat dominus ejus. Vos autem dixi amicos : quia omnia quæcumque audivi a Patre meo, nota feci vobis. Non vos me elegistis : sed ego elegi vos, et posui vos, ut eatis, et fructum afferatis : et fructus vester maneat : ut quodcumque petieritis Patrem in nomine meo, det vobis.

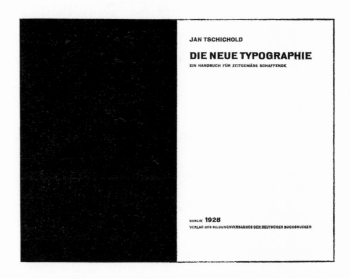

JAN TSCHICHOLD

DIE NEUE TYPOGRAPHIE
EIN HANDBUCH FÜR ZEITGEMÄSS SCHAFFENDE

BERLIN 1928
VERLAG DES BILDUNGSVERBANDES DER DEUTSCHEN BUCHDRUCKER

1. *50 years Bauhaus* arranged by Wurttembergischer Kunstverein, Stuttgart, 1968. Royal Academy of Arts, London.

frivolous, dream-like period which was in such marked contrast to the solemnities or heavy-handed humour of the Bauhaus. The pageant was played out by bizarre characters like the flamboyant and usually semi-naked creole Josephine Baker and at the Folies Bergère by the ageing, befeathered Mistinguette. Jean Cocteau was the *enfant terrible* of the time, Honegger was writing a tone poem, *Pacific 231*, based on the sound of a steam locomotive and Léger was painting his 'mechanical' compositions.

In 1922, the discovery by Howard Carter and Lord Carnarvon of Tutankhamen's tomb, in the Valley of the Kings near Luxor, set a new fashion for Egyptian ornaments. In 1925 *L'Exposition des Arts Décoratifs et Industriels* was held in Paris. The decorative motifs for '*Les Arts Décos*' were a mixture of Tutankhamen-inspired ornament and the zigzag line of the Charleston. *Les Arts Décos* underlined the end of traditional design. Novelty was everything. Meanwhile the rich, smart set took the *Train Bleu* south or hurtled down the *Route Sept* in their long-bonneted Hispano-Suizas and Isotta-Fraschinis.

Kees van Dongen painted their portraits, Max Jacob was the poet of the epoch and in literature, André Gide, according to F. Scott Fitzgerald, was 'the master'. If Gide was the master, Fitzgerald was certainly the Boswell of the age.

In fine printing, Vollard was still producing *éditions de luxe*. His first and loveliest book, *Parallèlement*, illustrated with Bonnard lithographs, had been produced in 1900. In 1924 the same artist etched the illustrations for Vollard's edition of Octave Mirabeau's *Dingo*. Other artists such as Picasso, Juan Gris and Rouault were illustrating limited editions for numerous publishers, who had caught on to the profitable idea of the *édition de luxe*. In 1926 Raoul Dufy, the artist most representative of the epoch, lithographed the illustrations for Apollinaire's *Le Poète Assassiné*, for Au Sans Pareil.

On the poster hoardings, Adolphe Jean-Marie Mouron, a Ukrainian-born Frenchman, who worked under the name of Cassandre, made use of various motifs from contemporary painting and added a personal humour of his own. Cassandre was not only the most inventive poster artist of his time (perhaps of any time), but also contributed as much to modern graphics as did the new typographers of the Bauhaus.

Du Côté de chez Swann had first been published in 1913. In 1927 Marcel Proust's *A la Recherche du temps perdu*, came to a close with *Le Temps Retrouvé*. It was 'a history of an epoch and a history of a conscience.' Two years later, '*Le Krache de Wall Street et la fête est fini*'. Scott Fitzgerald wrote its obituary in *Echoes of the Jazz Age* with these somewhat extravagant words, 'The most expensive orgy in history was over'.

In the year of the Wall Street crash, A. Tolmer's *Mise en Page* was published in Paris. This was a cheerful, ill-disciplined book, with more of *Art Déco* than of the Bauhaus in its make up.

However various Cubist, Suprematist and Constructivist clichés were shown and also a lively use of photo-collage. Tolmer, an enterprising printer and publisher, was prodigal with his ideas and this book rather than Tschichold's disciplined *Die Neue Typographie* became the bible of the advertising agencies in the 1930's. The demand for novelty that *Art Déco* strove to meet, combined with the anarchy of Dada, had left a somewhat shaky structure on which to base the design of printing or anything else.

The Dutch painter, Piet Mondrian, from 1921 onwards had brought back balanced harmony into design, for he showed how very harmonious asymmetry could be. His beautifully planned, yet intuitive, grid paintings had had a marked influence on the Bauhaus and led to a new formality of grid structure for typography.

In England, in the years immediately following the 1914–18 war, there was a buoyant feeling in the air, and this to a modest degree affected printing and publishing. Oliver Simon, one of the pioneers of the English revival of good printing, wrote in his *Printer and Playground* 'It was (and still is) difficult for an amateur to enter the printing trade. English printing of the early 1920's would nevertheless have been the poorer if several adventurous spirits had not found ways and means of entry.' These amateurs included Oliver Simon himself working under Harold Curwen at the Curwen Press, Francis Meynell, the son of a poet and a publisher, at the Pelican Press (a one room establishment in London), Herbert Simon and Harry Carter at the Kynoch Press, a subsidiary of I.C.I., and Stanley Morison and Walter Lewis at C. W. Hobson's short-lived Cloister Press at Heaton Mersey. They were all to go on to great things. The private presses had provided the inspiration but as Oliver Simon said 'Many of their books, forced into a Renaissance mould, had an air of unreality about them.' He felt that modern machinery used with intelligence allied to imagination could produce books with their own kind of beauty and help to mould a new typographic style. In the United States, Updike, Bruce Rogers and W. A. Dwiggins and T. M. Cleland had already succeeded in producing fine work in this manner. Later, the Simons at the Curwen Press and Meynell with his Nonesuch Press were triumphantly to confirm these hopeful words.

This English typographic movement was very different from either the *Die Neue Typographie* or *Art Déco* and though its impetus came from the work of Morris, Emery Walker, Cobden-Sanderson and the other Private Press printers, it had absolutely nothing of Morris's medievalism and very little of the Doves Press Jensonist heritage. Francis Meynell, whilst at the Pelican Press, had already shown a fondness for flowery borders, arabesques and the typefaces and styles of seventeenth-century French printers. Oliver Simon's style was more austere but still made great play with rather more formal borders, influenced by

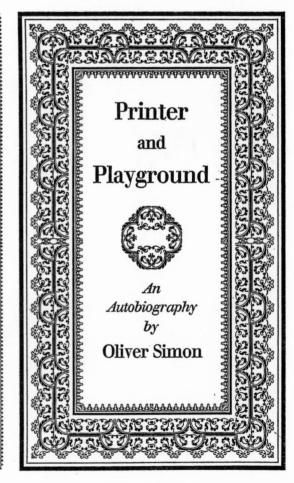

Top: Monotype Walbaum, a revival of an early 19th-century
Neo-Classic typeface and Lutetia, designed by Jan van Krimpen in
1924

Below: Drawing by Eric Gill for Monotype's Gill Sans Italic,
1928 – 9

Walbaum
and Walbaum

LUTETIA
abcdefghjkmpqrstu

abcdefghijka

2. *The Double Crown Club*, Stanley Morison, privately printed 1969.

the work of Carl Ernst Poeschel, the Leipzig printer. In 1925, Simon bought a complete range of the Neo-Classic typeface Walbaum from the Berthold Foundry. The break with Private Press typography was complete.

England in the '20's was not all buoyancy. Unemployment led to hunger marches and indirectly to the General Strike of 1926. However the printing revival continued. The most potent influence came from Stanley Morison, who from 1922 onwards guided the Monotype Corporation through a remarkable, if backward-looking programme, of re-cutting typefaces which were based on the work of the great type-founders of the past, such as Griffo, Garamond, Van Dyck, Caslon, Baskerville, Ehrhardt and ultimately Walbaum, and even to commissioning new and equally classic faces from such modern designers as Jan van Krimpen and Eric Gill. With curious perversity in 1928, Morison persuaded Gill, a classical stone letter-cutter with no knowledge of type-founding, or liking for display types, to design a series of sans serif typefaces. Neither Morison nor Gill liked sans serifs. Morison actually wrote 'The reason why we have decided to stick to a seriffed form of typography is because we have discovered in the course of centuries that a serif does assist legibility. It is a rational thing to have and not a superstitious following of the ancients.' On the same theme he continued, 'It is useful to encourage a knowledge of history among typographers so that they emancipate themselves from the possibility of following doctrinaire – instead of rationalist – idealogues, who must have a style that corresponds with what they take to be a certain definite trend in the arts, irrespective of whether that trend is a strengthening or weakening of legibility'.[2] This is all very sound, yet, great man that he was, Morison had one or two blind spots. One was *Die Neue Typographie*. He was quite willing to use sans serifs, large and small, on the yellow paper jackets he designed for Gollancz in the 1930's. In terms of the written word these jackets were brutally effective. As pieces of design, as seen by the Bauhaus typographers, they were non-starters, but if Morison was not a designer in their eyes, he was a very logical typographer and a man of letters, in more senses than one.

In 1929, Morison published in *The Fleuron*, his *First Principles of Typography*. It is the most rational and intelligent thing that has ever been written about the typography of books. It does not, and does not attempt to, say anything about design which, as Lissitzky, Moholy-Nagy and Bayer have shown, can add another dimension to communication, and can help to elucidate and bring order into what might otherwise be visual and typographic chaos.

The 1929 Wall Street crash led to the trade depression of the 1930's. With mass unemployment there was even an attempt to get back to William Morris's ideas of handicraft, for labour-saving methods were at a discount.

In England and elsewhere, typography reverted to classical symmetry. From 1930 to 1945, typographically things stood still then there was a post-war boom and the *avant garde* doctrines of the '20's came back with renewed force, first in Switzerland, then in the United States and finally and a long time after in England, which had been through a romantic phase in painting, and in printing through a prolonged and nostalgic flirtation with nineteenth-century typefaces.

The 1920's were the formative, germinal years. In the forties, the lessons of the New Typography had to be relearned after nearly two decades in cold storage.

In 1945, in France, in spite of Existentialism, the old guard still ruled the painting roost. Picasso was pouring forth work. During the war he had completed his Buffon bestiary with a set of very fine sugar aquatints. Picasso once explained that the war-time spate of illustration in Paris was due to the difficulties of keeping warm at home. Lacourière's printing workshop was the one well-heated place in which they could work. In the late '40's, with the war behind him and the anticipatory horrors of Guernica forgotten, he was living an idyllic life near Antibes recapturing the gaiety of the '20's. All this was revealed in his dancing fauns and felicitous paintings of Françoise Gilot. In 1947, Matisse's book *Jazz*, filled with his *papiers collés* designs, further recalled the Jazz Age. Braque, Dufy and Rouault were also enjoying an Indian summer.

The nineteen-fifties began with the first commercially made computer appearing on the market. Computerized typesetting was already in sight and Switzerland led the world in printing technology and in typographic design. In Zurich, Adrian Frutiger started work on a new family of sans serif typefaces which he named Univers. In London, the Festival of Britain planned to herald a new epoch, proved to be the last nostalgic and somewhat tremulous kick of a decorative old age, typographically sweetened with Victoriana. New York, with Abstract Expressionists such as Jackson Pollock, William de Kooning and Mark Rothko, had at last wrenched the title of the centre of the world's art away from Paris. A new and highly doctrinaire design school was established at Ulm. There was a sudden burst of new signs on the motorways, airports and railways. For these, classic roman capitals were replaced by lower-case grotesques with very large x-heights and practically no ascenders or descenders. Most of these letter forms were derived from the Haas Type-foundry *Grotesk*.

Figurative painting, practically killed by abstraction, was given new life by Pop Art. But it was a figurative painting consciously brash and intentionally at the lowest level of graphic art. The strip cartoon, the pin-up, the breakfast cereal packet and the pin-table saloons were all grist to the mill of this vigorous movement. Printing once again, as it had done for Dada, was repaying its debt to the fine arts.

ABCDEFGHIJM
&abcdefghijkl
mnopqrstuvw

Top: *Neue Haas Grotesk* designed by Max Miedinger, 1957

Below: Road traffic signs designed by the Ministry of Transport in England 1963. The most interesting innovation is the omission of the stroke in the fraction

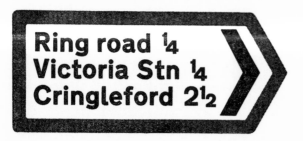

3. *Cybernetic Serendipity*, Jasia Reichardt, Studio International, 1968.

Op Art and Kinetic Art added optical illusion to painting and actual movement to sculpture. In 1960 the Boeing Airplane Company developed the use of computerized drawings for such purposes as to establish the possible range of movements a pilot might make in his cockpit. Such graphics can be made with a cathode ray tube, with an electronic beam electrically deflected across a phosphorescent screen.[3] So much for paint and canvas.

In typographics, a universal style came into being. It was a belatedly functional and not particularly exciting development of the German New Typography of the nineteen-twenties. Photo-typesetting and offset printing had eliminated the strict modular structure of Gutenberg's metal types. In print anything could now be printed, even rubber type. The actual difficulties of hot metal setting and imposition were forgotten. The strict discipline of spacing and layout that the metal chase, metal furniture and metal types imposed was lost. This loss of such limitations forced the typographic designer to create his own limitations, by grid layouts and so on. At least he was better off than the painters, who with no limitations sought with such difficulty to find solutions to the problems of today. At least the typographer had for the moment, letters and words to play with. And words that were conveying some message. He was, however, in danger of finding himself strait-jacketed like the modern architect by new sets of rules, as mathematical and as confining as anything Palladio laid down.

Printing has always reflected the times in which it has operated. On occasions it has helped to shape those times. Its pre-eminence both as the prime means of communicating and recording information, and as a reflection of its age is at last being challenged by audio-visual aids and data-processing electronic computers. The fact that whole worlds of information can be stored in one machine, and not stored away in distant and inaccessible racks but to hand immediately, makes one question the viability of the modern library and perhaps even of the printed book.

The 1963 *Report on Automation and the Library of Congress* put forward the idea that the catalogue should be scrapped and replaced by a vast automated memory. The reader would consult this by keyboard, or, for more complex enquiries, by push-button controls on cathode ray display tubes. Finally the information the student seeks is presented to him through photographic or electronic micro-reproduction. Not only would he be able to find out what books or papers there are on his own subjects but also a digest of what is actually in them. Tele-communication would allow immediate access to all the large libraries throughout the continent. So much for the printed book!

Yet, the codex, Alcuin's duplex alphabet and Gutenberg's metal typefaces are not entirely played out, only the forms are

Top: Typefaces produced for electronic scanning.
The Visible Word, Herbert Spencer, Royal College of Art, London,
1968

Centre: A new alphabet to meet the needs of cathode-ray
type-setting, designed by Wim Crouwel. *The Visible Word*

changing. Books are still handy things and Alcuin's Carolingian
hand has had quite a good run, even though the legibility of its
derivatives has been questioned from time to time; recurringly
the argument for a single alphabet crops up. The creation of
machine-readable letters may produce an answer to this argument. Machine-readable types would appear to have been
designed by engineers who were more familiar with square-
filling and doodling on graph paper than with the form of
letters, either classical or gothic. A more conventionally
acceptable sans serif typeface for computer use has been evolved
by Adrian Frutiger, working in collaboration with engineers,
for the European Computers Association. Judged by the same
designer's Univers, it is a poor thing. It is probable that a completely new alphabet, with no allegiance to the Caroline
miniscule or the Trajan Column, may be the proper answer.
Wim Crouwel's design for an alphabet designed solely to meet
the needs of cathode ray tube typesetting may be nearer the
mark. It would seem as if the engineers are taking over.

The declining influence of the fine arts on printing has resulted
from the destructive legacy of Dada and the introspective preoccupations of contemporary artists. The influence of artists
who once reached out for the stars is superseded by that of
cosmonauts who are on the threshold of visiting them. The
printer no longer looks to the painter or the architect to design
his title-pages and to lead the reader through Baroque portals
into the pages of Tyndale's *Bible* or into the works of contemporary or classical authors.

The world is changing and naturally enough so is art. The really
creative artist today has largely ceased to concern himself with
the production of pictures or sculpture as objects for sale, but
has turned to experiment with ideas. That his experiments may
result in utterly expendable *objets d'art* is of no great concern to
him. It is a return to content, to the fact that the thought behind
the picture is more important than the picture itself. Its importance lies in the fact that the idea can survive the material
destruction of the so-called works of art.

The same thing applies to printing. Printed books, once such
treasured objects, such gateways to wisdom and knowledge,
are becoming daily more ephemeral. The modern book is the
paperback. In many disciplines, books may even be outdated
before they have left the printing presses.

It would also seem as if a bleak utilitarianism is descending on
to the book pages, yet as 'typographic man' is replaced by
'electronic man', the visual needs of the new reader are going to
be met once again with pictures, perhaps applied to some new
shorthand typography. The situation is comparable to the
twelfth century, when illiterate peasants gazed at the windows
of Chartres and read the iconography as if it was a book. We
are back in a Gothic culture.

ABCDEFGHIJKLMNOP
QRSTUVWXYZ
1234567890

neu
alphabet

Below: Computer graphics, showing one of a series of drawings
giving the range of movements of a pilot in the cockpit of an
aeroplane. Produced by the Boeing Computer Graphic Organization.
This was one of the works exhibited in the *Cybernetic Serendipity*
Exhibition at the I.C.A. in 1968

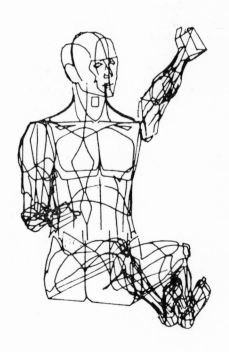

Bibliography

CHAPTER I
A History of the English Church and People, Bede. Tr. Leo Sherley-Price Penguin Books, Harmondsworth, Middlesex: 1955.
The Sequence of English Medieval Art, Walter Oakeshott. Faber and Faber, London: 1950.
The Invention of Printing in China, and its spread westwards, T. F. Carter. The Ronald Press Co, New York: 1955.
A History of Europe (2 vols.) H. A. L. Fisher, First published 1935. Collins Fontana Library, London: 1960.
The Waning of the Middle Ages, J. H. Huizinga. (Originally pub. 1924.) Penguin Books: 1965; Doubleday, New York.
The Civilization of Charlemagne, Jacques Boussard. World University Library, Weidenfeld and Nicolson, London: 1968.
The Awakening of Europe, Philippe Wolff, trs. Anne Carver. Penguin Books: 1968.

CHAPTER 2
Five Hundred Years of Printing, S. H. Steinberg. Penguin Books: 1955.
Gothic, George Henderson. Penguin Books: 1967.
Printing Types: their history, forms and use, D. B. Updike. Harvard University Press, Cambridge, Mass: 1922.
History of England, G. M. Trevelyan. Longmans, Green & Co, London: 1926. Doubleday, New York.

CHAPTER 3
The Italian Renaissance and its historical background, Denys Hay. Cambridge University Press: 1961.
Renaissance Handwriting, Alfred Fairbank and Berthold Wolpe. Faber and Faber, London: 1960.
The Renaissance in Italy, John Addington Symonds. 1875–86.
Four Centuries of Fine Printing (2nd Ed) Stanley Morison. Benn, London: 1949.
The Fifteenth Century: the Prospect of Europe, Margaret Aston. Thames and Hudson, London: 1968. Harcourt Brace and World, New York: 1968.
Academies of Art Past and Present, Nikolaus Pevsner. Cambridge University Press: 1940.
A Concise History of Art (2 vols.), Germain Bazin, Thames and Hudson: 1958.

CHAPTER 4
Printing and the Mind of Man, ed. John Carter and P. H. Muir. Cassell and Co., London: 1967; Holt, Rhinhart & Winston, New York.
Reformation and Society in Sixteenth Century Europe, A. G. Dickens. Thames and Hudson, London: 1966; Harcourt Brace and World, New York.
A History of Book Illustration, David Bland. Faber and Faber, London: 1969, University of California Press: 1969.

CHAPTER 5
Dutch Civilization in the Seventeenth Century and other essays, J. H. Huizinga. Collins, London: 1968; Ungar, New York: 1968.
Christopher Plantin, Colin Clair. Cassell and Co., London: 1960; Hillary House, New York: 1960.

CHAPTER 6
The English Common Reader, Richard D. Altick. University of Chicago Press: 1957. Paperback edition: 1963.
British Architects and Craftsmen, Sacheverell Sitwell. Batsford: London: 1945.
Man not Citizen: Erasmus in our Time, Hans Redeker. Trs. H. Romeijn, Boymans van Beuningen Museum, Rotterdam: 1969.

CHAPTER 7
English Social History, G. M. Trevelyan. Longmans, Green and Co., London: 1942; McKay, New York: 1965.
London Tradesman's Cards of the 18th century, Ambrose Heal. Batsford, London: 1925; Dover, New York: 1967.
The Age of Reason, Harold Nicolson. Constable, London, 1960; Panther Books: 1968; Doubleday, New York: 1961.

CHAPTER 7 *continued*
A History of the Old English Letter Foundries, T. B. Reed. Ed. A. F. Johnson. Faber and Faber, London: 1952; Boston Book and Art Shop, Boston.
The English Writing Masters, Ambrose Heal. Cambridge University Press: 1931.
John Bell, Stanley Morison. Cambridge University Press: 1931.

CHAPTER 8
From Baroque to Rococo, Nicolas Powell. Faber and Faber, London: 1959.
Baroque Churches of Central Europe, John Bourke. Faber and Faber, London: 1958.
Fournier on Type-founding: the Text of Manuel Typographique, Tr. Harry Carter, Soncino Press, London: 1930; Burt Franklin, New York: 1930.

CHAPTER 9
Neo-Classicism, Hugh Honour. Penguin Books Ltd, Harmondsworth, 1968 and New York: 1968.
Architecture in Britain 1530–1830, John Summerson, Penguin Books, 1965.
An Illustrated History of Interior Decoration, Mario Praz, trs. W. Weaver. Thames and Hudson: 1964.

CHAPTER 10
Nature of Gothic, John Ruskin, from *The Stones of Venice*, first published 1847; Hill and Wang, New York.
Pioneers of Modern Design, Nikolaus Pevsner, Penguin Books, Harmondsworth: 1960. Penguin, New York: 1964.
A Memoir of Thomas Bewick, written by himself, 1822–28. Longman, Green, Longman and Roberts, London: 1862. Southern Illinois University Press, Carbondale, Illinois.
Vincent Figgins Type Specimens: 1801 *and* 1815, Berthold Wolpe, Printing Historical Society, London: 1967.
Victorian Book Design and Colour Printing, Ruari McLean. Faber and Faber, London: 1963. Oxford University Press, New York: 1963.
The Pre-Raphaelite Tragedy, William Gaunt. Jonathan Cape, London: 1942; Schocken, New York.
19th Century Ornamented Typefaces and Title-pages, Nicolette Gray. Faber and Faber, London: 1938.
Printed Ephemera, John Lewis, Faber and Faber, London: 1962. Paperback edition 1969.
Caslon Architectural, Berthold Wolpe: an article in *Alphabet*, ed. R. S. Hutchings. James Moran, London: 1964.

CHAPTER 11
Art Nouveau, ed. Peter Selz and Mildred Constantine. Museum of Modern Art. Dist. Doubleday and Co., New York: 1959.
Art Nouveau, Mario Amaya. Studio Vista, London: 1966; Dutton, New York: 1966.
The Art Nouveau Book in Britain, John Russell Taylor, Methuen, London: 1966; M. I. T. Press, Cambridge, Mass.: 1967.
The Twentieth Century Book, John Lewis. Studio Vista, London: 1967; Reinhold, New York.
William Morris as Designer, Ray Watkinson. Studio Vista, London: 1967; Reinhold, New York.

CHAPTER 12
Dada, Monograph of a Movement, ed. Willy Verkauf. Tiranti, London: 1957.
Bauhaus 1919–1928, ed. Herbert Bayer, Walter Gropius, Isa Gropius. Museum of Modern Art, New York: 1938.
Bauhaus, Hans M. Wingler, Massachusetts Institute of Technology, Boston: 1969.
The Gutenberg Galaxy, Marshall McLuhan. University of Toronto Press: 1962.
Pioneers of Modern Typography, Herbert Spencer. Lund Humphries, London: 1969.
Cybernetic Serendipity, Jasia Reichardt. Studio International: 1968.
The Visible Word, Herbert Spencer. Royal College of Art, London: 1968.

Index

Note: numerals in italics refer to the captions of the plates

224